D0531799

Taste of Home's
Favorite Brand
Name Recipes
2002

Taste of Home Books

Copyright © 2002 Publications International, Ltd.
All rights reserved. This publication may not be reproduced or quoted in whole or in part by any means whatsoever without written permission from:

Louis Weber, CEO
Publications International, Ltd.
7373 North Cicero Avenue
Lincolnwood, IL 60712

Permission is never granted for commercial purposes.

All recipes and photographs that contain specific brand names are copyrighted by those companies and/or associations, unless otherwise specified. All photographs *except* those on pages 6 bottom left, 9, 11, 20 bottom left, 26, 27, 37, 42 bottom left, 53, 59, 63, 66 top left, 73, 75, 83, 92 top right, 92 bottom right, 105, 107, 108 top left, 108 bottom left, 111, 115, 117, 119, 122, 129, 139, 145, 150, 153, 163, 165, 169, 178, 185, 191 and 205 copyright © Publications International, Ltd.

Favorite Brand Name Recipes is a trademark of Publications International, Ltd.

DOLE® is a registered trademark of Dole Food Company, Inc.

™/© M&M's, M and the M&M's Characters are trademarks of Mars, Incorporated. © Mars, Inc. 2002.

Carnation, Libby's, Nestlé, Ortega and Toll House are registered trademarks of Nestlé.

TACO BELL® and HOME ORIGINALS® are trademarks owned and licensed by Taco Bell Corp.

Butter Flavor CRISCO® all-vegetable shortening and Butter Flavor CRISCO® No-Stick Cooking Spray are artificially flavored.

Editor: Heidi Reuter Lloyd
Food Editor: Janaan Cunningham
Associate Food Editor: Diane Werner
Senior Recipe Editor: Sue A. Jurack
Recipe Editor: Janet Briggs

Front cover photography by Reiman Publications.
Food Photography: Dan Roberts
Food Photography Artist: Vicky Marie Moseley
Photo Studio Manager: Anne Schimmel

Pictured on the front cover *(clockwise from top left):* Garlic 'n Lemon Roast Chicken *(page 136),* Asparagus with Citrus Dressing *(page 54)* and Cherry Glazed Chocolate Torte *(page 197).*

Pictured on the back cover *(clockwise from top):* French Bistro Ham *(page 142),* Layer After Layer Lemon Pie *(page 188)* and Fruit Salad with Orange Poppy Seed Dressing *(page 22).*

ISBN: 0-7853-6690-3

Library of Congress Control Number: 2001098903

Manufactured in China.

8 7 6 5 4 3 2 1

Some of the products listed in this publication may be in limited distribution.

Microwave Cooking: Microwave ovens vary in wattage. Use the cooking times as guidelines and check for doneness before adding more time.

Taste of Home's Favorite Brand Name Recipes 2002

A Collection of Favorite Recipes
From Our Family to Yours

TRUST is a key ingredient when you're trying a new cookbook. This innovative book, *Taste of Home's Favorite Brand Name Recipes 2002,* is a book you can doubly trust.

First, all 326 down-home recipes were hand-picked by the home economists at *Taste of Home,* the No. 1 cooking magazine in America. Second, every recipe features name-brand foods you've used with confidence for years.

This book is packed with guaranteed-good recipes. We spent time collecting family-pleasing, name-brand favorites so that you don't have to. For instance:

• When we wanted a main dish your family could really sink its teeth into, we chose a recipe from the National Pork Board.

• When we wanted a home-style entrée that was a bit on the light side, we got together to talk turkey and selected a recipe from Butterball®.

Chicken Gumbo (p. 148)

• And when we decided we needed a few chocolate recipes your family would melt over, we sifted through quite a pile, choosing recipes from Baker's®, Hershey®s and Nestlé®.

326 Grade-A Recipes

The result is a fabulous collection of recipes. Every single recipe has been kitchen-tested and stamped with an "A" for awesome.

This book will take you from the start of a family meal to the finish, giving you plenty of choices for appealing appetizers, delicious desserts and everything in between—soups, salads, entrées, side dishes and breads.

With 326 selections, you'll never run out of clever combinations. You can mix and match to your heart's content. And your family will be happy, too.

Cheesecake-Topped Brownies (p. 186)

How to Find a Recipe

This book is indexed two ways. If you look under any major ingredient, you'll find a list of the recipes that feature it.

For example, if you know you want to serve chicken tonight, turn to "chicken" in the general index and ponder the many tasty options.

The alphabetical index starts on page 220, so once you and your family have discovered a few favorites, you can easily find them by name the next time you want to make them.

You'll also find 150 big, full-color photos that will whet your appetite, inspire you and help you decide the perfect meal to make. Happy cooking with *Taste of Home's Favorite Brand Name Recipes 2002.*

Appetizers & Snacks

Barbecue Beef Ribettes

(Pictured at left)

    1 clove garlic, minced
    1 tablespoon vegetable oil
  1/2 cup ketchup
  1/3 cup A.1.® Original or A.1.® BOLD & SPICY Steak Sauce
  1/4 cup chili sauce
    2 tablespoons packed light brown sugar
    2 thin slices fresh lemon
  1/2 teaspoon liquid hot pepper seasoning
2-1/2 pounds beef ribs, cut into 2-inch pieces

In medium saucepan, over low heat, cook garlic in oil until tender. Stir in ketchup, steak sauce, chili sauce, sugar, lemon and hot pepper seasoning; cook 1 to 2 minutes or until heated through. Reserve 2/3 cup for serving with cooked ribs. Set aside remaining sauce for basting ribs.

Arrange ribs on rack in large roasting pan. Bake at 400°F for 30 minutes.

Brush ribs generously with 1/4 cup basting sauce. Grill ribs over medium heat or broil 6 inches from heat source 20 to 25 minutes or until ribs are tender, turning and basting often with remaining basting sauce. Serve with reserved 2/3 cup sauce. Garnish as desired.　　*Makes 8 appetizer servings*

Clockwise from top left: *Cheesy Quesadillas (p. 14), Barbecue Beef Ribettes, Ortega® Green Chile Guacamole (p. 18) and Crispie Cheese Twists (p. 10)*

Take-Along Snack Mix

Awesome Antipasto

>   1 jar (16 ounces) mild cherry peppers, drained
>   2 cans (4-1/2 ounces each) artichoke hearts, drained
> 1/2 pound asparagus spears, cooked
> 1/2 cup pitted black olives
>   1 red onion, cut into wedges
>   1 green bell pepper, sliced into rings
>   1 red bell pepper, sliced into rings
>   1 bottle (8 ounces) Italian salad dressing
>   1 cup shredded Parmesan cheese, divided
>   1 package (6 ounces) HILLSHIRE FARM® Hard Salami

Layer cherry peppers, artichoke hearts, asparagus, olives, onion and bell peppers in 13×9-inch glass baking dish.

Pour dressing and 1/3 cup cheese over vegetables. Cover; refrigerate 1 to 2 hours.

Drain vegetables, reserving marinade. Arrange vegetables and Hard Salami in rows on serving platter. Drizzle with reserved marinade. Top with remaining 2/3 cup cheese.   *Makes 6 servings*

Take-Along Snack Mix

(Pictured above)

>   1 tablespoon butter or margarine
>   2 tablespoons honey
>   1 cup toasted oat cereal, any flavor
> 1/2 cup coarsely broken pecans
> 1/2 cup thin pretzel sticks, broken in half
> 1/2 cup raisins
>   1 cup "M&M's"® Chocolate Mini Baking Bits

In large heavy skillet over low heat, melt butter; add honey and stir until blended. Add cereal, nuts, pretzels and raisins, stirring until all pieces are evenly coated. Continue cooking over low heat about 10 minutes, stirring frequently. Remove from heat; immediately spread on waxed paper until cool. Add "M&M's"® Chocolate Mini Baking Bits. Store in tightly covered container.

Makes about 3-1/2 cups mix

Warm Vegetable & Seafood Dip

>   1 envelope LIPTON® RECIPE SECRETS® Vegetable Soup Mix*
>   1 container (16 ounces) sour cream
>   1 can (6 ounces) imitation crabmeat, cooked shrimp or 1 cup frozen cooked crabmeat, thawed
>   3 ounces cream cheese, softened
>   1 teaspoon lemon juice

Also terrific with Lipton® Recipe Secrets® Savory Herb with Garlic Soup Mix.

1. Preheat oven to 325°F. In 1-quart casserole, combine all ingredients.

2. Bake uncovered 30 minutes or until heated through.

3. Serve with your favorite dippers.

Makes 3 cups dip

Black Bean Spirals

(Pictured below)

1 can (15 ounces) black beans, rinsed, drained
6 flour tortillas (10-inch)
1 package (8 ounces) PHILADELPHIA® Cream Cheese, softened
1 cup KRAFT® Shredded Cheddar *or* Monterey Jack Cheese
1/2 cup BREAKSTONE'S® or KNUDSEN® Sour Cream
1/4 teaspoon onion salt
TACO BELL® HOME ORIGINALS®* Thick 'N Chunky Salsa.

TACO BELL and HOME ORIGINALS are registered trademarks of Taco Bell Corp.

PLACE beans in food processor container fitted with steel blade or blender container; cover. Process until smooth. Spread layer of beans on each tortilla.

PLACE cheeses, sour cream and onion salt in food processor container fitted with steel blade or blender container; cover. Process until smooth. Spread cheese mixture over beans.

ROLL tortillas up tightly. Refrigerate 30 minutes. Cut into 1/2-inch slices. Serve with TACO BELL® HOME ORIGINALS® Thick 'N Chunky Salsa.

Makes 20 servings

Great Substitute: Substitute 1 can (16 ounces) TACO BELL® HOME ORIGINALS® Refried Beans for puréed black beans.

Helpful Hint

To soften cream cheese quickly, remove it from the wrapper and place it in a medium microwave-safe bowl. Microwave it on MEDIUM (50% power) for 15 to 20 seconds or until the cheese is slightly softened.

Black Bean Spirals

Hot Artichoke Dip

(Pictured at right)

1 package (8 ounces) PHILADELPHIA® Cream
    Cheese, softened
1 can (14 ounces) artichoke hearts, drained,
    chopped
1/2 cup KRAFT® Real Mayonnaise
1/2 cup (2 ounces) KRAFT® 100% Grated
    Parmesan Cheese
2 tablespoons finely chopped fresh basil *or*
    1 teaspoon dried basil leaves
2 tablespoons finely chopped red onion
1 clove garlic, minced
1/2 cup chopped tomato

MIX cream cheese and all remaining ingredients
except tomato with electric mixer on medium speed
until well blended.

SPOON into 9-inch pie plate.

BAKE at 350°F for 25 minutes. Sprinkle with tomato.
Serve with assorted cut-up vegetables or baked pita
bread wedges. *Makes 3-1/4 cups dip*

Note: To make baked pita bread wedges, cut 3 split
pita breads each into 8 triangles. Place on cookie
sheet. Bake at 350°F for 10 to 12 minutes or until
crisp.

Zesty Bruschetta

1 envelope LIPTON® RECIPE SECRETS® Savory
    Herb with Garlic Soup Mix
6 tablespoons olive or vegetable oil*
1 loaf French or Italian bread (about 18 inches
    long), sliced lengthwise
2 tablespoons shredded or grated Parmesan
    cheese

Substitution: Use 1/2 cup margarine or butter, melted.

Preheat oven to 350°F. Blend savory herb with garlic
soup mix and oil. Brush onto bread, then sprinkle
with cheese.

Bake 12 minutes or until golden. Slice, then serve.
Makes 1 loaf, about 18 pieces

Crispie Cheese Twists

(Pictured on page 6)

1/2 cup grated Parmesan cheese
3/4 teaspoon LAWRY'S® Seasoned Pepper
1/2 teaspoon LAWRY'S® Garlic Powder with
    Parsley
1 package (17-3/4 ounces) frozen puff pastry,
    thawed
1 egg white, lightly beaten

Preheat oven to 350°F. In small bowl, combine
Parmesan cheese, Seasoned Pepper and Garlic
Powder with Parsley. Unfold pastry sheets onto
cutting board. Brush pastry lightly with egg white;
sprinkle each sheet with 1/4 of the cheese mixture.
Lightly press into pastry; turn over and repeat. Cut
each sheet into 12 (1-inch-wide) strips; twist. Place
on greased cookie sheet. Bake 15 minutes or until
golden brown. *Makes 2 dozen twists*

Serving Suggestion: Serve in a napkin-lined basket.
Place layer of plastic wrap over napkin to protect it.

Classic Chicken Puffs

1 box UNCLE BEN'S® Long Grain & Wild Rice
    Original Recipe
2 cups cubed cooked TYSON® Fresh Chicken
1/2 can (10-3/4 ounces) condensed cream of
    mushroom soup
1/3 cup chopped green onions
1/3 cup diced pimientos or diced red bell pepper
1/3 cup diced celery
1/3 cup chopped fresh parsley
1/3 cup chopped slivered almonds
1/4 cup milk
1 box frozen prepared puff pastry shells, thawed

COOK: CLEAN: Wash hands. Prepare rice according
to package directions. When rice is done, add
remaining ingredients (except pastry shells). Mix
well. Reheat 1 minute. Fill pastry shells with rice
mixture.

SERVE: Serve with a mixed green salad and
balsamic vinaigrette, if desired.

CHILL: Refrigerate leftovers immediately.
Makes 6 servings

Hot Artichoke Dip

7-Layer Mexican Dip

7-Layer Mexican Dip

(Pictured at left)

1 package (8 ounces) PHILADELPHIA® Cream
　　Cheese, softened
1 tablespoon TACO BELL® HOME ORIGINALS®*
　　Taco Seasoning Mix
1 cup guacamole
1 cup TACO BELL® HOME ORIGINALS®* Thick 'N
　　Chunky Salsa
1 cup shredded lettuce
1 cup KRAFT® Shredded Mild Cheddar Cheese
1/2 cup chopped green onions
2 tablespoons sliced pitted ripe olives

*TACO BELL and HOME ORIGINALS are registered trademarks owned and licensed by Taco Bell Corp.

MIX cream cheese and seasoning mix. Spread onto bottom of 9-inch pie plate or quiche dish.

LAYER guacamole, salsa, lettuce, cheese, onions and olives over cream cheese mixture; cover. Refrigerate.

SERVE with NABISCO® Crackers or tortilla chips.
Makes 6 to 8 servings

Great Substitutes: If your family doesn't like guacamole, try substituting 1 cup TACO BELL® HOME ORIGINALS® Refried Beans.

Cheesy Stuffed Eggs

6 hard-cooked eggs
1/4 cup EASY CHEESE® Sharp Cheddar Pasteurized
　　Process Cheese Spread
2 tablespoons KRAFT® Mayonnaise
2 tablespoons GREY POUPON® Dijon Mustard
2 tablespoons finely chopped parsley
　　Additional EASY CHEESE® Pasteurized Process
　　　Cheese Spread, for garnish
　　Chopped pimientos, for garnish

1. Halve eggs lengthwise. Scoop yolks into bowl; set egg white halves aside.

2. Mash yolks; blend in cheese spread, mayonnaise, mustard and parsley. Spoon or pipe mixture into egg white halves. Cover; refrigerate until serving time.

3. Serve topped with additional cheese spread and pimientos if desired. *Makes 12 appetizers*

Caponata

1 pound eggplant, cut into 1/2-inch cubes
3 large cloves garlic, minced
1/4 cup olive oil
1 can (14-1/2 ounces) DEL MONTE® Dried
　　Tomatoes with Basil, Garlic & Oregano
1 medium green pepper, finely chopped
1 can (2-1/4 ounces) sliced ripe olives, drained
2 tablespoons lemon juice
1 teaspoon dried basil, crushed
1 baguette French bread, cut into 1/4-inch slices

1. Cook eggplant and garlic in oil in large skillet over medium heat 5 minutes. Season with salt and pepper, if desired.

2. Stir in remaining ingredients except bread. Cook, uncovered, 10 minutes or until thickened.

3. Cover and chill. Serve with bread.
Makes approximately 4-1/2 cups

Festive Cocktail Meatballs

(Pictured below)

1-1/2 pounds ground beef
1 cup MINUTE® Rice
1 can (8 ounces) crushed pineapple in juice
1/2 cup finely shredded carrot
1/3 cup chopped onion
1 egg, slightly beaten
1 teaspoon ground ginger
1 bottle (8 ounces) prepared French dressing
2 tablespoons soy sauce

MIX ground beef, rice, pineapple, carrot, onion, egg and ginger in medium bowl. Form 1-inch meatballs. Place on greased baking sheets. Bake at 400°F for 15 minutes or until browned.

MEANWHILE, mix together dressing and soy sauce. Serve meatballs with dressing mixture.
Makes 50 to 60 meatballs

Chocolate Swizzle Nog

2 cups milk
1 (14-ounce) can EAGLE® BRAND Sweetened Condensed Milk (NOT evaporated milk)
2 tablespoons unsweetened cocoa powder
1/2 teaspoon vanilla or peppermint extract
Whipped cream or whipped topping

1. In medium saucepan over medium heat, combine milk, Eagle Brand and cocoa. Heat through, stirring constantly. Remove from heat; stir in vanilla.

2. Serve warm in mugs; top with whipped cream. Store covered in refrigerator. *Makes 4 servings*

Helpful Hint

If you want to trim the fat in any Eagle® Brand recipe, just use Eagle® Brand Fat Free or Low Fat Sweetened Condensed Milk instead of the original Eagle® Brand.

Festive Cocktail Meatballs

Spicy Marinated Shrimp

(Pictured at right)

1 green onion, finely chopped
2 tablespoons olive oil
2 tablespoons fresh lemon juice
2 tablespoons prepared horseradish
2 tablespoons ketchup
1 tablespoon finely chopped chives
1 teaspoon TABASCO® brand Pepper Sauce
1 clove garlic, minced
1 teaspoon Dijon mustard
    Salt to taste
2 pounds medium shrimp, cooked, peeled and
    deveined

Combine all ingredients except shrimp in large bowl. Add shrimp and toss to coat. Cover; chill 4 to 6 hours or overnight. Place shrimp mixture in serving bowl; serve with toothpicks.   *Makes 30 to 40 shrimp*

Cheesy Quesadillas

(Pictured on page 6)

1/2 pound ground beef
  1 medium onion, chopped
1/4 teaspoon salt
  1 can (4.5 ounces) chopped green chilies,
      drained
  1 jar (26 to 28 ounces) RAGÚ® Hearty
      Robusto!™ Pasta Sauce
  8 (6-1/2-inch) flour tortillas
  1 tablespoon olive or vegetable oil
  2 cups shredded Cheddar and/or mozzarella
      cheese (about 8 ounces)

1. Preheat oven to 400°F. In 12-inch skillet, brown beef with onion and salt over medium-high heat; drain. Stir in chilies and 1/2 cup Ragú Pasta Sauce; set aside.

2. Evenly brush one side of 4 tortillas with half of the oil. On cookie sheets, arrange tortillas, oil-side down. Evenly top with 1/2 of the cheese, beef filling, then remaining cheese. Top with remaining 4 tortillas, then brush tops with remaining oil.

3. Bake 10 minutes or until cheese is melted. To serve, cut each quesadilla into 4 wedges. Serve with remaining sauce, heated.   *Makes 4 servings*

Hot Broccoli Dip

1 (1-1/2-pound) round sourdough bread loaf
1/2 cup finely chopped celery
1/2 cup chopped red pepper
1/4 cup finely chopped onion
  2 tablespoons butter or margarine
  1 pound (16 ounces) VELVEETA® Pasteurized
      Prepared Cheese Product, cut up
  1 (10-ounce) package frozen chopped broccoli,
      thawed, drained
1/4 teaspoon dried rosemary leaves, crushed

Cut slice from top of bread loaf; remove center, leaving 1-inch shell. Cut removed bread into bite-size pieces. Cover shell with top. Place on cookie sheet with bread pieces. Bake at 350°F, 15 minutes or until hot. In large skillet, sauté celery, pepper and onion in butter. Reduce heat to low. Add prepared cheese product; stir until melted. Stir in remaining ingredients; heat thoroughly, stirring constantly. Spoon into bread loaf. Serve hot with toasted bread pieces and vegetable dippers.

Makes 6 to 8 servings

MICROWAVE DIRECTIONS: Prepare bread loaf as directed. Combine celery, pepper, onion and butter in 2-quart microwave-safe bowl. Microwave on HIGH 1 minute. Add remaining ingredients; microwave on HIGH 5 to 6 minutes or until hot, stirring after 3 minutes. Spoon into bread loaf. Serve hot with toasted bread pieces and vegetable dippers.

Helpful Hint

Prepare cut-up vegetable dippers ahead of serving time. Slice vegetables, such as carrots, celery and zucchini as desired. Place the carrots and celery in separate bowls; cover the vegetables with cold water. Refrigerate until ready to use. Place zucchini sticks in a small resealable plastic food storage bag and refrigerate until ready to use.

Tangy Pineapple Fondue

(Pictured at right)

1 (8-ounce) can crushed pineapple in its own
    juice, undrained
1 cup apple juice
1/4 cup A.1.® Steak Sauce
1/4 cup firmly packed light brown sugar
1 tablespoon cornstarch
1 medium pineapple, cut into chunks
1 (10.7-ounce) package prepared pound cake,
    cut into 1-inch cubes
1 pint strawberries, halved
1 large Granny Smith apple, cored and cut into
    chunks

Mix crushed pineapple, apple juice, steak sauce, brown sugar and cornstarch in small saucepan until blended. Cook and stir over medium heat until boiling; reduce heat. Simmer 1 minute; keep warm.

Alternately thread pineapple chunks and cake cubes onto 16 (10-inch) metal skewers. Grill kabobs over medium heat until lightly toasted, about 3 to 5 minutes, turning occasionally. Remove pineapple chunks and cake cubes from skewers; arrange on large platter with remaining fruit. Serve with warm sauce for dipping.
Makes 16 servings

Helpful Hint

To prevent cut apples from browning when exposed to air, brush the cut sides with a small amount of lemon or other citrus juice. Or, place the pieces in lemon water, a mixture of six parts water and one part lemon juice.

Easy Vegetable Squares

2 (8-ounce) cans refrigerated crescent rolls
    (16 rolls)
1 (8-ounce) package cream cheese, softened
1 (3-ounce) package cream cheese, softened
1/3 cup mayonnaise or salad dressing
1 teaspoon dried dill weed
1 teaspoon buttermilk salad dressing mix (1/4 of
    0.4-ounce package)
3 cups desired toppings (suggestions follow)
1 cup shredded Wisconsin Cheddar, Mozzarella,
    or Monterey Jack cheese

For crust, unroll crescent rolls and pat into 15-1/2×10-1/2×2-inch baking pan. Bake according to package directions. Cool.

Meanwhile, in a small mixing bowl stir together cream cheese, mayonnaise, dill weed, and salad dressing mix. Spread evenly over cooled crust. Sprinkle with desired toppings and shredded Cheddar, Mozzarella or Monterey Jack cheese.
Makes 32 appetizer servings

Topping Options: Finely chopped broccoli, cauliflower or green pepper; seeded and chopped tomato; thinly sliced green onion, black olives or celery; or shredded carrots.

Favorite recipe from **Wisconsin Milk Marketing Board**

Hot Spiced Cider

2 quarts apple cider
2/3 cup KARO® Light or Dark Corn Syrup
3 cinnamon sticks
1/2 teaspoon whole cloves
1 lemon, sliced
    Cinnamon sticks and lemon slices (optional)

1. In medium saucepan combine cider, corn syrup, cinnamon sticks, cloves and lemon slices.

2. Bring to boil over medium-high heat. Reduce heat; simmer 15 minutes. Remove spices.

3. If desired, garnish each serving with a cinnamon stick and lemon slice.
Makes about 10 servings

Wisconsin Wings

(Pictured at right)

18 RITZ® Crackers, finely crushed (about 3/4 cup
  crumbs)
1/3 cup KRAFT® Grated Parmesan Cheese
  1 teaspoon dried oregano leaves
1/2 teaspoon garlic powder
1/2 teaspoon paprika
1/8 teaspoon coarse ground black pepper
  2 pounds chicken wings, split and tips removed
1/3 cup GREY POUPON® Dijon Mustard

1. Mix cracker crumbs, Parmesan cheese, oregano,
garlic powder, paprika and pepper in shallow dish;
set aside.

2. Coat chicken wing pieces with mustard; roll in
crumb mixture to coat. Place on greased baking
sheet.

3. Bake at 350°F for 35 to 40 minutes or until golden
brown, turning pieces over halfway through baking
time. Serve warm.   *Makes 12 servings*

Tip: Crush crackers quickly by placing them in a
sealed plastic food storage bag, then running a
rolling pin over the bag to pulverize them.

Peach Fizz

3 fresh California peaches, peeled, halved, pitted
  and sliced
1 can (6 ounces) pineapple juice
1/4 cup frozen limeade or lemonade concentrate
1/4 teaspoon almond extract
  Finely crushed ice
3 cups club soda, chilled

Add peaches to food processor or blender. Process
until smooth to measure 2 cups purée. Stir in
pineapple juice, limeade and almond extract. Fill
12-ounce glasses 2/3 full with crushed ice. Add
1/3 cup peach base to each. Top with club soda.
Stir gently. Serve immediately.   *Makes 6 servings*

Favorite recipe from **California Tree Fruit
Agreement**

Golden Harvest Punch

4 cups MOTT'S® Apple Juice
4 cups orange juice
3 liters club soda
1 quart orange sherbet
5 pound bag ice cubes (optional)

Combine apple juice, orange juice and club soda in
punch bowl. Add scoops of sherbet or ice.
                    Makes 25 servings

Ortega® Green Chile Guacamole

(Pictured on page 6)

2 medium very ripe avocados, seeded, peeled
  and mashed
1/2 cup (4-ounce can) ORTEGA® Diced Green
  Chiles
2 large green onions, chopped
2 tablespoons olive oil
1 teaspoon lime juice
1 clove garlic, finely chopped
1/4 teaspoon salt
  Tortilla chips

COMBINE avocados, chiles, green onions, olive oil,
lime juice, garlic and salt in medium bowl. Cover;
refrigerate for at least 1 hour. Serve with chips.
                    Makes 2 cups dip

Tip: This all-time favorite dip can be used in tacos,
burritos, tamales, chimichangas or combined with
Ortega® Salsa Prima™ for a spicy salad dressing.

Helpful Hint

*Firm avocados require additional
ripening at home. To speed
ripening, put avocados in a
paper bag. Store them at room
temperature for a few days until
they yield to gentle pressure,
then use them promptly or
refrigerate them.*

Salads

"Red, White and Blue" Mold

(Pictured at left)

2-3/4 cups boiling water
  1 package (4-serving size) JELL-O® Brand Strawberry Flavor
     Gelatin Dessert, or any red flavor
  1 package (4-serving size) JELL-O® Brand Berry Blue Flavor
     Gelatin Dessert
  1 cup cold water
1-1/2 cups sliced strawberries
  1 package (4-serving size) JELL-O® Brand Lemon Flavor
     Gelatin Dessert
  1 pint (2 cups) vanilla ice cream, softened
1-1/2 cups blueberries

STIR 1 cup of the boiling water into each of the red and blue gelatins in separate medium bowls at least 2 minutes until completely dissolved. Stir 1/2 cup of the cold water into each bowl.

PLACE bowl of red gelatin in larger bowl of ice and water. Stir until thickened, about 8 minutes. Stir in strawberries. Pour into 9×5-inch loaf pan. Refrigerate 7 minutes.

MEANWHILE, stir remaining 3/4 cup boiling water into lemon gelatin in medium bowl at least 2 minutes until completely dissolved. Spoon in ice cream until melted and smooth. Spoon over red gelatin in pan. Refrigerate 7 minutes.

MEANWHILE, place bowl of blue gelatin in larger bowl of ice and water. Stir until thickened, about 7 minutes. Stir in blueberries. Spoon over lemon gelatin in pan.

REFRIGERATE 4 hours or until firm. Unmold. Garnish as desired. *Makes 12 servings*

Clockwise from top left: *Italian Rotini Salad (p. 30), Layered Chicken Salad (p. 22), "Red, White and Blue" Mold and Sirloin Citrus Salad (p. 24)*

Fruit Salad with Orange Poppy Seed Dressing

(Pictured at right and on back cover)

1/4 cup orange juice
3 tablespoons cider vinegar
3 tablespoons *French's®* Dijon Mustard
2 tablespoons honey
1 tablespoon *French's®* Worcestershire Sauce
1 teaspoon grated orange peel
1/2 teaspoon salt
1/2 cup canola or corn oil
1 tablespoon poppy seeds
6 cups fruit: such as orange segments; cantaloupe, watermelon and/or honeydew melon balls; blueberries; blackberries; grapes; star fruit and/or strawberry slices; nectarine wedges
Lettuce leaves

To prepare dressing, place juice, vinegar, mustard, honey, Worcestershire, orange peel and salt in blender or food processor. Cover and process until well blended. Gradually add oil in steady stream, processing until very smooth. Stir in poppy seeds.

Arrange fruit on lettuce leaves on large platter. Spoon dressing over fruit just before serving.

Makes 6 side-dish servings
(about 1-1/2 cups dressing)

Coleslaw Supreme

4 cups shredded green cabbage
2 cups shredded red cabbage
1 can (about 8 ounces) sliced peaches, drained and chopped
1/2 cup sliced celery
1/3 cup chopped green onion
1/4 cup chopped peanuts
1/4 cup French dressing
1/2 teaspoon LAWRY'S® Garlic Salt
1/4 teaspoon celery seed

In large bowl, combine all ingredients; mix well. Refrigerate at least 30 minutes.

Makes 4 to 6 servings

Serving Suggestion: Serve with sandwiches and barbecued foods.

Hint: Substitute 1/2 package (16 ounces) preshredded coleslaw mix for the 6 cups shredded cabbage.

Layered Chicken Salad

(Pictured on page 20)

2 cans (14.5 ounces each) CONTADINA® Recipe Ready Diced Tomatoes, undrained
4 cups torn salad greens
2 cups sliced fresh mushrooms
4 cups cubed cooked chicken
1 cup sliced red onion
1 package (16 ounces) frozen peas, thawed
1/2 cup sliced cucumber
1-1/2 cups mayonnaise
1 teaspoon seasoned salt
3/4 teaspoon dried tarragon leaves, crushed
1/8 teaspoon ground black pepper

1. Drain tomatoes, reserving 2 tablespoons juice. Layer ingredients in large salad bowl as follows: greens, mushrooms, drained tomatoes, chicken, onion, peas and cucumber.

2. Combine mayonnaise, reserved juice, seasoned salt, tarragon and pepper in small bowl; blend well.

3. Spread mayonnaise mixture over top of salad; cover with plastic wrap. Chill for several hours or overnight. *Makes 6 to 8 servings*

Honey of a Dressing

1/3 cup red wine vinegar
1/3 cup honey
1 teaspoon crushed dried oregano leaves
1/2 teaspoon salt
1/8 teaspoon ground red pepper

Combine vinegar and honey in small bowl; mix well. Stir in remaining ingredients.

Makes about 3/4 cup dressing

Favorite recipe from **National Honey Board**

Fruit Salad with Orange Poppy Seed Dressing

Spiral Pasta Salad

(Pictured at right)

8 ounces tri-color spiral pasta, cooked according to package directions
1 can (12 ounces) STARKIST® Tuna, drained and broken into chunks
1 cup slivered pea pods
1 cup chopped yellow squash or zucchini
1 cup asparagus cut into 2-inch pieces
1/2 cup slivered red onion
1/2 cup sliced pitted ripe olives

DIJON VINAIGRETTE
1/3 cup white wine vinegar
1/4 cup olive or vegetable oil
2 tablespoons water
2 teaspoons Dijon mustard
1 teaspoon dried basil, crushed
1/4 teaspoon pepper
Lettuce leaves

For salad, rinse pasta in cool water; drain well. In a large bowl toss together pasta, tuna, pea pods, squash, asparagus, onion and olives. For dressing, in a shaker jar combine remaining ingredients except lettuce. Cover and shake until well blended. Pour over salad; toss well. Serve on lettuce-lined plates.

Makes 5 servings

Great American Potato Salad

3/4 cup MIRACLE WHIP® Salad Dressing
1 teaspoon KRAFT® Pure Prepared Mustard
1/2 teaspoon celery seed
1/2 teaspoon salt
1/8 teaspoon pepper
4 cups cubed cooked potatoes
2 hard-cooked eggs, chopped
1/2 cup chopped onion
1/2 cup celery slices
1/2 cup chopped sweet pickle

• MIX salad dressing, mustard and seasonings in large bowl. Add remaining ingredients; mix lightly. Cover; refrigerate several hours or until chilled.

Makes 6 servings

Sirloin Citrus Salad

(Pictured on page 20)

1 pound boneless beef top sirloin steak,* cut 1 inch thick
Citrus Vinaigrette (recipe follows)
1 tablespoon olive oil
Salt (optional)
4 cups torn romaine lettuce
2 oranges, peeled and separated into segments
1/4 cup walnuts, toasted
Sliced strawberries (optional)

*Recipe may also be prepared using beef top round steak cut 1 inch thick or flank steak.

Prepare Citrus Vinaigrette; reserve. Cut beef steak into 1/8-inch-thick strips; cut each strip in half. Heat oil in large nonstick skillet over medium-high heat. Add 1/2 of the beef; stir-fry 1 to 2 minutes. Remove with slotted spoon; season with salt to taste, if desired. Repeat with remaining beef. Toss lettuce, beef and oranges in large bowl. Sprinkle with walnuts. Drizzle with Citrus Vinaigrette. Garnish with strawberries, if desired. Serve immediately.

Makes 4 servings

Citrus Vinaigrette: Thoroughly combine 2 tablespoons *each* orange juice and red wine vinegar, 1 tablespoon olive oil, 2 teaspoons honey and 1-1/4 teaspoons Dijon mustard.

Favorite recipe from **North Dakota Beef Commission**

Helpful Hint

Potatoes and pasta can be dressed with either a vinaigrette-type dressing or a creamy mayonnaise-type dressing. Add a vinaigrette dressing to hot potatoes and pasta if you want them to absorb more dressing for added flavor. Cool the mixture before adding other vegetables or herbs. Mayonnaise should be combined with room temperature ingredients to prevent the mayonnaise from separating.

Caramel Apple Salad

(Pictured below)

3 Granny Smith or other green apples, diced
3 red apples, diced
6 bars (2.07 ounces each) chocolate-covered caramel peanut nougat, chopped
1 tub (8 ounces) COOL WHIP® Whipped Topping, thawed

MIX apples and chopped candy bars in large serving bowl until well blended. Gently stir in whipped topping.

REFRIGERATE until ready to serve.

Makes 20 servings

Caramel Apple Salad

24-Hour Ham Fiesta Salad

1 avocado, chopped
1/4 cup mayonnaise or salad dressing
2 tablespoons diced canned green chilies
2 tablespoons lemon juice
1 clove garlic, minced
1/2 teaspoon chili powder
1/4 teaspoon salt
4 cups torn iceberg, Boston or Bibb lettuce
1/2 cup (2 ounces) shredded Monterey Jack cheese with jalapeño peppers
1 cup red kidney beans, rinsed and drained
1-1/2 cups chopped HILLSHIRE FARM® Ham
2 tomatoes, cut into thin wedges
1/2 cup sliced pitted black olives
3/4 cup slightly crushed tortilla chips

In blender or food processor, combine avocado, mayonnaise, chilies, lemon juice, garlic, chili powder and salt. Cover and blend until smooth; set aside.

Place lettuce in bottom of large salad bowl. Layer cheese, beans, Ham, tomatoes and olives over lettuce. Spread avocado mixture evenly over top of salad, sealing to edge of bowl. Cover tightly. Chill 4 to 24 hours.

Sprinkle with tortilla chips before serving.

Makes 4 servings

Italian Pasta Salad

3 cups (8 ounces) tri-color rotini, cooked, drained
2 cups broccoli flowerets
1 (8-ounce) bottle KRAFT® House Italian Dressing
1 cup KRAFT® 100% Grated Parmesan Cheese
1/2 cup chopped red pepper
1/2 cup pitted ripe olives
1/2 cup sliced red onion

TOSS all ingredients. Refrigerate until chilled.

Makes 8 servings

Santa Fe Potato Salad

Santa Fe Potato Salad

(Pictured above)

5 medium white potatoes
1/2 cup vegetable oil
1/4 cup red wine vinegar
1 package (1.0 ounce) LAWRY'S® Taco Spices & Seasonings
1 can (7 ounces) whole kernel corn, drained
2/3 cup sliced celery
2/3 cup shredded carrots
2/3 cup chopped red or green bell pepper
2 cans (2-1/4 ounces each) sliced black olives, drained
1/2 cup chopped red onion
2 tomatoes, wedged and halved

In large saucepan, cook potatoes in boiling water to cover until tender, about 40 minutes; drain. Cool slightly; cut into cubes. In small bowl, combine oil, vinegar and Taco Spices & Seasonings. Add to warm potatoes and toss gently to coat. Cover; refrigerate at least 1 hour. Gently fold in remaining ingredients. Refrigerate until thoroughly chilled.

Makes 10 servings

Serving Suggestion: Serve in lettuce-lined bowl with hamburgers or deli sandwiches.

> ### *Helpful Hint*
>
> *At home, store potatoes in a cool, dark, dry, well-ventilated place. Do not refrigerate potatoes. It is important to protect potatoes from light which can cause them to turn green and lose quality.*

Confetti Barley Salad

(Pictured at right)

4 cups water
1 cup dry pearl barley
1/3 cup GREY POUPON® Dijon Mustard
1/3 cup olive oil
1/4 cup red wine vinegar
2 tablespoons chopped parsley
2 teaspoons chopped fresh rosemary leaves *or*
   1/2 teaspoon dried rosemary leaves
2 teaspoons grated orange peel
1 teaspoon sugar
1-1/2 cups diced red, green or yellow bell peppers
1/2 cup sliced green onions
1/2 cup sliced pitted ripe olives
   Fresh rosemary and orange and tomato slices,
   for garnish

1. Heat water and barley to a boil in 3-quart saucepan over medium-high heat; reduce heat. Cover; simmer for 45 to 55 minutes or until tender. Drain and cool.

2. Whisk mustard, oil, vinegar, parsley, rosemary, orange peel and sugar in small bowl until blended; set aside.

3. Mix barley, bell peppers, green onions and olives in large bowl. Stir in mustard dressing, tossing to coat well. Refrigerate several hours to blend flavors. To serve, spoon barley mixture onto serving platter; garnish with rosemary and orange and tomato slices. *Makes 6 to 8 servings*

Warm Spinach and Rice Chicken Salad

3 TYSON® Individually Fresh Frozen® Boneless,
   Skinless Chicken Breasts
1 box UNCLE BEN'S® COUNTRY INN® Chicken
   Flavored Rice
1/2 cup Italian salad dressing, divided
6 cups chopped fresh spinach
3 plum tomatoes, chopped
1/4 cup pitted black olives, cut into halves

PREP: CLEAN: Wash hands. Remove protective ice glaze from frozen chicken by holding under cool running water 1 to 2 minutes. Brush chicken with 2 teaspoons salad dressing. CLEAN: Wash hands.

COOK: Grill or broil chicken, turning once, 20 to 25 minutes or until internal juices run clear. (Or insert instant-read meat thermometer in thickest part of chicken. Temperature should read 170°F.) Meanwhile, prepare rice according to package directions. Combine hot cooked rice with remaining salad dressing, spinach, tomatoes and olives; stir until spinach is lightly wilted.

SERVE: Place rice mixture on individual serving plates; top with sliced chicken.

CHILL: Refrigerate leftovers immediately.
Makes 3 servings

Holiday Fruit Salad

3 packages (3 ounces each) strawberry flavor
   gelatin
3 cups boiling water
2 ripe DOLE® Bananas
1 package (16 ounces) frozen strawberries
1 can (20 ounces) DOLE® Crushed Pineapple
1 package (8 ounces) cream cheese, softened
1 cup dairy sour cream or plain yogurt
1/4 cup sugar
   Crisp DOLE® Lettuce leaves

• In large bowl, dissolve gelatin in boiling water. Slice bananas into gelatin mixture. Add frozen strawberries and undrained pineapple. Reserve half of the mixture at room temperature. Pour remaining mixture into 13×9-inch pan. Refrigerate 1 hour or until firm.

• In mixer bowl, beat cream cheese with sour cream and sugar; spread over chilled layer. Gently spoon reserved gelatin mixture on top. Refrigerate until firm, about 2 hours.

• Cut into squares; serve on lettuce-lined salad plates. Garnish with additional pineapple and mint leaves, if desired. *Makes 12 servings*

Salmon Broccoli Waldorf Salad

(Pictured at right)

> 1 bag (16 ounces) BIRDS EYE® frozen Broccoli
>   Cuts
> 1 large red delicious apple, chopped
> 1/4 cup thinly sliced green onions
> 1/2 cup bottled creamy roasted garlic, ranch or
>   blue cheese dressing
> 1 can (14-3/4 ounces) salmon, drained and
>   flaked

• In large saucepan, cook broccoli according to package directions; drain and rinse under cold water in colander.

• In large bowl, toss together broccoli, apple, onions and dressing. Gently stir in salmon; add pepper to taste.   *Makes 4 servings*

Pasta Waldorf Salad: Increase salad dressing to 1 cup. Add 6 cups cooked pasta with the salmon.

Serving Suggestion: Serve over lettuce leaves and sprinkle with toasted nuts.

Birds Eye® Idea: To prevent cut fruits and vegetables, such as apples and artichokes, from discoloring, try rubbing them with a lemon wedge.

Helpful Hint

Apples will keep in a cool, dry place for a week or two. For longer storage, place apples in a plastic bag and store in the refrigerator. Apples in good condition can last up to six weeks in the refrigerator. Check them occasionally and discard any that have begun to spoil as one rotten apple can ruin them all.

Roasted Chicken Salad

> 2 cups cubed TYSON® Roasted Chicken
> 4 tablespoons mayonnaise
> 3 tablespoons sweet relish
> 1 tablespoon finely chopped celery
> 1 teaspoon finely chopped onion
> 1/4 teaspoon mustard
> 1/8 teaspoon garlic salt
>   Salt and black pepper to taste

PREP: CLEAN: Wash hands. In large bowl, combine all ingredients except chicken; mix well. Stir in chicken. Cover; chill thoroughly.

SERVE: Serve on a bed of lettuce leaves, in tomato cups or on kaiser rolls.

CHILL: Refrigerate leftovers immediately.
                                                Makes 2 servings

Italian Rotini Salad

(Pictured on page 20)

> 1 (12-ounce) package tricolor rotini pasta,
>   cooked and drained
> 1 pound cooked roast beef, cut into 1/2-inch
>   cubes (about 2 cups)
> 2 cups broccoli flowerettes, blanched
> 4 ounces provolone cheese, cut into 1/4-inch
>   cubes (about 1 cup)
> 1/3 cup purchased roasted red peppers, coarsely
>   chopped
> 3/4 cup A.1.® Original or A.1.® BOLD & SPICY
>   Steak Sauce
> 1/2 cup purchased Italian dressing

Mix pasta, beef, broccoli, cheese and peppers in large nonmetal bowl. Blend steak sauce and dressing in small bowl; pour over pasta mixture, tossing to coat well. Refrigerate at least 1 hour before serving.   *Makes 8 servings*

Tag-Along Fruit Salad

(Pictured at right)

CITRUS DRESSING
- 1/4 cup CRISCO® Oil*
- 1/4 cup orange juice
- 2 tablespoons lemon juice
- 2 tablespoons sugar
- 1/4 teaspoon paprika

SALAD
- 1 can (20 ounces) pineapple chunks in juice, drained
- 2 cups seedless green grapes
- 1-1/4 cups miniature marshmallows**
- 1 cup fresh orange sections
- 1 cup sliced fresh pears***
- 1 cup sliced banana***
- 1 cup sliced apples***
- 1/2 cup maraschino cherries, halved

Use your favorite Crisco Oil product.

**1 cup raisins may be substituted for marshmallows.*

***Add Citrus Dressing to sliced pears, bananas and apples immediately after slicing to prevent discoloration.*

1. *For dressing,* combine oil, orange juice, lemon juice, sugar and paprika in container with tight-fitting lid. Shake well.

2. Combine pineapple, grapes, marshmallows, oranges, pears, banana, apples and cherries in large bowl. Shake dressing. Pour over salad. Toss to coat. Cover. Refrigerate. Garnish, if desired.

Makes 10 servings

Helpful Hint

To ripen bananas, store them at room temperature. To speed the ripening process, place the bananas in an unsealed paper bag at room temperature. To prevent ripe bananas from spoiling, store them, tightly wrapped, in the refrigerator. Although the peel will turn brown, the fruit will retain its creamy color for about three days.

German Potato Salad

- 4 cups sliced peeled Colorado potatoes
- 4 slices bacon
- 3/4 cup chopped onion
- 1/4 cup sugar
- 3 tablespoons all-purpose flour
- 1-1/2 teaspoons salt
- 1 teaspoon celery seeds
- 1/4 teaspoon black pepper
- 1 cup water
- 3/4 cup vinegar
- 2 hard-cooked eggs, chopped

Cook potatoes in boiling water until tender; drain. Meanwhile, cook bacon in medium skillet. Drain on paper towels; cool and crumble. Cook and stir onion in drippings until tender. Combine sugar, flour, salt, celery seeds and pepper; blend in water and vinegar. Stir into onion in skillet; heat until bubbly. Pour over combined potatoes, bacon and eggs; toss. Serve immediately.   *Makes 6 servings*

Favorite recipe from **Colorado Potato Administrative Committee**

Blue Cheese Chicken Salad

- 1 can (14-1/2 ounces) DEL MONTE® Diced Tomatoes with Garlic & Onion
- 1/2 pound boneless, skinned chicken breasts, cut into strips
- 1/2 teaspoon dried tarragon
- 6 cups torn assorted lettuces
- 1/2 medium red onion, thinly sliced
- 1/2 medium cucumber, thinly sliced
- 1/3 cup crumbled blue cheese
- 1/4 cup Italian dressing

1. Drain tomatoes, reserving liquid. In large skillet, cook reserved liquid until thickened, about 5 minutes, stirring occasionally.

2. Add chicken and tarragon; cook until chicken is no longer pink, stirring frequently.

3. Cool. In large bowl, toss chicken and tomato liquid with remaining ingredients.

Makes 4 servings

Cobb Salad

Sweet Potato Salad

1-1/2 pounds sweet potatoes or yams, scrubbed, quartered lengthwise and cut crosswise into 3/4 inch pieces (2 large or 3 medium potatoes)
   3 tablespoons cider vinegar
   2 tablespoons sweet pickle relish
   2 teaspoons Dijon mustard
1/2 teaspoon salt
1/4 teaspoon freshly ground black pepper
1/2 cup CRISCO® Oil*
   2 scallions or green onions, trimmed and thinly sliced
1/4 cup finely chopped red bell pepper (optional)

*Use your favorite Crisco Oil product.

1. Place potato slices in vegetable steamer.** Place steamer over 2 inches of water in large pot. Cover pot. Bring to a boil on high heat. Steam potatoes 10 to 15 minutes, or until tender when pierced with knife. Remove steamer from pan. Peel potatoes when cool enough to handle (about 10 minutes). Place potatoes in mixing bowl.

2. Combine vinegar, pickle relish, mustard, salt and pepper in jar with tight-fitting lid. Shake well. Add oil. Shake well again.

3. Toss warm potatoes with dressing. Add scallions and red pepper, if used. Serve at room temperature or chilled.   *Makes 4 servings*

**Boil for 10 to 15 minutes if steamer is not available.

Note: This salad can be made up to one day in advance and refrigerated, tightly covered with plastic wrap.

Cobb Salad

(Pictured at left)

   4 skinless boneless chicken breast halves, cooked, cooled
2/3 cup vegetable oil
1/3 cup HEINZ® Distilled White or Apple Cider Vinegar
   1 clove garlic, minced
   2 teaspoons dried dill weed
1-1/2 teaspoons granulated sugar
1/2 teaspoon salt
1/4 teaspoon pepper
   8 cups torn salad greens, chilled
   1 large tomato, diced
   1 medium green bell pepper, diced
   1 small red onion, chopped
3/4 cup crumbled blue cheese
   6 slices bacon, cooked, crumbled
   1 hard-cooked egg, chopped

Shred chicken into bite-size pieces. For dressing, in jar, combine oil, vinegar, garlic, dill, sugar, salt and pepper; cover and shake vigorously. Pour 1/2 cup dressing over chicken; toss well to coat. Toss greens with remaining dressing. Line each of 4 large individual salad bowls with greens; mound chicken mixture on greens. Arrange mounds of tomato, green pepper, onion, cheese, bacon and egg on greens.   *Makes 4 servings*

Mixed Spring Vegetable Salad

8 ounces fresh green beans, trimmed and cut into thirds
1 medium zucchini (about 1/2 pound), sliced
1 large tomato *or* 3 plum tomatoes, sliced
3 tablespoons FILIPPO BERIO® Extra Virgin Olive Oil
3 tablespoons lemon juice
Salt and freshly ground black pepper

Cook or steam green beans and zucchini separately until tender-crisp. Cover; refrigerate until chilled. Stir in tomato. Just before serving, drizzle olive oil and lemon juice over vegetables. Season to taste with salt and pepper. *Makes 6 servings*

Helpful Hint

Salad greens and raw vegetables are best served very cold to ensure crispness. Serving green salads on chilled plates will help keep them crisp.

Beef Caesar Salad

(Pictured below)

2 pounds boneless beef sirloin, top round or flank steak
1 bottle (8 ounces) creamy Caesar salad dressing
1/4 cup *French's*® Worcestershire Sauce
1/4 cup *French's*® Dijon Mustard
1 teaspoon grated lemon peel
2 tablespoons lemon juice
8 cups romaine lettuce leaves, washed and torn

1. Place steak in resealable plastic food storage bag. Combine remaining ingredients *except* lettuce. Pour *3/4 cup* sauce over steak. Seal bag; marinate steak in refrigerator 30 minutes. Reserve remaining sauce for dressing.

2. Broil or grill steak 15 minutes for medium-rare. Let stand 15 minutes. Slice steak; serve with dressing over lettuce. *Makes 8 servings*

Beef Caesar Salad

Orange-Berry Salad

(Pictured at right)

1/2 cup prepared HIDDEN VALLEY® Original
     Ranch® salad dressing
  2 tablespoons orange juice
  1 teaspoon grated orange peel
1/2 cup heavy cream, whipped
  1 can (11 ounces) mandarin orange segments
  2 packages (3 ounces each) strawberry- or
     raspberry-flavored gelatin
  1 can (16 ounces) whole-berry cranberry sauce
1/2 cup walnut pieces
     Mint sprigs
     Whole fresh strawberries and raspberries

In large bowl, whisk together salad dressing, orange juice and peel. Fold in whipped cream; cover and refrigerate. Drain oranges, reserving juice. Add water to juice to measure 3 cups; pour into large saucepan and bring to a boil. Stir in gelatin until dissolved. Cover and refrigerate until partially set. Fold orange segments, cranberry sauce and walnuts into gelatin. Pour into lightly oiled 6-cup ring mold. Cover and refrigerate until firm; unmold. Garnish with mint, fresh strawberries and raspberries. Serve with chilled dressing.   *Makes 8 servings*

Spinach and Fried Chicken Salad

1-1/2 pounds boneless, skinless chicken breasts, cut
       into 1-1/2-inch nuggets (or purchase the
       chicken breast nuggets already cut up in the
       supermarket poultry section)
  3/4 teaspoon salt, divided
  1/2 teaspoon freshly ground black pepper, divided
  1/2 cup all-purpose flour
    3 eggs
  1/4 cup milk
    1 cup bread crumbs
  3/4 pound fresh spinach, stems discarded, rinsed
       and dried
    2 carrots, peeled and cut into thin strips
    1 red bell pepper, seeds and ribs removed, and
       cut into thin slices
  1/2 red onion, peeled and cut into thin rings
    3 tablespoons honey
    4 tablespoons Dijon mustard
  1/3 cup cider vinegar
    2 cups CRISCO® Oil,* divided

*Use your favorite Crisco Oil product.

1. Rinse chicken. Pat dry. Season chicken with 1/2 teaspoon salt and 1/4 teaspoon pepper. Place flour on sheet of plastic wrap or wax paper. Beat eggs with milk. Place bread crumbs on another sheet of plastic wrap or wax paper.

2. Dip chicken pieces in flour. Shake to remove any excess. Dip in egg mixture. Roll in bread crumbs. Refrigerate 10 minutes.

3. Arrange vegetables in large shallow bowl. Combine honey, mustard, vinegar, 1/4 teaspoon salt and 1/4 teaspoon pepper in jar with a tight-fitting lid. Shake well. Add 1 cup oil. Shake well again.

4. Heat remaining 1 cup oil in 10 or 12-inch skillet to 375°F. Add chicken pieces. Do not crowd skillet. Fry 6 to 8 minutes, or until chicken is no longer pink in center. Turn, if necessary, with slotted spoon. Remove from pan with slotted spoon. Drain on paper towels.

5. Arrange chicken on top of vegetables. Drizzle dressing over all. Serve immediately.
          Makes 4 servings

Note: The salad is even quicker to make if you purchase the already breaded chicken nuggets in the poultry case or the freezer case. The dressing can be made up to 2 days in advance and refrigerated.

Helpful Hint

To easily unmold a gelatin salad, follow these steps: First, use moistened fingertips to gently pull the gelatin away from the edges of the mold. Next, dip the mold into a large bowl of warm water for about 10 seconds, immersing it almost to the rim. Then cover the mold with a wet serving plate and invert. (The wet plate lets you slide the gelatin to the center.) Finally, give the mold a gentle shake or two. If it does not slide out at once, return it to the bowl of water for a few seconds.

Orange-Berry Salad

Border Black Bean Chicken Salad

(Pictured at right)

1/4 cup olive oil, divided
1-1/2 pounds boneless skinless chicken breasts, cut into 2-inch strips
1 clove garlic, minced
1/2 jalapeño pepper, seeded and finely chopped
1-1/4 teaspoons salt, divided
4 cups torn romaine lettuce
1 can (15 to 16 ounces) black beans, drained and rinsed
1 cup peeled and seeded cucumber cubes
1 cup red bell pepper strips
1 cup chopped tomato
1/2 cup chopped red onion
1/3 cup tomato vegetable juice
2 tablespoons fresh lime juice
1/2 teaspoon ground cumin
1/2 cup chopped pecans, toasted
Fresh parsley, for garnish

Heat 2 tablespoons oil in large skillet over medium heat until hot. Add chicken; stir-fry 2 minutes or until no longer pink in center. Add garlic, jalapeño and 3/4 teaspoon salt; stir-fry 30 seconds. Combine chicken mixture, lettuce, beans, cucumber, red pepper, tomato and onion in large salad bowl. Combine tomato juice, lime juice, remaining 2 tablespoons oil, cumin and remaining 1/2 teaspoon salt in small jar with lid; shake well. Add to skillet; heat over medium heat until slightly warm. Pour warm dressing over chicken mixture; toss to coat. Sprinkle with pecans. Garnish with parsley. Serve immediately. *Makes 4 servings*

Favorite recipe from **National Chicken Council**

Helpful Hint

To make a tossed salad ahead of time, place the firm vegetables and the meat or poultry in the bottom of the salad bowl and add the salad dressing. Top with the salad greens but do not toss. Chill this mixture for up to two hours. Toss the salad just before serving.

Classic Vinaigrette

1/4 cup FILIPPO BERIO® Olive Oil
1/4 cup white wine vinegar
1 teaspoon Dijon mustard
1/4 teaspoon sugar
Salt and freshly ground black pepper

In small screw-topped jar, combine olive oil, vinegar, mustard and sugar. Shake vigorously until well blended. Season to taste with salt and pepper. Store dressing in refrigerator up to 1 week. Shake well before using. *Makes about 1/2 cup dressing*

Garlic Vinaigrette: Add 1 small, halved clove garlic to oil mixture; let stand 1 hour. Discard garlic. Store and serve as directed.

Lemon Vinaigrette: Use 2 tablespoons lemon juice in place of vinegar; add finely grated peel of 1 small lemon to oil mixture. Store and serve as directed.

Herb Vinaigrette: Whisk 1 to 2 tablespoons finely chopped fresh herbs (basil, oregano or chives) into dressing just before serving. Store and serve as directed.

Shallot Vinaigrette: Add 1 to 2 finely chopped shallots to oil mixture; let stand at least 1 hour before serving. Store and serve as directed.

Cranberry Waldorf Fluff

1-1/2 cups cranberries, finely chopped
1 cup JET-PUFFED® Miniature Marshmallows
1/4 cup sugar
1-1/2 cups finely chopped apple
1/2 cup MIRACLE WHIP® Salad Dressing
1/4 cup chopped walnuts
1/8 teaspoon ground cinnamon

• MIX cranberries, miniature marshmallows and sugar. Cover; refrigerate several hours or until chilled.

• ADD remaining ingredients; mix lightly.
Makes 6 servings

Crab Salad with Chiles and Cilantro

(Pictured at right)

> 1 cup sour cream
> 1/2 cup (4-ounce can) ORTEGA® Diced Green
>   Chiles
> 1/2 cup finely chopped onion
> 1/4 cup chopped fresh cilantro
> 2 tablespoons lime juice
> 1/2 teaspoon salt
> 1 pound fresh or chopped imitation crabmeat

COMBINE sour cream, chiles, onion, cilantro, lime juice and salt in medium bowl; add crabmeat. Toss to coat well; cover. Chill for at least 1 hour.

SERVE with crackers or tortilla chips or use as a topping for salads.   *Makes 4 servings*

Tip: Serve this salad atop ORTEGA® Tostada Shells or inside ORTEGA® Taco Shells for an easy elegant seafood meal!

Mexican Pork Salad

> 1 pound boneless pork loin, cut into
>   3×1/2×1/4-inch strips
> 4 cups shredded lettuce
> 1 medium orange, peeled, sliced and quartered
> 1 medium avocado, peeled, seeded and diced
> 1 small red onion, sliced and separated into rings
> 1 tablespoon vegetable oil
> 1 teaspoon chili powder
> 3/4 teaspoon salt
> 1/2 teaspoon dried oregano leaves, crushed
> 1/4 teaspoon ground cumin

Place lettuce on serving platter. Arrange orange, avocado and red onion over lettuce. Heat oil in large skillet; add chili powder, salt, oregano and cumin. Add pork loin strips and stir-fry over medium-high heat 5 to 7 minutes or until pork is tender. Spoon hot pork strips over lettuce mixture. Serve immediately.   *Makes 4 servings*

Favorite recipe from **National Pork Producers Council**

Ambrosia Mold

> 1 can (8 ounces) crushed pineapple in juice,
>   undrained
> 2 cups boiling water
> 1 package (8-serving size) or 2 packages
>   (4-serving size) JELL-O® Brand Orange Flavor
>   Gelatin Dessert
> 1-3/4 cups thawed COOL WHIP® Whipped Topping
> 1 can (11 ounces) mandarin orange segments,
>   drained
> 1-1/2 cups miniature marshmallows
> 1/2 cup BAKER'S® ANGEL FLAKE® Coconut
>   (optional)

DRAIN pineapple, reserving juice. Add cold water to juice to make 1 cup.

STIR boiling water into gelatin in large bowl at least 2 minutes until completely dissolved. Stir in measured pineapple juice and water. Refrigerate about 1-1/4 hours or until slightly thickened (consistency of unbeaten egg whites).

STIR in whipped topping with wire whisk until smooth. Refrigerate 10 minutes or until mixture will mound. Stir in pineapple, oranges, marshmallows and coconut. Spoon into 6-cup mold.

REFRIGERATE 3 hours or until firm. Unmold.
   Makes 10 servings

Easy Parmesan Dressing

> 1/4 cup red or white wine vinegar
> 2 teaspoons jarred minced garlic *or* 1 large clove
>   garlic, peeled and minced
> 1/2 teaspoon Italian seasoning
> 1/2 teaspoon salt
> 1/4 teaspoon freshly ground black pepper
> 1/4 cup grated Parmesan cheese
> 3/4 cup CRISCO® Oil*

*Use your favorite Crisco Oil product.

Combine vinegar, garlic, Italian seasoning, salt and pepper in jar with tight-fitting lid. Shake well. Add Parmesan cheese and Crisco Oil. Shake well again.
   Makes 1 cup dressing

Side Dishes

Cheesy Potato Pancakes
(Pictured at left)

1-1/2 quarts prepared instant mashed potatoes, cooked dry and
      cooled
1-1/2 cups (6 ounces) shredded Wisconsin Colby or Muenster
      cheese
    4 eggs, lightly beaten
1-1/2 cups all-purpose flour, divided
   3/4 cup chopped fresh parsley
   1/3 cup chopped fresh chives
1-1/2 teaspoons dried thyme, rosemary or sage leaves
    2 eggs, lightly beaten

1. In large bowl, combine potatoes, cheese, 4 beaten eggs,
3/4 cup flour and herbs; mix well. Cover and refrigerate at
least 4 hours before molding and preparing.

2. To prepare, form 18 (3-inch) patties. Dip patties in 2 beaten
eggs and dredge in remaining 3/4 cup flour. Cook each patty in
nonstick skillet over medium heat 3 minutes per side or until
crisp, golden brown and heated through.

3. Serve warm with eggs or omelets, or serve with sour cream
and sliced pan-fried apples or applesauce.
Makes 4 to 6 servings

Variation: Substitute Wisconsin Cheddar or Smoked Cheddar
for Colby or Muenster.

Favorite recipe from **Wisconsin Milk Marketing Board**

Clockwise from top left: *Acorn Squash Filled
with Savory Spinach (p. 52), Roasted Mixed
Vegetables (p. 64), Garlic Black Beans & Rice
(p. 50) and Cheesy Potato Pancakes*

Campbell's® Parmesan Potatoes

Pearls o' Barley Salad

2 cups water
1/2 cup **QUAKER® Scotch Brand Pearled Barley** *
1/8 teaspoon salt (optional)
1/2 cup (2 ounces) cubed Swiss cheese
1/2 medium cucumber, cut into matchstick pieces
1/3 cup sliced celery
1/3 cup sliced green onions
1/4 cup finely chopped fresh parsley
1/4 cup sliced green olives
1/4 cup Italian salad dressing
1/4 teaspoon dried oregano leaves, crumbled
1/8 to 1/4 teaspoon ground red pepper
    Fresh spinach leaves, rinsed, trimmed
2 to 3 tablespoons dry roasted sunflower kernels

*Quick Method: Use 2/3 cup QUAKER® Scotch Brand Quick Pearled Barley; decrease simmer time to 10 to 12 minutes. Proceed as directed.

Bring water to a boil; stir in barley and salt. Cover and reduce heat. Simmer 45 to 50 minutes or until tender. Remove from heat; let stand 5 minutes.

In large bowl, combine barley with remaining ingredients except spinach leaves and sunflower kernels. Cover and refrigerate several hours or overnight. Serve on large platter or individual plates lined with spinach leaves. Sprinkle with sunflower kernels. Garnish with tomato wedges, if desired.

Makes 8 servings

Campbell's® Parmesan Potatoes

(Pictured above)

1 can (10-3/4 ounces) **CAMPBELL'S® Condensed Cheddar Cheese Soup**
1/2 cup milk
1/2 cup grated Parmesan cheese
1/4 teaspoon pepper
4 medium white potatoes, cut in 1-inch pieces (about 4 cups)
1 can (2.8 ounces) *French's® Taste Toppers™* **French Fried Onions (1-1/3 cups)**

1. In greased shallow 2-quart baking dish mix soup, milk, cheese and pepper. Stir in potatoes and *1/2 can Taste Toppers*.

2. Bake at 400°F for 40 minutes or until potatoes are tender. Sprinkle remaining *Taste Toppers* over potatoes. Bake 5 minutes more or until *Taste Toppers* are golden.

Makes 4 servings

Helpful Hint

Barley, native to Ethiopia, is available in several forms. Hulled barley has only the husk removed so that its bran and germ are intact. Scotch barley and barley grits have been further processed by grinding or cracking. All of these forms can be found in health food stores. The most common form of barley is pearled, meaning that it has been polished many times to remove the bran and most of the germ. Pearled barley is also available in a quick-cooking form. Pearl and quick-cooking barley are readily available in supermarkets.

Carrots with Raisin Sauce

(Pictured below)

2 bags (16 ounces each) BIRDS EYE® frozen
    Sliced Carrots
1/4 cup brown sugar
1 tablespoon cornstarch
2/3 cup water
1/2 cup raisins
2 teaspoons cider vinegar

• Cook carrots according to package directions;
drain.

• Blend brown sugar and cornstarch in small
saucepan.

• Add remaining ingredients; cook over low heat
until sauce is thickened and raisins are plump.

• Toss carrots with sauce.

Makes about 8 servings

Easy Picnic Beans

1 small onion, chopped
2 teaspoons vegetable oil
2 cans (16 ounces each) HEINZ® Vegetarian
    Beans
1/4 cup HEINZ® Tomato Ketchup
1 tablespoon brown sugar (optional)
1 teaspoon HEINZ® Worcestershire Sauce

Sauté onion in oil until tender. Stir in beans and
remaining ingredients. Simmer, uncovered, 10 to
15 minutes or until desired consistency, stirring
occasionally.

Makes 4 servings (about 3-1/2 cups)

Carrots with Raisin Sauce

Garden-Style Risotto

(Pictured at right)

1 can (14-1/2 ounces) low-sodium chicken broth
1-3/4 cups water
2 cloves garlic, finely chopped
1 teaspoon dried basil leaves, crushed
1/2 teaspoon dried thyme leaves, crushed
1 cup arborio rice
2 cups packed DOLE® Fresh Spinach, torn
1 cup DOLE® Shredded Carrots
3 tablespoons grated Parmesan cheese

• Combine broth, water, garlic, basil and thyme in large saucepan. Bring to boil; meanwhile, prepare rice.

• Place rice in large, nonstick saucepan sprayed with vegetable cooking spray. Cook and stir rice over medium heat about 2 minutes or until rice is browned.

• Pour 1 cup boiling broth into saucepan with rice; cook, stirring constantly, until broth is almost absorbed (there should be some broth left).

• Add enough broth to barely cover rice; continue to cook, stirring constantly, until broth is almost absorbed. Repeat adding broth and cooking, stirring constantly, until broth is almost absorbed, about 15 minutes; add spinach and carrots with the last addition of broth.

• Cook 3 to 5 minutes more, stirring constantly, or until broth is almost absorbed and rice and vegetables are tender. Do not overcook. (Risotto will be saucy and have a creamy texture.) Stir in Parmesan cheese. Serve warm.

Makes 6 servings

Garden Pilaf: Substitute 1 cup uncooked long grain white rice for arborio rice and reduce water from 1-3/4 cups to 1/2 cup. Prepare broth as directed above with 1/2 cup water; meanwhile, brown rice as directed above. Carefully add browned rice into boiling broth. Reduce heat to low; cover and cook 15 minutes. Stir in vegetables; cover and cook 4 to 5 minutes longer or until rice and vegetables are tender. Stir in Parmesan cheese.

Kentucky Cornbread & Sausage Stuffing

1/2 pound BOB EVANS® Original Recipe Roll
    Sausage
3 cups fresh bread cubes, dried or toasted
3 cups crumbled prepared cornbread
1 large apple, peeled and chopped
1 small onion, chopped
1 cup chicken or turkey broth
2 tablespoons minced fresh parsley
1 teaspoon salt
1 teaspoon rubbed sage or poultry seasoning
1/4 teaspoon black pepper

Crumble sausage into small skillet. Cook over medium heat until browned, stirring occasionally. Place sausage and drippings in large bowl. Add remaining ingredients; toss lightly. Use to stuff chicken loosely just before roasting. Or, place stuffing in greased 13×9-inch baking dish. Add additional broth for moister stuffing, if desired. Bake in 350°F oven 30 minutes. Leftover stuffing should be removed from bird and stored separately in refrigerator. Reheat thoroughly before serving.

Makes enough stuffing for 5-pound chicken,
8 side-dish servings

Serving Suggestion: Double this recipe to stuff a 12- to 15-pound turkey.

Helpful Hint

If you're planning to stuff a chicken or turkey, don't do it until just before roasting to avoid growth of harmful bacteria. Baking the stuffing in a separate dish instead of inside the chicken or turkey will reduce the cooking time for the bird, as the oven heat can circulate more freely when the cavity is not full.

Asian Rice & Squash Noodles with Peanut Sauce

(Pictured at right)

2 boxes UNCLE BEN'S® COUNTRY INN®
   Oriental Fried Rice
1 medium spaghetti squash
4 tablespoons peanut butter
2 tablespoons soy sauce
1 tablespoon grated gingerroot
6 green onions, sliced

PREP: CLEAN: Wash hands. Carefully cut squash in half lengthwise. Remove seeds and place flesh-side down in microwavable baking dish. Add 1/2 cup water; cover with plastic wrap.

COOK: Microwave squash at HIGH 9 to 10 minutes or until skin is firm but soft. Remove from dish and allow to cool until safe to handle. Spoon out flesh into bowl (it will come out in strands like spaghetti). Meanwhile, prepare rice according to package directions. In large nonstick skillet, combine peanut butter, soy sauce and gingerroot. Heat slightly; add squash and rice. Mix thoroughly.

SERVE: Garnish rice and squash mixture with green onions.

CHILL: Refrigerate leftovers immediately.

Makes 6 servings

Tip: Squash can also be baked in 350°F oven 45 to 50 minutes (omit plastic wrap).

Baked Tomatoes

4 medium tomatoes
1/2 cup dry bread crumbs
1 tablespoon chopped fresh basil *or* 1 teaspoon
   dried basil leaves
1/2 teaspoon salt
1/2 teaspoon dried oregano leaves
1/4 teaspoon freshly ground black pepper
1 clove garlic, minced (optional)
2 tablespoons FILIPPO BERIO® Olive Oil

Preheat oven to 375°F. Cut off stems and a thin slice from bottom of each tomato. Cut each tomato in half crosswise. Place in shallow casserole, cut side up. In small bowl, mix bread crumbs, basil, salt, oregano, pepper and garlic, if desired. Stir in olive oil. Spoon evenly over tomatoes. Bake 15 to 20 minutes or until lightly browned.

Makes 8 servings

Garlic Mashed Potatoes

6 medium all-purpose potatoes, peeled, if
   desired, and cut into chunks (about
   3 pounds)
Water
1 envelope LIPTON® RECIPE SECRETS® Garlic
   Mushroom Soup Mix*
1/2 cup milk
1/2 cup margarine or butter

*Also terrific with Lipton® Recipe Secrets® Savory Herb with Garlic, Onion-Mushroom, Onion or Golden Onion Soup Mix.

In 4-quart saucepan, cover potatoes with water; bring to a boil over high heat.

Reduce heat to low and simmer, uncovered, 20 minutes or until potatoes are very tender; drain.

Return potatoes to saucepan, then mash. Stir in remaining ingredients.   *Makes about 8 servings*

Creamed Spinach à la Lawry's®

4 slices bacon, finely chopped
1 cup finely chopped onions
1/4 cup all-purpose flour
2 teaspoons LAWRY'S® Seasoned Salt
1/2 teaspoon LAWRY'S® Seasoned Pepper
1/2 teaspoon LAWRY'S® Garlic Powder with
   Parsley
1-1/2 to 2 cups milk
2 packages (10 ounces each) frozen spinach,
   cooked and drained

In medium skillet, fry bacon until almost crisp. Add onions to bacon and cook until onions are tender, about 10 minutes. Remove from heat. Add flour, Seasoned Salt, Seasoned Pepper and Garlic Powder with Parsley; mix well. Gradually add milk, starting with 1-1/2 cups, and stir over low heat until thickened. Add spinach and mix thoroughly. If too thick, add additional milk.   *Makes 8 servings*

Serving Suggestion: Serve with prime ribs of beef.

*Asian Rice & Squash Noodles with
Peanut Sauce*

Hot Hush Puppies

(Pictured at right)

WESSON® Vegetable Oil
1-3/4 cups cornmeal
1/2 cup all-purpose flour
1 teaspoon sugar
3/4 teaspoon baking soda
1/2 teaspoon salt
1/2 teaspoon garlic salt
1/2 cup diced onion
1/2 to 1 (4-ounce) can diced jalapeño peppers
1 cup buttermilk
1 egg, beaten

Fill a large deep-fry pot or electric skillet to half its depth with Wesson® Oil. Heat oil to 400°F. Meanwhile, in a large bowl, sift together cornmeal, flour, sugar, baking soda, salt and garlic salt; blend well. Add onion and jalapeño peppers; stir until well blended. In small bowl, combine buttermilk and egg; add to dry ingredients. Stir until batter is moist and *all* ingredients are combined. Working in small batches, carefully drop batter by heaping tablespoons into hot oil. Fry until golden brown, turning once during frying. Remove and drain on paper towels. Serve with your favorite salsa or dipping sauce. *Makes 36 hush puppies*

Eggplant Pasta Bake

4 ounces bow-tie pasta
1 pound eggplant, diced
1 clove garlic, minced
1/4 cup olive oil
1-1/2 cups shredded Monterey Jack cheese
1 cup sliced green onions
1/2 cup grated Parmesan cheese
1 can (14-1/2 ounces) DEL MONTE® Diced Tomatoes with Basil, Garlic & Oregano

1. Preheat oven to 350°F. Cook pasta according to package directions; drain.

2. Cook eggplant and garlic in oil in large skillet over medium-high heat until tender.

3. Toss eggplant with cooked pasta, 1 cup Jack cheese, green onions and Parmesan cheese.

4. Place in greased 9-inch square baking dish. Top with undrained tomatoes and remaining 1/2 cup Jack cheese. Bake 15 minutes or until heated through. *Makes 6 servings*

Garlic Black Beans & Rice

(Pictured on page 42)

2 cups UNCLE BEN'S® NATURAL SELECT™ Chicken & Herb Rice
1 tablespoon olive oil
1/2 cup diced onion
1/2 cup diced green bell pepper
4 cloves garlic, minced
1 can (15 ounces) black beans, rinsed and drained
1 tablespoon fresh lime juice

COOK: CLEAN: Wash hands. In medium saucepan, heat oil until hot. Sauté onion, bell pepper and garlic 1 minute. Add rice and cook according to package directions. When rice has finished cooking, stir in beans and lime juice.

SERVE: Serve warm.

CHILL: Refrigerate leftovers immediately.

Makes 4 servings

Company Potatoes

1 package (28 ounces) frozen O'Brien potatoes, thawed
1 teaspoon LAWRY'S® Seasoned Salt
1/2 teaspoon LAWRY'S® Seasoned Pepper
1 can (10-3/4 ounces) condensed cream of chicken soup
1 cup dairy sour cream
1 cup (4 ounces) shredded cheddar cheese
1 cup seasoned dry bread crumbs
1/4 cup butter, melted

In 13×9×2-inch baking dish, combine first 6 ingredients and spread evenly. In small bowl, combine bread crumbs and butter; sprinkle over potatoes. Bake in 350°F oven 45 to 60 minutes. *Makes 8 servings*

Serving Suggestion: Serve with baked ham and peas.

Hot Hush Puppies

Saucy Skillet Potatoes

1 tablespoon margarine or butter
1 cup chopped onion
1/2 cup HELLMANN'S® or BEST FOODS® Real or
    Light Mayonnaise or Low Fat Mayonnaise
    Dressing
1/3 cup cider vinegar
1 tablespoon sugar
1 teaspoon salt
1/4 teaspoon freshly ground pepper
4 medium potatoes, cooked, peeled and sliced
1 tablespoon chopped parsley
1 tablespoon crumbled cooked bacon or real
    bacon bits

1. In large skillet, melt margarine over medium heat. Add onion; cook 2 to 3 minutes or until tender-crisp.

2. Stir in mayonnaise, vinegar, sugar, salt and pepper. Add potatoes; cook, stirring constantly, 2 minutes or until hot (do not boil).

3. Sprinkle with parsley and bacon.

Makes 6 to 8 servings

Brussels Sprouts with Almonds and Dijon Mustard

1 box (10 ounces) BIRDS EYE® frozen Brussels
    Sprouts
1-1/2 tablespoons sliced almonds (toasted, if desired)
1-1/2 teaspoons butter or margarine, melted
1-1/2 teaspoons Dijon mustard

• Cook brussels sprouts according to package directions; drain.

• Combine with remaining ingredients; mix well. Serve hot with salt and pepper to taste.

Makes 3 to 4 servings

Acorn Squash Filled with Savory Spinach

(Pictured on page 42)

4 small acorn squash
2 tablespoons FILIPPO BERIO® Olive Oil
1 (10-ounce) package frozen chopped spinach,
    thawed and drained
1 cup ricotta cheese
1 tablespoon grated Parmesan cheese
1/4 teaspoon freshly ground black pepper
1/8 teaspoon salt
1/8 teaspoon ground nutmeg

Preheat oven to 325°F. Cut squash crosswise in half. Scoop out seeds and fibers; discard. Brush insides and outsides of squash halves with olive oil. Place in large shallow roasting pan. Bake, uncovered, 35 to 40 minutes or until tender when pierced with fork.

In medium bowl, combine spinach, ricotta cheese, Parmesan cheese, pepper, salt and nutmeg. Spoon equal amounts of spinach mixture into squash halves. Bake, uncovered, an additional 10 to 15 minutes or until heated through.

Makes 8 servings

To Microwave: Prepare squash as directed above. Place in large shallow microwave-safe dish. Cover with vented plastic wrap. Microwave on HIGH (100% power) 10 to 12 minutes or until squash are softened, rotating dish halfway through cooking. Prepare filling; spoon into squash halves. Cover with vented plastic wrap; microwave on HIGH 6 to 8 minutes or until filling is hot and squash are tender when pierced with fork.

Helpful Hint

Softening an acorn squash in your microwave can make slicing it much easier. First, pierce the rind in a few places to allow steam to escape. Next, place the squash in the microwave and heat at HIGH 1 to 2 minutes. Let it stand about 3 minutes and then slice it as the recipe directs.

Barley with Corn and Red Pepper

Barley with Corn and Red Pepper

(Pictured above)

1/2 cup WISH-BONE® Italian Dressing*
1 medium red pepper, chopped
1/2 cup chopped onion
1 cup uncooked pearled barley
1-3/4 cups chicken broth
1-1/4 cups water
2 tablespoons finely chopped coriander
 (cilantro) or parsley
1 tablespoon lime juice
1/2 teaspoon ground cumin
1/8 teaspoon ground black pepper
1 can (7 ounces) whole kernel corn, drained

Also terrific with WISH-BONE® Robusto Italian or Lite Italian Dressing.

In large saucepan, heat Italian dressing and cook red pepper with onion over medium heat, stirring occasionally, 5 minutes or until tender. Stir in barley and cook, stirring constantly, 1 minute. Stir in broth, water, coriander, lime juice, cumin and pepper. Simmer covered 50 minutes or until barley is done. (Do not stir while simmering.) Stir in corn.

Makes about 6 servings

Helpful Hint

Coriander, or cilantro, is a green leafy herb with a distinctive flavor and a pungent aroma. Cilantro looks very much like flat-leaf parsley.

Zesty Zucchini and Bean Casserole

(Pictured at right)

    3 tablespoons olive oil, divided
3/4 pound yellow squash, quartered lengthwise
        and sliced
3/4 pound zucchini, quartered lengthwise and
        sliced
    1 red onion, chopped
    1 can (19 ounces) white cannellini beans or
        chick-peas, drained and rinsed
    1 tub (15 ounces) marinara sauce
1/4 cup chopped fresh basil *or* 2 teaspoons dried
        basil leaves
    3 tablespoons *French's*® Hearty Deli Brown
        Mustard, divided
1-1/2 cups fresh whole wheat bread crumbs*

To make fresh bread crumbs, place 3 slices of day-old bread in food processor; process until fine crumbs form.

1. Preheat oven to 400°F. Heat 1 tablespoon oil in large skillet over medium-high heat. Add squash, zucchini and onion. Cook 5 to 8 minutes or until crisp-tender, stirring often. Stir in beans, marinara sauce, basil and 1 tablespoon mustard. Bring to a boil. Spoon into shallow 2-quart baking dish.

2. Mix bread crumbs, remaining 2 tablespoons oil and 2 tablespoons mustard in small bowl; toss to coat evenly. Sprinkle bread crumbs over vegetables. Bake 20 minutes or until heated through and vegetables are tender.   *Makes 8 servings*

Classic Macaroni and Cheese

    2 cups elbow macaroni
    3 tablespoons butter or margarine
1/4 cup chopped onion (optional)
    2 tablespoons all-purpose flour
1/2 teaspoon salt
1/8 teaspoon pepper
    2 cups milk
    2 cups (8 ounces) SARGENTO® Chef Style or
        Fancy Mild Cheddar Shredded Cheese,
        divided

Cook macaroni according to package directions; drain. In medium saucepan, melt butter and cook onion, if desired, about 5 minutes or until tender. Stir in flour, salt and pepper. Gradually add milk and cook, stirring occasionally, until thickened. Remove

from heat. Add 1-1/2 cups cheese and stir until melted. Mix cheese sauce with cooked macaroni. Place in 1-1/2-quart casserole; top with remaining 1/2 cup cheese. Bake at 350°F 30 minutes or until bubbly and cheese is golden.   *Makes 6 servings*

Asparagus with Citrus Dressing

(Pictured on front cover)

    1 pound asparagus
    3 tablespoons orange juice
    2 tablespoons lemon juice
    2 teaspoons granulated sugar
    1 teaspoon Dijon mustard
1/2 teaspoon salt
1/4 teaspoon freshly ground black pepper
1/3 cup CRISCO® Oil*
    2 finely chopped hard-cooked egg yolks,
        optional

Use your favorite Crisco Oil product.

1. Snap off the tough asparagus ends. Discard. Peel ends of spears with sharp paring knife, if desired.

2. Pour 2 inches of water into large skillet. Bring to a boil on high heat. Add asparagus. Boil uncovered 3 to 5 minutes, or until crisp-tender. Drain well. Transfer asparagus to serving plate.

3. Combine orange juice, lemon juice, sugar, mustard, salt and pepper in jar with tight-fitting lid. Shake well. Add oil. Shake well again. Pour as much dressing as wanted over warm asparagus. Sprinkle with egg yolk, if desired. Serve at room temperature.
          Makes 4 servings

> ### *Helpful Hint*
> *When purchasing fresh asparagus, select firm, smooth green stems with tightly closed tips; tips that are open are a sign of age. Look for even green shading along the whole length; ends that become lighter in color may be a sign of toughness.*

Zesty Zucchini and Bean Casserole

Brown Rice and Green Onion Pilaf

2 tablespoons FILIPPO BERIO® Olive Oil
3/4 cup chopped green onions, white part and about 2 inches of green part
1 cup uncooked brown rice
2-1/2 cups chicken broth, defatted (see note) or water
1/2 teaspoon salt
Additional green onion, green part sliced into matchstick-size strips (optional)

In heavy medium saucepan, heat olive oil over medium heat until hot. Add chopped green onions; cook and stir 3 to 4 minutes or until wilted. Add rice; cook and stir 3 to 4 minutes to coat rice with oil. Add chicken broth and salt; stir well. Bring to a boil. Cover; reduce heat to low and simmer 40 minutes or until rice is tender and liquid is absorbed. Garnish with additional green onion, if desired. *Makes 4 to 5 servings*

Note: To defat chicken broth, refrigerate can of broth for at least 1 hour. Open can; use a spoon to lift out any solid fat floating on surface of broth.

Glazed Brussels Sprouts and Pearl Onions

2 cups fresh brussels sprouts, trimmed
1 (10-ounce) package frozen pearl onions
3 tablespoons FLEISCHMANN'S® Original Margarine
1 pinch sugar
Salt and freshly ground black pepper, to taste

1. Cook brussels sprouts in boiling salted water in large saucepan for 8 minutes. Add onions; cook for 4 minutes. Drain.

2. Melt margarine in large skillet over medium-high heat.

3. Add brussels sprouts mixture and sugar; cook and stir until onions are golden. Season with salt and pepper to taste. *Makes 4 servings*

Country Corn Bake

2 cans (11 ounces each) Mexican-style whole kernel corn, drained*
1 can (10-3/4 ounces) condensed cream of potato soup
1/2 cup milk
1/2 cup thinly sliced celery
1-1/3 cups *French's® Taste Toppers*™ French Fried Onions, divided
1/2 cup (2 ounces) shredded Cheddar cheese
2 tablespoons bacon bits**

Or, substitute 1 bag (16 ounces) frozen whole kernel corn, thawed and drained.

**Or, substitute 2 slices crumbled, cooked bacon.*

Preheat oven to 375°F. Combine corn, soup, milk, celery, *2/3 cup **Taste Toppers**,* cheese and bacon bits in large bowl. Spoon mixture into 2-quart square baking dish. Cover; bake 30 minutes or until hot and bubbly. Stir; sprinkle with remaining *2/3 cup **Taste Toppers***. Bake, uncovered, 3 minutes or until **Taste Toppers** are golden.

Makes 4 to 6 servings

Helpful Hint

To prepare celery, separate the ribs from the stalk. Rinse the ribs under cold running water to remove any sand and dirt, rubbing lightly with a fingertip to loosen the soil at the bottom of the rib. Trim off and save the leaves to flavor soups or stocks. Darker green outer ribs may be stringy, but do not discard them. Remove the strings and use the ribs for cooking. To remove tough strings, snap a short piece from the top of a rib that has been trimmed below the joint, leaving the short piece attached. Pull the piece down the length of the rib. The strings and outer membrane will pull off.

Tart & Tasty Stuffing

(Pictured below)

   2 tablespoons butter or margarine
3/4 cup chopped celery
1/2 cup chopped onion
   1 teaspoon dried thyme leaves
1/4 teaspoon poultry seasoning
1/2 (14-ounce) package dried herb-seasoned
      stuffing cubes
3/4 cup chicken broth
   2 cups frozen unsweetened tart cherries, thawed
      and drained

Melt butter in medium saucepan over medium heat.
Add celery and onion; cook 2 to 3 minutes, or until
tender. Stir in thyme and poultry seasoning. Toss
together celery mixture, stuffing and broth. Gently
stir in cherries. Spoon into lightly greased 2-quart
casserole. Bake, covered, in preheated 350°F oven
30 minutes, or until hot.   *Makes 6 servings*

Favorite recipe from **Cherry Marketing Institute**

Marmalade-Crabapple Beets

1/3 cup KNOTT'S® Light Orange Marmalade
1/3 cup KNOTT'S® Crabapple Jelly
   1 tablespoon butter
   1 teaspoon grated fresh lemon peel
   2 (15.5-ounce) cans whole beets, drained well

1. In medium saucepan, bring Knott's Marmalade,
Knott's Crabapple Jelly, butter and lemon peel to a
boil. Add beets and continue boiling for 5 minutes;
stir often.

2. Remove from heat and let stand 3 minutes before
serving.   *Makes 8 (2-ounce) servings*

Helpful Hint

*Beet juice can stain wood and
plastic cutting boards, wooden
spoons, rubber scrapers and your
hands. Slice beets on a glass
plate and wear disposable plastic
gloves to eliminate staining.*

Tart & Tasty Stuffing

Cheesy Broccoli 'n Mushroom Bake

(Pictured at right)

2 packages (10 ounces each) frozen broccoli spears, thawed
1 can (10-3/4 ounces) condensed cream of mushroom soup
1/2 cup MIRACLE WHIP® Salad Dressing
1/2 cup milk
1 cup KRAFT® Shredded Cheddar Cheese
1/2 cup coarsely crushed croutons

• ARRANGE broccoli in 12×8-inch baking dish.

• WHISK together soup, salad dressing and milk. Pour over broccoli. Sprinkle with cheese and croutons.

• Bake at 350°F for 30 to 35 minutes or until thoroughly heated.   *Makes 6 to 8 servings*

Mixed Vegetable Saucepan Stuffing

1/2 cup *each:* chopped onion, celery, carrot and mushrooms
2 tablespoons margarine or butter
1 (14-1/2-ounce) can lower sodium chicken broth
1/3 cup GREY POUPON® COUNTRY DIJON® Mustard
1/2 teaspoon poultry seasoning
1/4 teaspoon rosemary leaves
5 cups dried bread stuffing cubes
1/3 cup PLANTERS® Walnuts, chopped
2 tablespoons chopped parsley

Sauté onion, celery, carrot and mushrooms in margarine in large saucepan over medium-high heat until tender. Stir in chicken broth, mustard, poultry seasoning and rosemary. Heat mixture to a boil; reduce heat. Cover and simmer for 5 minutes. Add bread cubes, walnuts and parsley, stirring to coat well. Cover; let stand for 5 minutes. Fluff with fork before serving.   *Makes 5 servings*

Herbed Wild Rice

1 tablespoon butter or margarine
3 cups sliced fresh mushrooms
1 cup uncooked wild rice blend
3/4 cup chopped onion
1 can (14-1/2 ounces) chicken broth
1/2 cup water
1 medium tomato, chopped
1 teaspoon dried basil
1 teaspoon dried oregano
1 teaspoon LAWRY'S® Lemon Pepper
3/4 teaspoon LAWRY'S® Garlic Powder with Parsley
1/2 teaspoon LAWRY'S® Seasoned Salt

In large saucepan, heat butter. Add mushrooms, rice and onion and cook over medium-high heat 5 minutes. Add remaining ingredients. Bring to a boil over medium-high heat; reduce heat to low. Cover; simmer 30 minutes or until liquid is absorbed and rice is tender.   *Makes 6 servings*

Serving Suggestion: For extra color, sprinkle finished dish with chopped fresh parsley, if desired.

Sesame Peanut Noodles with Green Onions

1 tablespoon peanut or vegetable oil
1 teaspoon finely chopped garlic
1/4 cup SKIPPY® Peanut Butter
1 teaspoon soy sauce
2-1/4 cups water
1 package LIPTON® Noodles & Sauce—Chicken Flavor
1/2 cup sliced green onions
2 tablespoons sesame seeds, toasted (optional)

In medium saucepan, heat oil and cook garlic over medium heat 30 seconds. Stir in peanut butter and soy sauce; cook until melted. Add water and bring to a boil. Stir in noodles & sauce—chicken flavor, then simmer, stirring frequently, 10 minutes or until noodles are tender. Stir in green onions and 1 tablespoon sesame seeds. To serve, sprinkle with remaining 1 tablespoon sesame seeds.

Makes about 4 servings

Home-Style Baked Beans

(Pictured at right)

2 strips bacon, finely chopped
1 large green or red bell pepper, seeded and chopped
1 small onion, chopped
3 cans (1 pound each) pork and beans
1/2 cup *French's®* Worcestershire Sauce
1/2 cup *French's®* Hearty Deli Brown Mustard
1/2 cup packed brown sugar
  Additional chopped bell pepper
  Shredded cheese

MICROWAVE DIRECTIONS
Place bacon, pepper and onion in microwave-safe 3-quart bowl. Cover loosely with waxed paper. Microwave on HIGH 5 minutes or until bacon is partially cooked. Stir in beans, Worcestershire, mustard and sugar. Microwave, uncovered, on HIGH 20 minutes or until heated through and mixture is slightly thickened, stirring twice. Garnish with additional pepper and cheese. Serve warm.

Makes 8 to 10 side-dish servings

Conventional Oven Directions: Preheat oven to 400°F. Cook and stir bacon, pepper and onion in large skillet over medium heat until bacon is crisp; transfer to 3-quart casserole dish. Stir in remaining ingredients except additional pepper and cheese. Bake 45 to 50 minutes, stirring occasionally. Garnish as directed.

Wild Zucchini Patties

  3/4 cup all-purpose flour
  3/4 teaspoon baking powder
  1/2 teaspoon baking soda
  1/8 teaspoon salt
  3/4 cup buttermilk
  3 teaspoons vegetable oil
1-1/4 cups grated zucchini
  1 cup cooked wild rice
  3/4 cup shredded Parmesan cheese
  1 jar (4-1/2 ounces) mushrooms, finely chopped
  1/2 jar (4 ounces) diced pimiento
  2 teaspoons dried basil leaves
    Vegetable cooking spray

In medium bowl, combine flour, baking powder, baking soda and salt. In small bowl, combine buttermilk and oil; add to dry ingredients, stirring

just until dry ingredients are moistened. Stir in remaining ingredients. Coat large nonstick griddle with cooking spray; place over medium heat until hot. Spoon 2 tablespoons zucchini mixture onto griddle, spreading into 2-inch rounds; cook 3 minutes on each side or until browned.

Makes 18 patties

Favorite recipe from **Minnesota Cultivated Wild Rice Council**

Confetti Corn

  6 medium tomatoes
  2 tablespoons butter or margarine
1/3 cup chopped green onions
1/3 cup chopped red bell pepper
  1 package (10 ounces) frozen corn, thawed
  2 tablespoons vinegar
  2 tablespoons chopped fresh cilantro
  1 teaspoon LAWRY'S® Garlic Salt

Cut 1/4 inch off top of tomatoes. Hollow out, reserving pulp. Chop pulp into chunks; set aside. In medium skillet, heat butter. Add green onions and bell pepper and cook over medium-high heat until tender. Add corn, vinegar, tomato pulp, cilantro and Garlic Salt; mix well. Heat 5 minutes or until flavors are blended. Place tomato shells in baking dish and heat in 350°F oven 5 minutes. Spoon tomato-corn mixture into shells.

Makes 6 servings

Helpful Hint

To chop an onion, peel the skin. Cut the onion in half through the root end with a utility knife. Place the onion half, cut side down, on a cutting board. Cut the onion into slices perpendicular to the root end, holding the onion with your fingers to keep it together. Turn the onion half and cut it crosswise. Repeat with the remaining half.

Home-Style Baked Beans

Vegetables & Wild Rice

Cheesy Mashed Potatoes and Turnips

  2 pounds all-purpose potatoes, peeled
  1 pound turnips, peeled
1/4 cup milk
1/2 cup shredded Cheddar cheese
1/4 cup butter or margarine
  1 teaspoon TABASCO® brand Pepper Sauce
1/2 teaspoon salt

In large saucepan over high heat, combine potatoes and turnips with enough water to cover. Bring to a boil and reduce heat to low; cover and simmer 25 to 30 minutes or until vegetables are tender. Drain. Return vegetables to saucepan; heat over high heat for a few seconds to eliminate any excess moisture, shaking saucepan to prevent sticking.

In small saucepan over medium heat, bring milk to a simmer. In large bowl, mash vegetables. Stir in warmed milk, cheese, butter, TABASCO® Sauce and salt.
Makes 8 servings

Note: This dish may be made up to 2 days in advance and reheated in microwave or double boiler above simmering water.

Vegetables & Wild Rice

(Pictured above)

  1 box UNCLE BEN'S® Long Grain & Wild Rice
    Roasted Garlic
2-1/3 cups water
  2 tablespoons butter or margarine
  1 cup corn, fresh or frozen
  1 medium tomato, chopped
  4 strips bacon, cooked and crumbled
  3 tablespoons chopped green onions

COOK: CLEAN: Wash hands. In medium skillet, combine water, butter, rice and contents of seasoning packet. Bring to a boil. Cover tightly and simmer 15 minutes. Add corn and simmer 15 minutes or until water is absorbed. Stir in tomato and bacon. Sprinkle with green onions.

SERVE: Serve with garlic toast, if desired.

CHILL: Refrigerate leftovers immediately.
Makes 6 servings

Helpful Hint

If turnips are purchased with tops attached, remove and store them separately. Store turnips in a plastic bag in the refrigerator for up to two weeks. Store turnip greens, unwashed, in the refrigerator in a plastic bag for several days. When cooking turnips or turnip greens, do not use aluminum or iron pans; the metal may darken the flesh of the turnips or impart a metallic flavor to the greens.

Swiss Vegetable Medley

(Pictured below)

1 can (10-3/4 ounces) condensed cream of
    mushroom soup
1/3 cup sour cream
1/4 teaspoon ground black pepper
1 bag (16 ounces) frozen vegetable combination,
    such as broccoli, cauliflower and red bell
    pepper, thawed and drained
1-1/3 cups *French's® Taste Toppers™* French Fried
    Onions, divided
1 cup (4 ounces) shredded Swiss cheese, divided

Preheat oven to 350°F. Combine soup, sour cream
and ground pepper in 2-quart shallow baking dish;
stir until well blended. Add vegetables, *2/3 cup*
Taste Toppers and 1/2 cup cheese; mix well.

Cover; bake 30 minutes or until heated through and
vegetables are tender. Stir; sprinkle with remaining
*2/3 cup **Taste Toppers*** and cheese. Bake 5 minutes
or until ***Taste Toppers*** are golden.

Makes 6 servings

Creamy Rice with Bacon

1 clove garlic, minced
1 tablespoon butter or margarine
1 can (14-1/2 ounces) chicken broth
1 package (8 ounces) PHILADELPHIA® Cream
    Cheese, cubed
1 cup long grain rice, uncooked
1/2 cup frozen tiny peas, thawed, drained
2 slices OSCAR MAYER® Bacon, crisply cooked,
    crumbled

COOK and stir garlic in butter in medium saucepan
until tender. Stir in broth. Bring to boil; reduce heat
to low. Add cream cheese; stir until cream cheese is
melted.

STIR in remaining ingredients; cover. Cook for
20 minutes, stirring occasionally. Serve with
Parmesan cheese, if desired.

Makes 4 servings

Swiss Vegetable Medley

Festive Sweet Potato Combo

(Pictured at right)

> 2 cans (15 ounces each) sweet potatoes or yams, drained
> 1-1/3 cups *French's® Taste Toppers*™ French Fried Onions, divided
> 1 large apple, sliced into thin wedges
> 2 cans (8 ounces each) crushed pineapple, undrained
> 3 tablespoons packed light brown sugar
> 3/4 teaspoon ground cinnamon

Preheat oven to 375°F. Grease 2-quart shallow baking dish. Layer sweet potatoes, *2/3 cup **Taste Toppers*** and half of the apple wedges in prepared baking dish.

Stir together pineapple with liquid, sugar and cinnamon in medium bowl. Spoon pineapple mixture over sweet potato mixture. Arrange remaining apple wedges over pineapple layer.

Cover; bake 35 minutes or until heated through. Uncover; sprinkle with remaining *2/3 cup **Taste Toppers***. Bake 3 minutes or until **Taste Toppers** are golden. *Makes 6 servings*

Cheesy Shells

> 1 package (16 ounces) BARILLA® Medium Shells
> 3/4 cup (12 ounces) pasteurized prepared cheese, cubed
> 1 cup heavy whipping cream
> 1 teaspoon garlic powder
> 1 teaspoon dry mustard
> 1 teaspoon paprika
> Salt and pepper

1. Begin cooking pasta shells according to package directions.

2. Meanwhile, heat cheese and cream in medium saucepan over medium heat until cheese melts, stirring frequently. Stir in garlic, mustard and paprika.

3. Drain pasta shells; return to cooking pot. Pour cheese mixture over shells; stir to coat. Add salt and pepper to taste. *Makes 8 servings*

Roasted Mixed Vegetables

(Pictured on page 42)

> 4 large red skin potatoes, cut into wedges (about 2 pounds)
> 3 large carrots, peeled and cut into 1-1/2-inch pieces (about 2 cups)
> 3 large parsnips, peeled and cut into 1-1/2-inch pieces (about 2 cups)
> 2 large onions, cut into wedges
> 1 tablespoon dried rosemary leaves
> 2 teaspoons garlic powder
> 1/4 cup FLEISCHMANN'S® Original Margarine, melted

1. Mix potatoes, carrots, parsnips and onions with rosemary and garlic powder in large bowl.

2. Drizzle with melted margarine, tossing to coat well. Spread in a 13×9×2-inch baking pan.

3. Bake at 450°F for 40 to 45 minutes or until fork-tender, stirring occasionally. *Makes 8 servings*

Wild Rice Apple Side Dish

> 1 cup uncooked wild rice
> 3-1/2 cups chicken broth
> 1/2 teaspoon ground nutmeg
> 1 cup dried apple slices
> 1 cup chopped onion
> 1 jar (4.5 ounces) sliced mushrooms, drained
> 1/2 cup thinly sliced celery

In large saucepan, simmer wild rice, broth and nutmeg 20 minutes. Add remaining ingredients; cover and simmer 20 to 30 minutes, stirring occasionally, until wild rice reaches desired doneness. *Makes 6 servings*

Favorite recipe from **Minnesota Cultivated Wild Rice Council**

Soups

Ravioli Soup

(Pictured at left)

8 ounces sweet Italian sausage, casing removed
1 clove garlic, crushed
2 (14-1/2-ounce) cans lower sodium chicken broth
2 cups water
1 (9-ounce) package frozen miniature cheese-filled ravioli
1 (15-ounce) can garbanzo beans, drained
1 (14-1/2-ounce) can stewed tomatoes
1/3 cup GREY POUPON® Dijon Mustard
1/2 teaspoon dried oregano leaves
1/4 teaspoon coarsely ground black pepper
1 cup torn fresh spinach leaves
Grated Parmesan cheese

1. Brown sausage and cook garlic in 4-quart heavy pot over medium heat until tender, stirring to break up sausage, about 5 minutes. Pour off excess fat; remove sausage mixture from pot and set aside.

2. Heat chicken broth and water to a boil in same pot over medium-high heat. Add ravioli; cook for 4 to 5 minutes or until tender. Stir in beans, stewed tomatoes, sausage mixture, mustard, oregano and pepper; heat through. Stir in spinach and cook until wilted, about 1 minute. Serve topped with Parmesan cheese. *Makes 8 servings*

Clockwise from top left: *Easy Ham & Veg•All®
Chowder (p. 80), Veg•All® Italian Soup (p. 88),
Ravioli Soup and Cheesy Broccoli Soup (p. 82)*

Beef Barley Soup

(Pictured at right)

1/2 pound ground beef
2-1/2 cups water
  1 can (14-1/2 ounces) stewed tomatoes, cut up
  3 medium carrots, sliced
3/4 cup sliced mushrooms
1/2 cup quick barley, uncooked
  2 cloves garlic, minced
  1 teaspoon dried oregano leaves, crushed
1/2 pound (8 ounces) VELVEETA® Pasteurized
    Prepared Cheese Product, cut up
  Salt and pepper

1. Brown meat in large saucepan; drain. Stir in water, tomatoes, carrots, mushrooms, barley, garlic and oregano.

2. Bring to boil. Reduce heat to low; cover. Simmer 10 minutes or until barley is tender.

3. Add Velveeta; stir until melted. Season to taste with salt and pepper.   *Makes 6 (1-cup) servings*

Farmer's Cold Tater Soup

2 to 3 Colorado potatoes, peeled
2 large onions, minced
2 leeks, minced (white parts only)
4 cups water
1 cup canned chicken broth
1 tablespoon butter, melted
1 tablespoon flour
2 cups hot milk*
  Chopped chives for garnish

For a richer soup, replace 1 cup milk with 1 cup half-and-half.

Combine potatoes, onions, leeks and water in large saucepan over high heat. Bring to a boil. Reduce heat to medium-low. Simmer 25 minutes or until potatoes are tender. Process vegetables in blender or food processor until smooth; return to saucepan. Add broth. Combine butter and flour until blended. Stir into potato mixture. Bring to a boil. Boil 1 minute. Stir in hot milk. Cool soup to room temperature; refrigerate until cold. Garnish with chopped chives.   *Makes 4 to 6 servings*

Favorite recipe from **Colorado Potato Administrative Committee**

Creamy Reuben Soup

1/2 cup chopped onion
1/4 cup chopped celery
  3 tablespoons butter or margarine
1/4 cup unsifted flour
  3 cups water
  4 teaspoons beef-flavored bouillon *or* 4 beef
    bouillon cubes
1/2 pound corned beef, shredded
  1 cup FRANK'S® or SNOWFLOSS® Kraut, well
    drained
  3 cups half-and-half
  3 cups (12 ounces) shredded Swiss cheese,
    divided
  6 to 8 slices rye or pumpernickel bread, toasted
    and cut into quarters

1. In large saucepan cook onion and celery in butter until tender.

2. Stir in flour until smooth.

3. Gradually stir in water and bouillon and bring to boil. Reduce heat and simmer uncovered 5 minutes.

4. Add corned beef, kraut, half-and-half and 1 cup cheese.

5. Cook over low heat for 30 minutes until slightly thickened, stirring frequently.

6. Ladle into 8 oven-proof bowls. Top each with toasted bread and 1/4 cup cheese. Broil until cheese melts. Serve immediately.   *Makes 8 servings*

Helpful Hint

A good soup pot is one that is heavy and conducts and distributes heat evenly. Copper is the ideal metal, though its cost puts it out of range for most cooks. Good alternatives are Calphalon, aluminum, or stainless steel with a copper or aluminum core.

Chicken Vegetable Soup

(Pictured at right)

1 bag SUCCESS® Rice
5 cups chicken broth
1-1/2 cups chopped uncooked chicken
1 cup sliced celery
1 cup sliced carrots
1/2 cup chopped onion
1/4 cup chopped fresh parsley
1/2 teaspoon black pepper
1/2 teaspoon dried thyme leaves, crushed
1 bay leaf
1 tablespoon lime juice

Prepare rice according to package directions.

Combine broth, chicken, celery, carrots, onion, parsley, pepper, thyme and bay leaf in large saucepan or Dutch oven. Bring to a boil over medium-high heat, stirring once or twice. Reduce heat to low; simmer 10 to 15 minutes or until chicken is no longer pink in center. Remove bay leaf; discard. Stir in rice and lime juice. Garnish, if desired.

Makes 4 servings

Minestrone Soup

1 can (14-1/2 ounces) Italian-style stewed tomatoes
2 cans (14-1/2 ounces each) low-sodium chicken broth
1/2 cup uncooked fine egg noodles or tiny pasta for soup
1 can (15-1/2 ounces) red kidney beans
1 bag (16 ounces) BIRDS EYE® frozen Mixed Vegetables
Grated Parmesan cheese

• Drain tomatoes, reserving liquid. Chop tomatoes into bite-size pieces.

• Bring broth, noodles, tomatoes and reserved liquid to boil in large saucepan over high heat. Cook, uncovered, over medium-high heat 6 minutes.

• Add beans and vegetables. Cover and cook 5 minutes or until heated through.

• Sprinkle individual servings with cheese.

Makes 4 servings

Tuscan Pasta and Beans

1 package (8 ounces) pasta, uncooked
2 to 3 teaspoons minced garlic
1 tablespoon vegetable oil
1 can (14-1/2 ounces) chicken broth
1 box (10 ounces) BIRDS EYE® frozen Chopped Spinach
1 can (15 ounces) white beans, drained
Crushed red pepper flakes
Grated Parmesan cheese

• In large saucepan, cook pasta according to package directions; drain.

• In large skillet, sauté garlic in oil over medium-high heat until garlic is tender. Add broth and spinach; cook according to spinach package directions.

• Stir in beans and pasta. Cook, uncovered, over medium-high heat until heated through.

• Season with pepper flakes and cheese to taste.

Makes 4 servings

Variation: Add 1/2 pound Italian sausage, casings removed and sliced, with the garlic. Cook until sausage is browned. Continue as directed.

Serving Suggestion: Serve with crusty Italian bread to soak up this flavorful broth.

Helpful Hint

To quickly peel a clove of garlic, place the clove on a cutting board. Slightly crush the clove under the flat side of a chef's knife blade; peel away the skin with your fingers. One medium clove of garlic yields about 1/2 teaspoon minced garlic.

Nacho Cheese Soup

(Pictured at right)

1 package (about 5 ounces) dry au gratin
    potatoes
1 can (about 15 ounces) whole kernel corn,
    undrained
2 cups water
1 cup salsa
2 cups milk
1-1/2 cups (6 ounces) SARGENTO® Taco Blend
    Shredded Cheese
1 can (about 2 ounces) sliced ripe olives, drained
    Tortilla chips (optional)

In large saucepan, combine potatoes, dry au gratin
sauce mix, corn with liquid, water and salsa. Heat to
a boil; reduce heat. Cover and simmer 25 minutes or
until potatoes are tender, stirring occasionally. Add
milk, cheese and olives. Cook until cheese is melted
and soup is heated through, stirring occasionally.
Garnish with tortilla chips. *Makes 6 servings*

Chilled Carrot Soup

2 tablespoons vegetable oil
1 cup chopped onion (1 large)
1-1/2 teaspoons curry powder
3-1/2 cups low sodium chicken broth
1 pound carrots, sliced (4 cups)
2 stalks celery, sliced (1 cup)
1 bay leaf
1/2 teaspoon ground cumin
1/2 teaspoon TABASCO® brand Pepper Sauce
1 tablespoon cornstarch
2 cups yogurt

Heat oil in large saucepan over medium-high heat;
cook and stir onion and curry powder over medium
heat 3 to 5 minutes or until onion is translucent.
Reduce heat to low. Add chicken broth, carrots,
celery, bay leaf, cumin and TABASCO® Sauce; mix
well. Bring to a boil over high heat; reduce heat to
low and simmer 25 minutes or until vegetables are
tender. Remove bay leaf. Spoon mixture, in several
batches, into container of electric blender or food
processor; process until smooth. Add cornstarch
to yogurt and stir until well blended. Gradually add
yogurt to soup mixture, stirring after each addition.
Chill before serving. Serve with additional
TABASCO® Sauce, if desired. *Makes about 7 cups*

Hearty Minestrone Gratiné

1 cup diced celery
1 cup diced zucchini
1 can (28 ounces) tomatoes with liquid, chopped
2 cups water
2 teaspoons sugar
1 teaspoon dried Italian herb seasoning
1 can (15 ounces) garbanzo beans, drained
4 (1/2-inch) slices French bread, toasted
1 cup (4 ounces) SARGENTO® Light Mozzarella
    Shredded Cheese
2 tablespoons SARGENTO® Fancy Parmesan
    Shredded Cheese
Freshly chopped parsley

Spray a large saucepan or Dutch oven with nonstick
cooking spray. Over medium heat, sauté celery and
zucchini until tender. Add tomatoes, water, sugar
and herb seasoning. Simmer, uncovered, 15 to
20 minutes. Add garbanzo beans and heat an
additional 10 minutes. Meanwhile, heat broiler.
Place toasted French bread on broiler pan. Top with
Mozzarella cheese. Broil until cheese melts. Ladle
soup into bowls and top with French bread. Sprinkle
Parmesan cheese over each bowl and garnish with
parsley. Serve immediately. *Makes 4 servings*

Helpful Hint

*When purchasing fresh zucchini,
choose those that are heavy for
their size, firm and well shaped.
They should have a bright color
and be free of cuts and any soft
spots. Small zucchini are more
tender because they have been
harvested when they were young.
Refrigerate zucchini, unwashed,
in a perforated plastic bag for
up to 5 days.*

Vegetable and Shrimp Chowder

Vegetable and Shrimp Chowder

(Pictured above)

1-1/2 cups diced Spanish onions
  1/2 cup sliced carrots
  1/2 cup diced celery
    2 tablespoons margarine or butter
    2 cups peeled and diced baking potatoes
    1 (10-ounce) package frozen corn
    5 cups chicken broth
  1/2 pound small shrimp, peeled and deveined
  1/3 cup GREY POUPON® Dijon Mustard
  1/4 cup chopped parsley

1. Cook and stir onions, carrots and celery in margarine or butter in large saucepan over medium heat for 3 to 4 minutes or until tender. Add potatoes, corn and chicken broth; heat to a boil.

2. Reduce heat; simmer for 20 to 25 minutes or until potatoes are tender. Add shrimp, mustard and parsley; cook for 5 minutes more or until shrimp are cooked. Garnish as desired. Serve warm.

Makes 8 servings

Creamy Wild Rice Asparagus Soup

  1 box (10 ounces) frozen asparagus cuts, thawed
  2 tablespoons butter
  1 can (14-1/2 ounces) vegetable broth, divided
  2 cups half and half
  2 cups cooked wild rice
  1 teaspoon salt
  1/2 teaspoon white pepper
  1/2 teaspoon lemon juice
    Fresh chervil leaves, for garnish

Remove asparagus tips; set aside. In medium saucepan, sauté remaining asparagus in butter 2 minutes. Add broth to cover asparagus; simmer until tender. Pour mixture into blender; purée. Return puréed mixture to saucepan; add remaining broth, half and half, wild rice, asparagus tips, salt, pepper and lemon juice; heat through. Garnish with chervil, if desired. *Makes 6 servings*

Favorite recipe from **Minnesota Cultivated Wild Rice Council**

Greek Lemon Soup

    1 bag SUCCESS® Rice
1-1/2 cups chopped cooked chicken
    1 cup thinly sliced carrots
  1/2 cup thinly sliced celery
    2 cans (14-1/2 ounces *each*) chicken broth
  1/2 teaspoon fresh dill
  1/4 teaspoon salt
  1/4 teaspoon pepper
    1 egg
  1/4 cup lemon juice

Prepare rice according to package directions.

Meanwhile, combine chicken, carrots, celery and chicken broth in medium saucepan. Bring to a boil over medium-high heat. Reduce heat to low; simmer 10 minutes. Add rice, dill, salt and pepper.

Beat egg in small bowl. Gradually whisk in lemon juice. Gradually add to soup, stirring constantly; continue simmering until egg is cooked.

Makes 4 servings

Butternut Squash Soup

(Pictured below)

2 tablespoons butter or margarine
1 medium onion, chopped
2 cloves garlic, minced
3 medium carrots, diced
2 stalks celery, diced
1 butternut squash, peeled, seeded and diced
1 medium potato, peeled and diced
3 cans (14-1/2 ounces each) ready-to-serve
    chicken broth
1/2 cup honey
1/2 teaspoon dried thyme leaves, crushed
    Salt and pepper, to taste

In large pot, melt butter over medium heat. Stir in onion and garlic. Cook and stir until lightly browned, about 5 minutes. Stir in carrots and celery. Cook and stir until tender, about 5 minutes. Stir in squash, potato, chicken broth, honey and thyme. Bring mixture to a boil; reduce heat and simmer 30 to 45 minutes, or until vegetables are tender. Remove from heat and cool slightly. Working in small batches, transfer mixture to blender or food processor; process until smooth. Return puréed soup to pot. Season to taste with salt and pepper. Heat until hot and serve. *Makes 6 servings*

Favorite recipe from **National Honey Board**

Helpful Hint

Butternut squash, which weighs from two to five pounds, is cylindrical with a slightly bulbous base. The skin is creamy tan and the flesh is a yellowish-orange. The flavor is sweet and slightly nutty.

Butternut Squash Soup

Zesty Noodle Soup

(Pictured at right)

1 pound BOB EVANS® Zesty Hot Roll Sausage
1 (14-1/2-ounce) can whole tomatoes, undrained
1/2 pound fresh mushrooms, sliced
1 large onion, chopped
1 small green bell pepper, chopped
2-1/2 cups tomato juice
2-1/2 cups water
1/4 cup chopped fresh parsley
1 teaspoon lemon juice
1 teaspoon Worcestershire sauce
1 teaspoon celery seeds
1/2 teaspoon salt
1/2 teaspoon dried thyme leaves
1 cup uncooked egg noodles

Crumble sausage into 3-quart saucepan. Cook over medium-high heat until browned, stirring occasionally. Drain off any drippings. Add tomatoes with juice, mushrooms, onion and pepper; cook until vegetables are tender, stirring well to break up tomatoes. Stir in all remaining ingredients except noodles. Bring to a boil over high heat. Reduce heat to low; simmer, covered, 30 minutes. Add noodles; simmer just until noodles are tender, yet firm. Serve hot. Refrigerate leftovers. *Makes 6 servings*

Serving Suggestion: Serve with crusty French bread.

Helpful Hint

Wipe mushrooms with a damp paper towel, brush with a mushroom brush or soft toothbrush, or rinse briefly under cold running water to remove the dirt. Pat them dry before using. Never soak mushrooms in water because they absorb water and will become mushy. Trim and discard the stem ends. Slice mushrooms through their stems or chop.

Creamy Wild Rice and Turkey Soup

2 cups chopped cooked BUTTERBALL® Breast of Young Turkey
1 tablespoon olive oil
1 cup finely chopped carrots
1 cup finely chopped onion
1/2 cup finely chopped celery
2 cloves garlic, minced
2 cans (14-1/2 ounces each) chicken broth
2 cups cooked wild rice
1/2 cup whipping cream
Salt and black pepper

Heat oil in large saucepan over medium heat until hot. Cook and stir carrots, onion, celery and garlic until onion is soft. Add chicken broth, wild rice and turkey; heat 10 minutes. Add whipping cream; cook over low heat until heated through. Add salt and pepper to taste. *Makes 8 (1-cup) servings*

Hoppin' John Soup

1 bag SUCCESS® Brown Rice
1/4 pound spicy turkey sausage
1/2 cup chopped onion
1/2 pound turnips, peeled and chopped
2 carrots, peeled and chopped
1/2 teaspoon salt
1/2 teaspoon pepper
3 cups chicken broth
1/2 package (16 ounces) frozen black-eyed peas, thawed and drained
1/2 package (16 ounces) frozen chopped mustard greens, thawed and drained
1/2 teaspoon red pepper flakes

Prepare rice according to package directions.

Brown sausage in large saucepan or Dutch oven over medium-high heat; drain. Add onion, turnips, carrots, salt and pepper. Reduce heat to low; simmer 7 minutes. Add broth; simmer 5 minutes. Add rice, peas and greens; simmer 10 minutes, stirring occasionally. Sprinkle with red pepper flakes. *Makes 6 servings*

Fisherman's Soup

(Pictured at right)

1/8 teaspoon dried thyme, crushed
1/2 pound halibut or other firm white fish
2 tablespoons vegetable oil
1 medium onion, chopped
1 clove garlic, crushed
3 tablespoons all-purpose flour
2 cans (14-1/2 ounces each) low-salt chicken broth
1 can (15-1/4 ounces) DEL MONTE® Whole Kernel Golden Sweet Corn, No Salt Added, undrained
1 can (14-1/2 ounces) DEL MONTE Whole New Potatoes, drained and chopped

1. Sprinkle thyme over both sides of fish. In large saucepan, cook fish in 1 tablespoon hot oil over medium-high heat until fish flakes easily when tested with a fork. Remove fish from saucepan; set aside.

2. Heat remaining 1 tablespoon oil in same saucepan over medium heat. Add onion and garlic; cook until onion is tender. Stir in flour; cook 1 minute. Stir in broth; cook until thickened, stirring occasionally. Stir in corn and potatoes.

3. Discard skin and bones from fish; cut fish into bite-sized pieces.

4. Add fish to soup just before serving; heat through. Stir in chopped parsley or sliced green onions, if desired.   *Makes 4 to 6 servings*

Helpful Hint

Halibut is a firm lean fish. If it is unavailable, you may substitute cod, haddock, orange roughy or sole.

Old Virginia Chicken & Dumplings

1 large smoked ham hock
1 (4- to 5-pound) stewing chicken
1 small onion, sliced
1 carrot, sliced
2 ribs celery with leaves, sliced
2 teaspoons LAWRY'S® Seasoned Salt
6 tablespoons flour
1 teaspoon LAWRY'S® Seasoned Salt
1/4 teaspoon white pepper
1/4 cup butter or margarine
1/2 cup half & half
1 cup steamed, sliced carrots and green peas (optional)

DUMPLING MIX
2 cups all-purpose flour
1-1/2 to 2 teaspoons LAWRY'S® Seasoned Salt
4 teaspoons baking powder
1 tablespoon shortening
3/4 cup milk

In large soup pot, combine ham hock, chicken, onion, carrot, celery, 2 teaspoons Seasoned Salt and enough water to cover and cook over medium-low heat until chicken is done, about 2 hours. Remove ham and chicken from stock. When cool enough to handle, remove meat from bones; dice meat and reserve. Strain stock into 1 quart measure and if needed, add more water to make 1 quart of stock. In small bowl, combine flour, 1 teaspoon Seasoned Salt and white pepper. In soup pot, heat butter over medium heat; stir in seasoned flour and cook while stirring constantly 2 to 3 minutes. Slowly add stock, stirring constantly; cook 2 minutes. Add half & half, stirring until smooth and thickened. Add diced meat and carrots and peas, if desired; adjust seasoning. Meanwhile, sift together flour, 1/2 to 2 teaspoons Seasoned Salt and baking powder three times. Mix in shortening with pastry blender or fork. Add milk and mix just until blended. Do not overwork dough. Dip teaspoon into cold water then into dough, spooning dough onto top of gently bubbling chicken mixture. Cook, covered, 15 minutes without lifting the lid.   *Makes 4 servings*

Ravioli Soup

(Pictured at right)

1 package (9 ounces) fresh or frozen cheese
    ravioli or tortellini
3/4 pound hot Italian sausage, crumbled
1 can (14-1/2 ounces) DEL MONTE® Italian
    Recipe Stewed Tomatoes
1 can (14-1/2 ounces) beef broth
1 can (14-1/2 ounces) DEL MONTE® Italian
    Beans, drained
2 green onions, sliced

1. Cook pasta according to package directions;
drain.

2. Meanwhile, cook sausage in 5-quart pot over
medium-high heat until no longer pink; drain. Add
undrained tomatoes, broth and 1-3/4 cups water;
bring to boil.

3. Reduce heat to low; stir in pasta, green beans and
green onions. Simmer until heated through. Season
with pepper and sprinkle with grated Parmesan
cheese, if desired. *Makes 4 servings*

Cheeseburger Soup

1/2 pound ground beef
3-1/2 cups water
1/2 cup cherry tomato halves or chopped tomato
1 pouch LIPTON® Soup Secrets Ring-O-Noodle
    Soup Mix with Real Chicken Broth
4 ounces Cheddar cheese, shredded

Shape ground beef into 16 mini burgers.

In large saucepan, thoroughly brown burgers; drain.
Add water, tomatoes and soup mix; bring to a boil.
Reduce heat and simmer uncovered, stirring
occasionally, 5 minutes or until burgers are cooked
and noodles are tender. Stir in cheese.
Makes about 4 (1-cup) servings

Black Bean Soup

4-1/4 cups (three 15-ounce cans) black beans,
    undrained
1-1/2 cups (14-1/2-ounce can) chicken broth
1 tablespoon vegetable oil
1 cup (1 small) chopped onion
4 cloves garlic, finely chopped
2-1/2 cups ORTEGA® Thick & Chunky Salsa
2 tablespoons lime juice
1 tablespoon ground cumin
1/2 to 1 teaspoon crushed red pepper
1/2 cup plain yogurt

PLACE beans with liquid and chicken broth in food
processor; cover. Blend until smooth (may be done
in batches if necessary).

HEAT vegetable oil in large saucepan over medium-
high heat. Add onion and garlic; cook for 1 to
2 minutes or until onion is tender. Add bean
mixture, salsa, lime juice, cumin and red pepper.
Bring to a boil. Reduce heat to low; cover. Cook,
stirring occasionally, for 25 to 30 minutes. Serve
topped with dollop of yogurt.
Makes 8 to 10 servings

Tip: For a main-dish soup, add cooked chicken or
turkey and corn. Garnish with yogurt or sour cream
and chopped green onions.

Easy Ham & Veg•All® Chowder

(Pictured on page 66)

2 cans (15 ounces each) VEG•ALL® Original
    Mixed Vegetables, with liquid
1 can (10-3/4 ounces) condensed cream of
    potato soup
1 cup cooked ham, cubed
1/2 teaspoon dried basil
1/4 teaspoon black pepper

In medium saucepan, combine Veg•All, soup, ham,
basil, and black pepper. Heat until hot; serve.
Makes 4 to 6 servings

Cheesy Broccoli Soup

(Pictured on page 66)

1/4 cup chopped onion
1 tablespoon butter or margarine
1-1/2 cups milk
3/4 pound (12 ounces) VELVEETA® Pasteurized
    Prepared Cheese Product, cut up
1 package (10 ounces) frozen chopped broccoli,
    thawed, drained
    Dash pepper

1. Cook and stir onion in butter in large saucepan on medium-high heat until tender.

2. Add remaining ingredients; stir on low heat until Velveeta is melted and soup is thoroughly heated.

Makes 4 (3/4-cup) servings

Use Your Microwave: Microwave onion and butter in 2-quart microwaveable casserole or bowl on HIGH 30 seconds to 1 minute or until onion is tender. Add remaining ingredients; mix well. Microwave 6 to 8 minutes or until Velveeta is melted and soup is thoroughly heated, stirring every 3 minutes.

Vegetable Soup

Vegetable Soup

(Pictured below left)

2 tablespoons FILIPPO BERIO® Olive Oil
2 medium potatoes, peeled and quartered
2 medium onions, sliced
3 cups beef broth
8 ounces fresh green beans, trimmed and cut
    into 1-inch pieces
3 carrots, peeled and chopped
8 ounces fresh spinach, washed, drained,
    stemmed and chopped
1 green bell pepper, diced
2 tablespoons chopped fresh parsley
1 tablespoon chopped fresh basil *or* 1 teaspoon
    dried basil leaves
1/2 teaspoon ground cumin
1 clove garlic, finely minced
    Salt and freshly ground black pepper
    Polenta squares (optional)

In Dutch oven, heat olive oil over medium-high heat until hot. Add potatoes and onions; cook and stir 5 minutes. Add beef broth, green beans and carrots. Bring mixture to a boil. Cover; reduce heat to low and simmer 10 minutes, stirring occasionally. Add spinach, bell pepper, parsley, basil, cumin and garlic. Cover; simmer an additional 15 to 20 minutes or until potatoes are tender. Season to taste with salt and black pepper. Serve hot with polenta squares, if desired. *Makes 6 to 8 servings*

Chicken Tortellini Soup

1 can (48 ounces) chicken broth
1 package PERDUE® SHORT CUTS® Fresh Italian
    Carved Chicken Breast
1 package (9 ounces) fresh pesto or cheese
    tortellini or tortelloni
1 cup fresh spinach or arugula leaves, shredded
1/4 to 1/2 cup grated Parmesan cheese

In large saucepan over medium-high heat, bring broth to a boil. Add chicken and tortellini; cook 6 to 8 minutes, until pasta is tender, reducing heat to keep a gentle boil. Just before serving, stir in fresh spinach. Ladle soup into bowls and sprinkle with Parmesan cheese. *Makes 4 servings*

Southwest Chicken Soup

Southwest Chicken Soup

(Pictured above)

3 tablespoons vegetable oil
3 corn tortillas, cut into 1/2-inch strips
1/3 cup chopped onion
2/3 cup chopped green and red bell peppers
1 clove garlic, minced
1/4 cup all-purpose flour
2 (14-1/2-ounce) cans chicken broth
2 cups cubed cooked chicken
1 (15-ounce) can VEG•ALL® Mixed Vegetables, drained
2 teaspoons chili powder

1. Heat oil in large skillet; add tortilla strips and fry, stirring constantly, until golden. Drain on paper towel-lined plate.

2. Add onion and bell peppers to skillet; cook and stir until soft.

3. Add garlic and stir in flour; gradually stir in chicken broth.

4. Add remaining ingredients except tortilla strips; cook until thickened. Sprinkle with tortilla strips before serving. *Makes 4 to 6 servings*

Helpful Hint

Store unwashed sweet bell peppers in the refrigerator. Green peppers begin to lose their crispness after three to four days, and red peppers are even more perishable. Once cut, refrigerate peppers, wrapped in plastic wrap, and use them quickly.

Creamy Shell Soup

(Pictured at right)

4 cups water
3 or 4 chicken pieces
1 cup chopped onion
1/4 cup chopped celery
1/4 cup minced fresh parsley *or* 1 tablespoon dried
  parsley flakes
1 bay leaf
1 teaspoon salt
1/4 teaspoon white pepper
2 medium potatoes, diced
4 or 5 green onions, chopped
3 chicken bouillon cubes
1/2 teaspoon seasoned salt
1/2 teaspoon poultry seasoning
4 cups milk
2 cups medium shell macaroni, cooked and
  drained
1/4 cup butter or margarine
1/4 cup all-purpose flour

Combine water, chicken, chopped onion, celery, minced parsley, bay leaf, salt and pepper in Dutch oven. Bring to a boil. Reduce heat to low; simmer until chicken is tender. Remove bay leaf; discard. Remove chicken; cool. Skin, debone and cut into small cubes; set aside.

Add potatoes, green onions, bouillon cubes, seasoned salt and poultry seasoning to broth. Simmer 15 minutes. Add milk, macaroni and chicken; return to a simmer.

Melt butter in skillet over medium heat. Add flour, stirring constantly, until mixture begins to brown. Add to soup; blend well. Let soup simmer on very low heat 20 minutes to blend flavors. Season to taste. Sprinkle with ground nutmeg and additional chopped parsley, if desired.　　*Makes 8 servings*

Favorite recipe from **North Dakota Wheat Commission**

Pantry Soup

2 teaspoons olive oil
8 ounces boneless skinless chicken, cubed
2 cans (14.5 ounces each) CONTADINA® Diced
  Tomatoes with Italian Herbs, undrained
3/4 cup chicken broth
3/4 cup water
1 cup garbanzo beans, undrained
1 cup kidney beans, undrained
1 package (16 ounces) frozen mixed vegetables
1/2 cup dry pasta (rotini or rotelle), cooked and
  drained
2 teaspoons lemon juice

1. Heat oil in 5-quart saucepan with lid; sauté chicken about 3 to 4 minutes or until cooked, stirring occasionally.

2. Mix in tomatoes, broth, water, garbanzo and kidney beans; cover and bring to a boil. Add mixed vegetables and pasta; bring to boil.

3. Reduce heat; cover and simmer 3 minutes or until vegetables are tender. Stir in lemon juice; serve with condiments, if desired.　　*Makes 6 to 8 servings*

Optional Condiments: Grated Parmesan cheese, chopped fresh basil or parsley, or croutons.

Pea Soup

2 tablespoons butter or margarine
1 medium onion, chopped
1 bag (16 ounces) BIRDS EYE® frozen Green Peas
1 can (14-1/2 ounces) chicken broth
1/2 teaspoon dried tarragon

• Melt butter in medium saucepan over medium-high heat. Add onion; cook until tender, about 3 minutes.

• Add peas, chicken broth and tarragon. Bring to boil; reduce heat to medium. Cover and cook 4 minutes.

• Transfer mixture to blender; blend until smooth. Strain, if desired. Serve hot or cold.
　　Makes about 3 servings

Cool Italian Tomato Soup

(Pictured at right)

1 can (14.5 ounces) CONTADINA® Recipe Ready
    Diced Tomatoes, undrained
2 cups tomato juice
1/2 cup half-and-half
2 tablespoons lemon juice
1 large cucumber, peeled, diced (about 2 cups)
1 medium green bell pepper, diced (about
    1/2 cup)
Chopped fresh basil (optional)
Croutons (optional)

1. Place tomatoes with juice, tomato juice, half-and-half and lemon juice in blender container; blend until smooth.

2. Pour into large bowl or soup tureen; stir in cucumber and bell pepper.

3. Sprinkle with basil and croutons just before serving, if desired.
Makes 6 cups

Hearty Tortellini Soup

1 small red onion, chopped
2 medium carrots, chopped
2 ribs celery, thinly sliced
1 small zucchini, chopped
2 plum tomatoes, chopped
2 cloves garlic, minced
2 cans (14-1/2 ounces *each*) chicken broth
1 can (15 ounces) red kidney beans, rinsed and
    drained
2 tablespoons *French's®* Worcestershire Sauce
1 package (9 ounces) refrigerated tortellini pasta

1. Heat *2 tablespoons oil* in 6-quart saucepot or Dutch oven over medium-high heat. Add vegetables, tomatoes and garlic. Cook and stir 5 minutes or until vegetables are crisp-tender.

2. Add broth, *1/2 cup water,* beans and Worcestershire. Heat to boiling. Stir in pasta. Return to boiling. Cook 5 minutes or until pasta is tender, stirring occasionally. Serve with crusty bread and grated Parmesan cheese, if desired.
Makes 4 servings

White Cheddar Seafood Chowder

2 tablespoons margarine or butter
1/2 cup chopped onion
2-1/4 cups water
1 package (6.2 ounces) PASTA RONI® Shells &
    White Cheddar
1 cup sliced carrots
1/2 teaspoon salt (optional)
3/4 pound fresh or thawed frozen firm white fish,
    cut into 1/2-inch pieces
1-1/4 cups milk
2 tablespoons chopped parsley (optional)

1. In 3-quart saucepan, melt margarine over medium heat. Add onion; sauté 1 minute.

2. Add water; bring to a boil over high heat.

3. Stir in pasta, carrots and salt.

4. Bring just to a boil. Reduce heat to medium. Boil, uncovered, stirring frequently, 12 minutes.

5. Add fish, milk, parsley and Special Seasonings. Continue cooking 3 to 4 minutes, stirring occasionally, or until pasta is desired tenderness and fish is opaque.
Makes 4 servings

Helpful Hint

Chowder is a type of milk- or cream-based soup closely associated with New England. It is most often made with clams, but lobster and cod are other favored seafood ingredients. Regional variations also exist, using chicken, corn or vegetables, but a thick, creamy soup of clams, potatoes and onions is the most common.

Chilly Cucumber Soup

(Pictured at right)

2 tablespoons butter
2 tablespoons all-purpose flour
4 large cucumbers, peeled, seeded and finely chopped (about 3-1/2 cups)
1/4 cup finely chopped parsley
1/4 cup finely chopped celery leaves
1 envelope LIPTON® RECIPE SECRETS® Golden Onion Soup Mix
2 cups water
2 cups (1 pint) light cream or half-and-half

In large saucepan, melt butter over medium heat; add flour and cook, stirring constantly, 3 minutes. Add cucumbers, parsley and celery leaves. Reduce heat to low and cook 8 minutes or until vegetables are tender. Stir in soup mix thoroughly blended with water. Bring to a boil over high heat. Reduce heat to low and simmer, covered, 15 minutes. Remove from heat, then cool.

In food processor or blender, purée soup mixture. Stir in cream; chill. Serve cold and garnish, if desired, with cucumber slices, celery leaves and lemon peel.   *Makes about 6 (1 cup) servings*

Helpful Hint

Cucumbers found in the supermarket produce section are often waxed to preserve the vegetable's moisture content. Wash cucumbers thoroughly in cold water in order to remove this waxy protective covering. Refrigerate whole cucumbers in a plastic bag for up to one week. To seed cucumbers, cut them in half lengthwise and scrape out the seeds with a small spoon.

Veg•All® Italian Soup

(Pictured on page 66)

2 tablespoons butter
1 cup diced onion
1 cup shredded cabbage
2 cups water
2 cans (14-1/2 ounces each) stewed tomatoes
1 can (15 ounces) VEG•ALL® Original Mixed Vegetables, drained
1 tablespoon chopped fresh parsley
1/2 teaspoon dried basil
1/2 teaspoon dried oregano
1/2 teaspoon black pepper

In large saucepan, melt butter. Stir in onion and cabbage. Heat for 2 minutes. Add water; cover and simmer for 10 minutes. Stir in tomatoes, Veg•All, and seasonings. Simmer for 10 minutes.

Makes 6 servings

Cabbage Soup

1 pound BOB EVANS® Italian or Original Recipe Roll Sausage
3 cups water
1 (14-1/2-ounce) can beef broth
1 (10-3/4-ounce) can condensed tomato soup
1 small head cabbage, coarsely chopped
1 medium onion, chopped
3/4 teaspoon salt
1/2 teaspoon black pepper
1/4 teaspoon paprika
1 bay leaf
1 (15-1/2-ounce) can dark red kidney beans, rinsed and drained
Parmesan cheese for garnish (optional)

Crumble and cook sausage in medium skillet until browned. Drain off any drippings. Combine sausage and all remaining ingredients except beans and cheese in large saucepan; bring to a boil over high heat. Reduce heat to low; cover and simmer 35 minutes or until cabbage is tender. Remove bay leaf. Add beans; cook until heated through. Serve in individual soup bowls and garnish with Parmesan cheese, if desired. Refrigerate leftovers.

Makes 8 servings

Tomato Chicken Gumbo

(Pictured at right)

6 chicken thighs
1/2 pound hot sausage links or Polish sausage, sliced
3 cups water
1 can (14-1/2 ounces) chicken broth
1/2 cup uncooked long-grain white rice
1 can (26 ounces) DEL MONTE® Traditional or Chunky Garlic and Herb Spaghetti Sauce
1 can (11 ounces) DEL MONTE® SUMMER CRISP™ Whole Kernel Golden Sweet Corn, drained
1 medium green bell pepper, diced

1. Preheat oven to 400°F. In large shallow baking pan, place chicken and sausage. Bake 35 minutes or until chicken is no longer pink in center. Cool slightly.

2. Remove skin from chicken; cut meat into cubes. Cut sausage into slices 1/2 inch thick.

3. Bring water and broth to boil in 6-quart pot. Add chicken, sausage and rice. Cover; cook over medium heat 15 minutes.

4. Stir in remaining ingredients; bring to boil. Cover; cook 5 minutes or until rice is tender. Serve with fresh hot biscuits.   *Makes 4 servings*

Tip: Add additional water or broth for a thinner gumbo. For spicier gumbo, serve with hot red pepper sauce.

Lentil Soup

1 tablespoon FILIPPO BERIO® Olive Oil
1 medium onion, diced
4 cups beef broth
1 cup dried lentils, rinsed and drained
1/4 cup tomato sauce
1 teaspoon dried Italian herb seasoning
  Salt and freshly ground black pepper

In large saucepan, heat olive oil over medium heat until hot. Add onion; cook and stir 5 minutes or until softened. Add beef broth; bring mixture to a boil. Stir in lentils, tomato sauce and Italian seasoning. Cover; reduce heat to low and simmer 45 minutes or until lentils are tender. Season to taste with salt and pepper. Serve hot.   *Makes 6 servings*

Corn and Potato Soup

2 tablespoons CRISCO® Oil*
1 medium onion, peeled and diced
1 tablespoon jarred minced garlic *or* 2 large cloves garlic, peeled and minced
3 ears fresh corn, husked, kernels cut from cobs
1 large Idaho or russet potato (about 1/2 pound), peeled and thinly sliced
1 can (14-1/2 ounces) chicken broth
1/4 teaspoon dried thyme leaves
3/4 cup half and half
1/2 teaspoon salt
1/4 teaspoon freshly ground black pepper

Use your favorite Crisco Oil product.

1. Heat oil in 2-quart saucepan on medium-high heat. Add onion and garlic. Sauté 3 minutes, or until onion is translucent.

2. Add corn, potato, broth, and thyme to pan. Bring to a boil. Cover pan. Reduce heat to low. Simmer 15 minutes, or until potato slices are breaking apart. Remove pan from heat. Mash soup with potato masher or fork; do not purée.

3. Add half and half, salt, and pepper to pan. Bring to a boil on medium heat. Simmer 3 minutes. Stir occasionally.   *Makes 4 servings*

Note: This soup can be made up to two days in advance and refrigerated, tightly covered. Reheat on low heat or in microwave oven.

Helpful Hint

To cut corn kernels from the cob, holding the tip of one ear, stand the corn upright on its stem end on a cutting board or in a shallow dish. Cut down the side of the cob with a utility knife, releasing the kernels without cutting the cob. Repeat while rotating the ear until all the kernels are removed.

Sandwiches

Ham and Swiss Sandwiches with Citrus Mayonnaise

(Pictured at left)

1/4 cup GREY POUPON® Dijon Mustard
1/4 cup mayonnaise*
1 tablespoon lime juice
1 tablespoon honey
1/2 teaspoon grated lime peel
1/4 teaspoon ground black pepper
8 (1/2-inch-thick) slices black bread
1 cup shredded lettuce
8 slices tomato
4 ounces sliced Swiss cheese
12 ounces sliced honey-baked ham

Low-fat mayonnaise may be substituted for regular mayonnaise.

Blend mustard, mayonnaise, lime juice, honey, lime peel and pepper in small bowl. Spread about 1 tablespoon mustard mixture on each bread slice.

On each of 4 bread slices, layer 1/4 cup lettuce, 2 tomato slices, 1 ounce cheese and 3 ounces ham. Top with remaining bread slices. Serve with remaining mustard mixture.

Makes 4 sandwiches

Clockwise from top left: *Hidden Valley® Wraps (p. 105), Nutty Albacore Salad Pita (p. 96), Best Ever Beef Hero (p. 104) and Ham and Swiss Sandwiches with Citrus Mayonnaise*

Buffet Cranberry Biscuits with Smoked Turkey

(Pictured at right)

1 BUTTERBALL® Fully Cooked Smoked Young
    Turkey, thawed, sliced thin
3-1/2 cups packaged biscuit mix
2 tablespoons butter or margarine
3/4 cup dried cranberries
1 cup milk

CRANBERRY BUTTER
    1/2 cup butter
    1/4 cup honey
    1/4 cup dried cranberries

Place biscuit mix in large bowl. Cut in butter with pastry blender until mixture resembles coarse crumbs. Stir in 3/4 cup cranberries; add milk. Stir until soft dough forms. Turn dough onto lightly floured surface; knead gently 10 times. Roll to 1/2-inch thickness. Cut 20 biscuits with 2-1/2-inch round cutter. Place on *ungreased* baking sheet. Bake in preheated 400°F oven 10 minutes or until golden brown.

To prepare Cranberry Butter, combine butter, honey and 1/4 cup cranberries in food processor; process just until blended.

To assemble sandwiches, split each biscuit in half. Spread each biscuit half generously with cranberry butter. Stack turkey on bottom of each biscuit. Place top half of biscuit on turkey.

Makes 20 buffet sandwiches

Note: Biscuits and butter can be made a few hours prior to serving.

Helpful Hint

When preparing biscuits, cut the shortening or butter into the dry ingredients with a pastry blender or two knives until the mixture forms coarse crumbs. Blending the fat in any further produces mealy biscuits. Mix the dough gently and quickly to achieve light and tender results. Overworking the dough makes the biscuits tough.

Grilled Vegetable Sandwiches

2 pounds assorted fresh vegetables*
1 envelope LIPTON® RECIPE SECRETS® Onion
    Soup Mix**
1/3 cup olive or vegetable oil
2 tablespoons balsamic or red wine vinegar
1/2 teaspoon dried basil leaves, crushed
4 (8-inch) pita breads, warmed
4 ounces crumbled Montrachet, shredded
    mozzarella, Jarlsberg, Monterey Jack or
    Cheddar cheese

Use any combination of the following, sliced: red, green or yellow bell peppers, mushrooms, zucchini or eggplant.

**Also terrific with Lipton® Recipe Secrets® Onion, Savory Herb with Garlic or Golden Onion Soup Mix.*

1. In large bowl, combine vegetables and soup mix blended with oil, vinegar and basil until evenly coated.

2. Grill or broil vegetables until tender. To serve, cut 1-inch strip off each pita. Fill with vegetables and sprinkle with cheese. Garnish, if desired, with shredded lettuce and sliced tomato.

Makes 4 servings

Easy Beef Barbecue

1 package KNORR® Recipe Classics™ Tomato
    Beef (Oxtail) Soup, Dip and Recipe Mix
1-1/2 cups water
    1/2 cup ketchup
    1 small onion, chopped
    2 tablespoons cider vinegar
    1 tablespoon firmly packed brown sugar
    1 tablespoon vegetable oil
    1 (1-pound) beef flank steak, thinly sliced or
        1 pound lean ground beef
    Sandwich rolls

• In small bowl, blend recipe mix, water, ketchup, onion, vinegar and brown sugar; set aside.

• In large skillet, heat oil over medium-high heat and brown steak in two batches.

• Stir in recipe mixture and steak. Bring to a boil over high heat. Reduce heat to low and simmer covered 10 minutes or until steak is tender. Serve over rolls.

Makes 6 servings

*Buffet Cranberry Biscuits
with Smoked Turkey*

Grilled Chicken Croissant with Roasted Pepper Dressing

Grilled Chicken Croissant with Roasted Pepper Dressing

(Pictured at left)

    1/2 cup *French's*® Dijon Mustard
      3 tablespoons olive oil
      3 tablespoons red wine vinegar
    3/4 teaspoon dried Italian seasoning
    3/4 teaspoon garlic powder
      1 jar (7 ounces) roasted red peppers, drained
      1 pound boneless skinless chicken breast halves
        Lettuce leaves
      4 croissants, split

Whisk together mustard, oil, vinegar and seasonings in small bowl until well blended. Pour 1/4 cup mixture into blender. Add peppers. Cover and process until mixture is smooth; set aside.

Brush chicken with remaining mustard mixture. Place chicken on grid. Grill over hot coals 15 minutes or until chicken is no longer pink in center, turning often. To serve, place lettuce leaves on bottom halves of croissants. Arrange chicken on top of lettuce. Spoon roasted pepper dressing over chicken. Cover with croissant top. Garnish as desired. *Makes 4 servings*

Nutty Albacore Salad Pitas

(Pictured on page 92)

      1 (3-ounces) pouch of STARKIST® Solid White
        Tuna, drained and flaked
    1/2 cup mayonnaise
    1/3 cup chopped celery
    1/4 cup raisins or seedless grape halves
    1/4 cup chopped walnuts, pecans or almonds
    1/2 teaspoon dried dill weed
        Salt and pepper to taste
      2 pita breads, halved
      4 curly leaf lettuce leaves

In medium bowl, combine tuna, mayonnaise, celery, raisins, nuts and dill; mix well. Add salt and pepper. Line each pita bread half with lettuce leaf; fill each with 1/4 of tuna mixture. *Makes 4 servings*

Open-Faced Italian Focaccia Sandwich

      2 cups shredded cooked chicken
    1/2 cup HIDDEN VALLEY® Original Ranch®
        Dressing
    1/4 cup diagonally sliced green onions
      1 piece focaccia bread, about 3/4 inch thick,
        10×7-inches
      2 medium tomatoes, thinly sliced
      4 cheese slices, such as provolone, Cheddar or
        Swiss
      2 tablespoons grated Parmesan cheese (optional)

Stir together chicken, dressing and onions in a small mixing bowl. Arrange chicken mixture evenly on top of focaccia. Top with layer of tomatoes and cheese slices. Sprinkle with Parmesan cheese, if desired. Broil 2 minutes or until cheese is melted and bubbly. *Makes 4 servings*

Note: Purchase rotisserie chicken at your favorite store to add great taste and save preparation time.

Bacon-Wrapped Bratwurst

(Pictured below)

8 links HILLSHIRE FARM® Bratwurst
2 tablespoons mustard
2 tablespoons chopped onion
2 slices Muenster cheese, each cut into 4 strips
8 slices HILLSHIRE FARM® Bacon, partially
    cooked and drained
    Prepared barbecue sauce
8 hot dog buns, toasted

Prepare grill for cooking. Slit Bratwurst lengthwise 3/4 inch deep. Evenly spread mustard inside each slit; evenly insert onion and cheese strips. Wrap each bratwurst with 1 slice Bacon; secure with toothpick. Grill 10 minutes, turning frequently and brushing with barbecue sauce. When bacon is crisp, remove toothpicks. Serve in buns.

Makes 4 servings

Caesar Chicken Sandwiches

3 tablespoons all-purpose flour
1/2 teaspoon ground black pepper
4 boneless skinless chicken breast halves
    Vegetable oil cooking spray
6 tablespoons lemon juice
4 cloves garlic, minced
4 teaspoons A.1.® Worcestershire Sauce
    Dash hot pepper sauce
2 tablespoons PLANTERS® Walnuts, toasted and
    chopped
4 teaspoons grated Parmesan cheese
4 romaine lettuce leaves
4 whole wheat sandwich rolls, sliced lengthwise

1. Mix flour and pepper. Coat chicken with flour mixture, shaking off excess. Spray 10-inch skillet with cooking spray for 2 seconds; lightly brown chicken on both sides over medium heat.

2. Blend lemon juice, garlic, Worcestershire and pepper sauce; pour over chicken. Cover; simmer for 15 minutes or until chicken is done. Sprinkle walnuts and cheese over chicken.

3. Arrange lettuce on rolls; top with chicken. Serve immediately. *Makes 4 sandwiches*

Bacon-Wrapped Bratwurst

Tex-Mex Chicken Fajitas

(Pictured at right)

1/2 cup LAWRY'S® Mesquite Marinade with Lime Juice
6 boneless skinless chicken breast halves (about 1-1/2 pounds), cut into strips
3 tablespoons plus 1-1/2 teaspoons vegetable oil, divided
1 small onion, sliced and separated into rings
1 medium-sized green bell pepper, cut into strips
3/4 teaspoon LAWRY'S® Garlic Powder with Parsley
1/2 teaspoon hot pepper sauce
1 medium tomato, cut into wedges
2 tablespoons chopped fresh cilantro
Flour tortillas, warmed
1 medium lime, cut into wedges

In large resealable plastic food storage bag, combine Mesquite Marinade with Lime Juice and chicken; seal bag. Marinate in refrigerator at least 30 minutes. In large skillet heat 1 tablespoon plus 1-1/2 teaspoons oil. Add onion, bell pepper, Garlic Powder with Parsley and hot pepper sauce and cook over medium-high heat 5 to 7 minutes or until onion is tender. Remove vegetable mixture from skillet; set aside. Heat remaining 2 tablespoons oil in same skillet. Remove chicken from marinade; discard used marinade. Add chicken to skillet and cook over medium-high heat 8 to 10 minutes or until chicken is no longer pink in center, stirring frequently. Return vegetable mixture to skillet with tomato and cilantro; heat through. Serve with flour tortillas and lime wedges. *Makes 4 to 6 servings*

Serving Suggestion: Top fajitas with dairy sour cream, guacamole, salsa and pitted ripe olives as desired.

Hint: One package (1.27 ounces) Lawry's® Spices & Seasonings for Fajitas, 1/4 cup lime juice and 1/4 cup vegetable oil can be substituted.

> ### *Helpful Hint*
> *A reamer is a hand-held tool, often wooden, that is inserted into a citrus fruit half and twisted to extract the juice.*

Quick and Easy Italian Sandwich

1 tablespoon olive or vegetable oil
1/2 pound mild Italian sausage, casing removed, sliced 1/2 inch thick
1 can (14.5 ounces) CONTADINA® Recipe Ready Diced Tomatoes with Italian Herbs, undrained
1/2 cup sliced green bell pepper
6 sandwich-size English muffins, split, toasted
1/4 cup (1 ounce) shredded Parmesan cheese, divided

1. Heat oil in medium skillet. Add sausage; cook 3 to 4 minutes or until no longer pink in center, stirring occasionally. Drain.

2. Add undrained tomatoes and bell pepper; simmer, uncovered, 5 minutes, stirring occasionally.

3. Spread 1/2 cup meat mixture on each of 6 muffin halves; sprinkle with Parmesan cheese. Top with remaining muffin halves. *Makes 6 servings*

Ranch Bacon and Egg Salad Sandwich

6 hard-cooked eggs, cooled and peeled
1/4 cup HIDDEN VALLEY® Original Ranch® Dressing
1/4 cup diced celery
3 tablespoons crisp-cooked, crumbled bacon*
1 tablespoon diced green onion
8 slices sandwich bread
Lettuce and tomato (optional)

Bacon pieces may be used.

Coarsely chop eggs. Combine with dressing, celery, bacon and onion in a medium mixing bowl; mix well. Chill until just before serving. Spread salad evenly on 4 bread slices; arrange lettuce and tomato on egg salad, if desired. Top with remaining bread slices. *Makes 4 sandwiches (about 2 cups salad)*

French Dip Sandwiches

(Pictured at right)

1/2 cup A.1.® Original or A.1.® BOLD & SPICY
  Steak Sauce, divided
1 tablespoon GREY POUPON® Dijon Mustard
4 steak rolls, split horizontally
8 ounces sliced cooked roast beef
1 (14-1/2-ounce) can beef broth

Blend 1/4 cup steak sauce and mustard; spread mixture evenly on cut sides of roll tops. Arrange 2 ounces beef on each roll bottom; replace roll tops over beef. Slice sandwiches in half crosswise, if desired.

Heat broth and remaining 1/4 cup steak sauce in small saucepan, stirring occasionally. Serve as a dipping sauce with sandwiches. Garnish as desired.

Makes 4 servings

Muffuletta

1 (9-3/4-ounce) jar green olive salad, drained
  and chopped
1/4 cup pitted black olives, chopped
1 large stalk celery, finely chopped
1-1/2 teaspoons TABASCO® brand Pepper Sauce,
  divided
1 (8-inch) round loaf crusty French *or* sourdough
  bread
3 tablespoons olive oil
4 ounces sliced salami
4 ounces sliced baked ham
4 ounces sliced provolone cheese

Combine green olive salad, black olives, celery and 1 teaspoon TABASCO® Sauce in medium bowl. Cut bread crosswise in half; remove some of soft inside from each half. Combine oil and remaining 1/2 teaspoon TABASCO® Sauce in small bowl. Brush mixture on inside of bread. Fill bottom with olive mixture. Top with salami, ham and provolone slices. Top with remaining bread half. Cut loaf into quarters.

Makes 4 to 6 servings

Note: To heat Muffuletta, preheat oven to 350°F. Before cutting, place sandwich on rack in oven and heat 10 minutes or until cheese is melted.

Seafood Salad Sandwiches

1 envelope LIPTON® RECIPE SECRETS® Vegetable
  Soup Mix
3/4 cup sour cream
1/2 cup chopped celery
1/4 cup mayonnaise
1 tablespoon fresh or frozen chopped chives
  (optional)
1 teaspoon lemon juice
  Hot pepper sauce to taste
1/8 teaspoon ground black pepper
2 packages (6 ounces each) frozen crabmeat,
  thawed and well drained*
4 hard rolls, halved
  Lettuce leaves

Variations: Use 1 package (12 ounces) frozen cleaned shrimp, cooked and coarsely chopped; or 2 packages (8 ounces each) sea legs, thawed, drained and chopped; or 1 can (12 ounces) tuna, drained and flaked; or 2 cans (6 ounces each) medium or large shrimp, drained and chopped; or 2 cans (6 ounces each) crabmeat, drained and flaked.

In large bowl, blend soup mix, sour cream, celery, mayonnaise, chives, lemon juice, hot pepper sauce and pepper. Stir in crabmeat; chill. To serve, line rolls with lettuce, then fill with crab mixture.

Makes 4 sandwiches

Cheesy Broccoli and Chicken Sandwiches

1 box (10 ounces) BIRDS EYE® frozen Broccoli
  with Cheese Sauce
4 teaspoons prepared mustard
4 slices bread, toasted
8 ounces boneless, skinless chicken breast,
  cooked and thinly sliced
1 tomato, thinly sliced
4 slices bacon, cooked crisp

• In medium saucepan, cook broccoli according to package directions.

• Meanwhile, spread mustard on 1 side of each bread slice.

• Arrange cooked chicken, tomato and bacon over mustard.

• Spoon broccoli with cheese sauce over top of each open-faced sandwich.

Makes 4 servings

Beefy Calzones

(Pictured at right)

    1 pound ground beef
1/4 cup finely chopped onion
1/4 cup finely chopped green bell pepper
    2 cloves garlic, minced
    1 (15-ounce) can tomato sauce
1/2 cup A.1.® THICK & HEARTY Steak Sauce
    1 teaspoon Italian seasoning
    2 (10-ounce) packages refrigerated pizza crust
      dough
    2 cups shredded mozzarella cheese (8 ounces)

In large skillet, over medium-high heat, cook beef, onion, pepper and garlic until beef is no longer pink, stirring to break up meat; drain. Keep warm.

In small skillet, over medium-high heat, heat tomato sauce, steak sauce and Italian seasoning to a boil. Reduce heat to low; simmer 5 minutes or until slightly thickened. Stir 1 cup tomato sauce mixture into beef mixture; set aside. Keep remaining tomato sauce mixture warm.

Unroll pizza dough from 1 package; divide into 4 equal pieces. Roll each piece into 6-inch square; spoon 1/3 cup reserved beef mixture onto center of each square. Top with 1/4 cup cheese. Fold dough over to form triangle. Press edges together, sealing well with tines of fork. Place on lightly greased baking sheets. Repeat with remaining dough, filling and cheese to make a total of 8 calzones. Bake at 400°F 20 minutes or until golden brown. Serve with warm sauce. Garnish as desired.

Makes 8 servings

Helpful Hint

Store garlic bulbs, loosely covered, in a cool, dark location with good air circulation. A specialized covered terra-cotta container with holes for air circulation is available for storing garlic bulbs. Bulbs may be stored up to ten days. After peeling, they may be tightly wrapped in plastic and refrigerated for a day or two.

Monte Cristo Sandwiches

1/3 cup HELLMANN'S® or BEST FOODS® Real or
      Light Mayonnaise or Low Fat Mayonnaise
      Dressing
1/4 teaspoon ground nutmeg
1/8 teaspoon freshly ground pepper
  12 slices white bread, crusts removed
    6 slices Swiss cheese
    6 slices cooked ham
    6 slices cooked chicken
    2 eggs
1/2 cup milk

1. In small bowl, combine mayonnaise, nutmeg and pepper; spread on one side of each bread slice.

2. Layer cheese, ham and chicken on 6 bread slices; top with remaining bread, mayonnaise sides down. Cut sandwiches diagonally into quarters.

3. In small bowl, beat together eggs and milk; dip sandwich quarters into egg mixture.

4. Cook on preheated greased griddle or in skillet, turning once, 4 to 5 minutes or until browned and heated through. *Makes 24 mini sandwiches*

Cheeseburger Joe

    1 pound ground beef
1/2 pound (12 ounces) VELVEETA® Pasteurized
      Prepared Cheese Product, cut up
1/4 cup catsup
    1 to 2 teaspoons onion powder
    1 teaspoon KRAFT® Pure Prepared Mustard
      (optional)
    6 hamburger buns, split

1. Brown meat in skillet; drain.

2. Add Velveeta, catsup, onion powder and mustard; reduce heat to medium-low. Stir until Velveeta is melted. Serve in buns. *Makes 6 servings*

Serving Suggestion: To make these sandwiches less messy, buy unsliced hamburger buns and cut off the top quarter of each bun. Hollow out the bottom part of the bun, then spoon Cheeseburger Joe into the bun and replace the top.

Beef Tip Steak Barbecue

1 pound beef round tip steaks, cut 1/8 to
    1/4 inch thick
1 tablespoon vegetable oil
1 large onion, halved lengthwise
1/2 cup A.1.® Original or A.1.® BOLD & SPICY
    Steak Sauce
1/3 cup chili sauce
1/4 cup water
1 tablespoon GREY POUPON® Dijon Mustard
4 hamburger buns or corn muffins, split

Cut steaks crosswise into 1/2-inch-wide strips; cut each strip in half. Heat oil in large skillet over medium-high heat. Stir-fry half the steak 30 to 60 seconds or to desired doneness; remove from skillet to large bowl. Repeat with remaining steak; remove from skillet to same bowl. Keep warm.

Cut onion halves into thin slices. Add to skillet; stir-fry 5 minutes or until tender. Mix steak sauce, chili sauce, water and mustard; add to onion. Reduce heat; simmer 5 minutes. Remove skillet from heat; stir in steak mixture. Spoon steak mixture onto bun bottoms; cover with tops. *Makes 4 servings*

Blazing Catfish Po' Boy

Blazing Catfish Po' Boys

(Pictured below left)

1-1/2 pounds catfish fillets
  3/4 cup yellow cornmeal
    1 egg
  1/3 cup *Frank's® RedHot®* Cayenne Pepper Sauce
    6 sandwich rolls, split in half
      Spicy Tartar Sauce (recipe follows)
    3 cups deli coleslaw

1. Cut fillets crosswise into 1-inch-wide strips. Combine cornmeal and *1/2 teaspoon salt* on sheet of waxed paper. Beat egg with *Frank's RedHot* in medium bowl. Dip fish pieces in egg mixture; shake off excess. Thoroughly coat with cornmeal mixture.

2. Heat *1-1/2 cups vegetable oil* in large deep skillet or electric fryer until hot (360°F). Cook fish, in batches, 5 minutes or until cooked through and golden on all sides, turning once. Drain on paper towels.

3. Hollow out rolls if necessary. Spread bottom of each roll with about *2 tablespoons* Spicy Tartar Sauce. Layer with *1/2 cup* coleslaw and a few pieces of fish. Cover with top of roll.

Makes 6 sandwiches

Spicy Tartar Sauce: Combine 2/3 cup prepared tartar sauce with 1/4 cup *Frank's RedHot*.

Best Ever Beef Heroes

(Pictured on page 92)

3 tablespoons mayonnaise
1 tablespoon Dijon mustard
2 teaspoons prepared horseradish
4 submarine or hoagie rolls, split
4 red leaf or romaine lettuce leaves
1 pound sliced deli roast beef
1 thin slice red onion, separated into rings
8 slices SARGENTO® Deli Style Sliced Swiss
    Cheese

1. Combine mayonnaise, mustard and horseradish; mix well. Spread on cut sides of rolls.

2. Fill rolls with lettuce, roast beef, onion rings and cheese. Close sandwiches; cut in half.

Makes 4 servings

Grilled Panini Sandwich

Grilled Panini Sandwiches

(Pictured above)

 8 slices country Italian, sourdough or other
  firm-textured bread
 8 slices SARGENTO® Deli Style Sliced
  Mozzarella Cheese
 1/3 cup prepared pesto
 4 large slices ripe tomato
 2 tablespoons olive oil

1. Top each of 4 slices of bread with a slice of cheese. Spread pesto over cheese. Arrange tomatoes on top, then another slice of cheese. Close sandwiches with remaining 4 slices bread.

2. Brush olive oil lightly over both sides of sandwiches. Cook sandwiches over medium-low coals or in a preheated ridged grill pan over medium heat 3 to 4 minutes per side or until bread is toasted and cheese is melted.

Makes 4 servings

Hidden Valley® Wraps

(Pictured on page 92)

 1 cup HIDDEN VALLEY® Original Ranch®
  Dressing
 1 package (8 ounces) cream cheese, softened
 10 ounces sliced turkey breast
 10 ounces Monterey Jack cheese slices
 2 large avocados, peeled and thinly sliced
 2 medium tomatoes, thinly sliced
  Shredded lettuce
 4 (12-inch) flour tortillas, warmed

Beat together dressing and cream cheese. Evenly layer half the turkey, Monterey Jack cheese, dressing mixture, avocados, tomatoes and lettuce in tortillas, leaving a 1-inch border around edges. Repeat layering with remaining ingredients. Fold right and left edges of tortillas into centers over the filling. Fold the bottom edge toward the center and roll firmly until completely wrapped. Place seam side down and cut in half diagonally.

Makes 4 servings

Shrimp Pitas

(Pictured at right)

3/4 cup olive oil
1/2 cup red wine vinegar
2 medium onions, chopped, divided
2 cloves garlic, minced, divided
2 teaspoons Italian seasoning, divided
1 pound medium shrimp, peeled and deveined
2 medium red or green bell peppers, julienned
4 cups fresh spinach leaves, stems removed and torn
3 cups cooked brown rice
1 teaspoon salt
1/2 teaspoon ground black pepper
3 pieces pita bread (about 6 inches), each cut in half

Combine olive oil, vinegar, 1/2 cup chopped onion, 1 clove garlic and 1 teaspoon Italian seasoning in large bowl. Add shrimp; stir until well coated. Cover and marinate in refrigerator 4 hours or overnight.

Thoroughly drain shrimp; discard marinade. Heat large skillet over medium-high heat until hot. Add shrimp, remaining onion, bell peppers, spinach and remaining 1 clove garlic; sauté 3 to 5 minutes or until shrimp are no longer pink and spinach is wilted. Add rice, remaining 1 teaspoon Italian seasoning, salt and black pepper. Cook and stir 2 to 3 minutes or until flavors are well blended. To serve, fill each pita with 1/2 to 3/4 cup rice mixture.

Makes 6 servings

Favorite recipe from **USA Rice Federation**

Eggplant & Pepper Cheese Sandwiches

1 (8-ounce) eggplant, cut into 18 slices
Salt and black pepper, to taste
1/3 cup GREY POUPON® COUNTRY DIJON® Mustard
1/4 cup olive oil
2 tablespoons red wine vinegar
3/4 teaspoon dried oregano leaves
1 clove garlic, crushed
6 (4-inch) pieces French bread, cut in half
1 (7-ounce) jar roasted red peppers, cut into strips
1-1/2 cups shredded mozzarella cheese (6 ounces)

1. Place eggplant slices on greased baking sheet, overlapping slightly. Sprinkle lightly with salt and pepper. Bake at 400°F for 10 to 12 minutes or until tender.

2. Blend mustard, oil, vinegar, oregano and garlic. Brush eggplant slices with 1/4 cup mustard mixture; broil eggplant for 1 minute.

3. Brush cut sides of French bread with remaining mustard mixture. Layer 3 slices eggplant, a few red pepper strips and 1/4 cup cheese on each bread bottom. Place on broiler pan with bread tops, cut-sides up; broil until cheese melts. Close sandwiches with bread tops and serve immediately; garnish as desired.

Makes 6 sandwiches

Kielbasa & Kraut Heroes

1 tablespoon vegetable oil
2 large red onions, cut in half lengthwise and thinly sliced
2 pounds kielbasa, thickly sliced
2 pounds sauerkraut, rinsed and well drained
1 can (12 ounces) beer or nonalcoholic malt beverage
1/2 cup *French's*® Hearty Deli Brown Mustard
1 tablespoon caraway seeds
8 hot dog or hero-style buns

1. Heat oil in large nonstick skillet over medium heat. Add onions; cook 5 minutes or just until tender, stirring often. Remove from skillet.

2. Add kielbasa to skillet; cook and stir 5 minutes or until lightly browned. Drain well. Stir in sauerkraut, beer, mustard and caraway seeds. Cook over low heat 10 minutes or until most of liquid is absorbed, stirring occasionally. Serve in buns.

Makes 8 servings

Tip: This recipe may be prepared ahead. To reheat, place mixture in 12×9-inch disposable foil pan; cover. Place on grid; cook over medium heat 15 minutes, stirring occasionally.

Breads

Savory Onion Focaccia

(Pictured at left)

1 pound frozen pizza or bread dough*
1 tablespoon olive oil
1 clove garlic, minced
1-1/3 cups *French's® Taste Toppers™* French Fried Onions,
    divided
1 cup (4 ounces) shredded mozzarella cheese
1/2 pound plum tomatoes (4 small), thinly sliced
2 teaspoons fresh chopped rosemary *or* 1/2 teaspoon dried
    rosemary
3 tablespoons grated Parmesan cheese

*Pizza dough may be found in frozen section of supermarket. Thaw in refrigerator before using.

Bring pizza dough to room temperature. Grease 15×10-inch jelly-roll pan. Roll or pat dough into rectangle same size as pan on floured board.** Transfer dough to pan.

Combine oil and garlic in small bowl; brush onto surface of dough. Cover loosely with kitchen towel. Let dough rise at room temperature 25 minutes. Prick dough with fork.

Preheat oven to 450°F. Bake dough 20 minutes or until edges and bottom of crust are golden. Sprinkle *1 cup* **Taste Toppers** and mozzarella cheese over dough. Arrange tomatoes over cheese; sprinkle with rosemary. Bake 5 minutes or until cheese melts.

Sprinkle with remaining *1/3 cup* **Taste Toppers** and Parmesan cheese. Bake 2 minutes or until **Taste Toppers** are golden. To serve, cut into rectangles.   *Makes 8 appetizer servings*

**If dough is too hard to roll, allow to rest on floured board.

Clockwise from top left: *Apple Crumb Coffeecake (p. 110), Gingerbread Streusel Raisin Muffins (p. 110), Savory Onion Focaccia and Freezer Rolls (p. 124)*

Cinnamon Honey Buns

(Pictured at right)

1/4 cup butter or margarine, softened and divided
1/2 cup honey, divided
1/4 cup chopped toasted nuts
2 teaspoons ground cinnamon
1 loaf (1 pound) frozen bread dough, thawed
    according to package directions
2/3 cup raisins

Grease 12 muffin cups with 1 tablespoon butter. To prepare topping, mix together 1 tablespoon butter, 1/4 cup honey and chopped nuts. Place 1 teaspoon topping in each muffin cup. To prepare filling, mix together remaining 2 tablespoons butter, remaining 1/4 cup honey and cinnamon. Roll out bread dough onto floured surface into 18×8-inch rectangle. Spread filling evenly over dough. Sprinkle with raisins. Starting with long side, roll dough into log. Cut log into 12 (1-1/2-inch) slices. Place 1 slice, cut-side up, into each prepared muffin cup. Set muffin pan in warm place; let dough rise 30 minutes. Place muffin pan on foil-lined baking sheet. Bake at 375°F 20 minutes or until buns are golden brown. Remove from oven; cool in pan 5 minutes. Invert muffin pan to remove buns.   *Makes 12 buns*

Favorite recipe from **National Honey Board**

Gingerbread Streusel Raisin Muffins

(Pictured on page 108)

1 cup raisins
1/2 cup boiling water
1/3 cup margarine or butter, softened
3/4 cup GRANDMA'S® Molasses (Unsulphured)
1 egg
2 cups all-purpose flour
1-1/2 teaspoons baking soda
1/2 teaspoon salt
1 teaspoon cinnamon
1 teaspoon ginger

TOPPING
1/3 cup all-purpose flour
1/4 cup firmly packed brown sugar
1/4 cup chopped nuts
3 tablespoons margarine or butter
1 teaspoon cinnamon

Preheat oven to 375°F. Grease bottoms only of 12 muffin cups or line with paper baking cups. In small bowl, cover raisins with boiling water; let stand 5 minutes. In large bowl, beat 1/3 cup margarine and molasses until fluffy. Add egg; beat well. Stir in 2 cups flour, baking soda, salt, 1 teaspoon cinnamon and ginger. Blend just until dry ingredients are moistened. Gently stir in raisins and water. Fill prepared muffin cups 3/4 full. For topping, combine all ingredients in small bowl. Sprinkle over muffins.

Bake 20 to 25 minutes or until toothpick inserted in centers comes out clean. Cool 5 minutes; remove from pan. Serve warm.   *Makes 12 muffins*

Apple Crumb Coffeecake

(Pictured on page 108)

2-1/4 cups all-purpose flour
1/2 cup sugar
1 envelope FLEISCHMANN'S® RapidRise™ Yeast
1/2 teaspoon salt
1/4 cup water
1/4 cup milk
1/3 cup butter or margarine
2 large eggs
2 cooking apples, cored and sliced
Crumb Topping (recipe follows)

In large bowl, combine 1 cup flour, sugar, undissolved yeast, and salt. Heat water, milk, and butter until very warm (120° to 130°F). Gradually add to dry ingredients. Beat 2 minutes at medium speed of electric mixer, scraping bowl occasionally. Add eggs and 1/2 cup flour. Beat 2 minutes at high speed, scraping bowl occasionally. Stir in remaining flour to make stiff batter. Spread evenly in greased 9-inch square pan. Arrange apple slices evenly over batter. Sprinkle Crumb Topping over apples. Cover; let rise in warm, draft-free place until doubled in size, about 1 hour.

Bake at 375°F for 35 to 40 minutes or until done. Cool in pan 10 minutes. Remove from pan; cool on wire rack.   *Makes 1 (9-inch) cake*

Crumb Topping: Combine 1/3 cup sugar, 1/4 cup all-purpose flour, 1 teaspoon ground cinnamon, and 3 tablespoons cold butter or margarine until crumbly.

Apple Sauce Coffee Ring

(Pictured below)

BREAD
- 1 package active dry yeast
- 1/3 cup plus 1 teaspoon granulated sugar, divided
- 1/4 cup warm water (105° to 115°F)
- 1/2 cup skim milk
- 1/2 cup MOTT'S® Natural Apple Sauce
- 1 egg
- 2 tablespoons margarine, melted and cooled
- 1 teaspoon salt
- 1 teaspoon grated lemon peel
- 5 cups all-purpose flour
- 1 teaspoon skim milk

FILLING
- 1-1/2 cups MOTT'S® Chunky Apple Sauce
- 1/2 cup raisins
- 1/3 cup firmly packed light brown sugar
- 1 teaspoon ground cinnamon

GLAZE
- 1 cup powdered sugar
- 2 tablespoons skim milk
- 1 teaspoon vanilla extract

Apple Sauce Coffee Ring

1. To prepare Bread, in large bowl, sprinkle yeast and 1 teaspoon granulated sugar over warm water; stir until yeast dissolves. Let stand 5 minutes or until mixture is bubbly. Stir in 1/2 cup milk, 1/2 cup apple sauce, remaining 1/3 cup granulated sugar, egg, margarine, salt and lemon peel.

2. Stir in flour, 1 cup at a time, until soft dough forms. Turn out dough onto floured surface; flatten slightly. Knead 5 minutes or until smooth and elastic, adding any remaining flour to prevent sticking if necessary. Shape dough into ball; place in large bowl sprayed with nonstick cooking spray. Turn dough over so that top is greased. Cover with damp towel; let rise in warm place 1 hour or until doubled in bulk.

3. Punch down dough. Roll out dough on floured surface into 15-inch square. Spray baking sheet with nonstick cooking spray.

4. To prepare Filling, in small bowl, mix 1-1/2 cups chunky apple sauce, raisins, brown sugar and cinnamon. Spread filling over dough to within 1/2 inch of edges. Roll up dough jelly-roll style. Moisten edge with water; pinch to seal seam. Moisten ends of dough with water; bring together to form ring. Pinch to seal seam. Place on prepared baking sheet. Make 1/8-inch-deep cuts across width of dough at 2-inch intervals around ring.

5. Let dough rise in warm place, uncovered, 30 minutes.

6. Preheat oven to 350°F. Brush top lightly with 1 teaspoon milk.

7. Bake 45 to 50 minutes or until lightly browned and ring sounds hollow when tapped. Remove from baking sheet; cool completely on wire rack.

8. To prepare Glaze, in small bowl, combine powdered sugar, 2 tablespoons milk and vanilla until smooth. Drizzle over top of ring. Cut into 24 slices.

Makes 24 servings

Helpful Hint

For an easy and special breakfast, freeze a fresh-baked, cooled coffee cake before adding the glaze; frost it after thawing. Thaw the unwrapped coffee cake at room temperature for two to three hours; or heat it, partially unwrapped, in a 375°F oven for 20 minutes.

Crispy Onion Crescent Rolls

Crispy Onion Crescent Rolls

(Pictured above)

1 can (8 ounces) refrigerated crescent dinner rolls
1-1/3 cups *French's*® Taste Toppers™ French Fried Onions, slightly crushed
1 egg, beaten

Preheat oven to 375°F. Line large baking sheet with foil. Separate refrigerated rolls into 8 triangles. Sprinkle center of each triangle with about 1-1/2 tablespoons ***Taste Toppers***. Roll-up triangles from short side, jelly-roll fashion. Sprinkle any excess ***Taste Toppers*** over tops of crescents.

Arrange crescents on prepared baking sheet. Brush with beaten egg. Bake 15 minutes or until golden brown and crispy. Transfer to wire rack; cool slightly. *Makes 8 servings*

Mexican Corn Bread

1/4 pound VELVEETA® Mexican Pasteurized Process Cheese Spread with Jalapeño Peppers, cubed
2 tablespoons milk
1 egg, beaten
1 (8-1/2-ounce) package corn muffin mix

• Preheat oven to 350°F.

• Stir together process cheese spread and milk in saucepan over low heat until process cheese spread is melted. Add with egg to muffin mix, mixing just until moistened. Pour into greased 8-inch square baking pan.

• Bake 20 minutes. *Makes 6 to 8 servings*

Variation: Substitute VELVEETA® Pasteurized Prepared Cheese Product for VELVEETA® Pasteurized Process Cheese Spread with Jalapeño Peppers.

Honey Sweet Potato Biscuits

(Pictured at right)

>2 cups all-purpose flour
>1 tablespoon baking powder
>1/2 teaspoon salt
>1/4 cup vegetable shortening
>1 tablespoon grated orange peel
>1 tablespoon grated lemon peel
>3/4 cup mashed cooked sweet potato (1 large sweet potato baked until tender, peeled and mashed)
>1/3 cup honey
>1/2 cup milk (about)

Combine flour, baking powder and salt in large bowl. Cut in shortening until mixture resembles small peas. Add orange and lemon peels, sweet potato and honey; mix well. Add enough milk to make soft, but not sticky, dough. Knead 3 or 4 times on lightly floured surface. Pat dough to 1-inch thickness and cut into 2-1/4-inch rounds. Place on ungreased baking sheet.

Bake in preheated 400°F oven 15 to 18 minutes or until lightly browned. Serve warm.

Makes 10 biscuits

Favorite recipe from **National Honey Board**

Cherry Swirl Coffee Cake

>1-1/4 cups milk
>1/2 cup shortening or margarine
>1/4 cup sugar
>1 teaspoon salt
>1 package (1/4 ounce) active dry yeast
>3-1/4 cups all-purpose flour
>2 eggs
>1/2 teaspoon vanilla
>1 cup (12-ounce jar) SMUCKER'S® Cherry Preserves
>1 cup powdered sugar
>Milk
>1/3 cup sliced almonds

In small saucepan, combine 1-1/4 cups milk, shortening, sugar and salt; bring just to a boil. Cool to lukewarm (105° to 115°F). Stir in yeast; transfer mixture to medium bowl.

Add 1 cup flour to milk mixture; beat well. Add eggs and vanilla; beat well. Stir in enough of the remaining flour to make a thick batter; beat until smooth. Cover and set in warm place until doubled in size, about 1 hour.

Stir batter down and pour into two greased 9-inch round cake pans; cover and set in warm place until doubled in size, about 1 hour. Make a swirl design on top of batter with a floured spoon; fill grooves with preserves, using 1/4 cup for each coffee cake.

Bake at 375°F for 30 to 35 minutes or until golden brown. Remove from pans; cool slightly on wire racks. Fill grooves with remaining preserves.

Mix powdered sugar with enough milk to make a thin glaze consistency; drizzle over warm coffee cakes. Sprinkle with almonds.

Makes 2 coffee cakes

Cranberry Orange Nut Muffins

>MAZOLA NO STICK® Cooking Spray
>1-1/2 cups flour
>1/2 cup sugar
>2 teaspoons baking powder
>1/2 teaspoon salt
>2 eggs
>1/2 cup KARO® Light Corn Syrup
>1/2 cup orange juice
>1/4 cup MAZOLA® Oil
>1 teaspoon grated orange peel
>1 cup fresh or frozen cranberries, chopped
>1/2 cup chopped walnuts

1. Preheat oven to 400°F. Spray 12 (2-1/2-inch) muffin pan cups with cooking spray.

2. In medium bowl, combine flour, sugar, baking powder and salt. In large bowl, combine eggs, corn syrup, orange juice, oil and orange peel. Stir in flour mixture until well blended. Stir in cranberries and walnuts. Spoon into prepared muffin pan cups.

3. Bake 18 to 20 minutes or until lightly browned and firm to touch. Cool in pan on wire rack 5 minutes; remove from pan. *Makes 12 muffins*

Bacon Brunch Buns

(Pictured at right)

1 loaf (1 pound) frozen bread dough
1/4 cup unsalted butter or margarine, melted
2 tablespoons (1/2 package) HIDDEN VALLEY®
    Original Ranch® with Bacon salad dressing
    mix
1 cup shredded Cheddar cheese
2 egg yolks
1-1/2 tablespoons cold water
3 tablespoons sesame seeds

Thaw bread dough following package directions. Preheat oven to 375°F. On floured board, roll dough into rectangle about 18×7 inches. In small bowl, whisk together butter and salad dressing mix. Spread mixture on dough; sprinkle with cheese. Roll up tightly, jelly-roll style, pinching seam to seal. Cut into 16 slices. Place slices cut-side down on greased jelly-roll pan. Cover with plastic wrap and let rise until doubled in bulk, about 1 hour. In small bowl, beat egg yolks and water; brush mixture over buns. Sprinkle with sesame seeds. Bake until golden brown, 25 to 30 minutes. Serve warm.

Makes 16 buns

Fiesta Corn Bread

2 cups all-purpose flour
1-1/2 cups white or yellow cornmeal
1-1/2 cups (6 ounces) shredded mild Cheddar cheese
1 cup (7-ounce can) ORTEGA® Diced Green
    Chiles
1/2 cup granulated sugar
1 tablespoon baking powder
1-1/2 teaspoons salt
1-1/2 cups (12 fluid-ounce can) NESTLÉ®
    CARNATION® Evaporated Milk
1/2 cup vegetable oil
2 large eggs, lightly beaten

PREHEAT oven to 375°F. Lightly grease 13×9-inch baking pan.

COMBINE flour, cornmeal, cheese, chiles, sugar, baking powder and salt in large bowl. Add evaporated milk, vegetable oil and eggs; stir just until moistened. Spread into prepared baking pan.

BAKE for 30 to 35 minutes or until wooden pick inserted in center comes out clean. Cool in pan on wire rack for 10 minutes; cut into squares. Serve warm. *Makes 24 servings*

Soft Pretzels

2-1/2 to 3 cups all-purpose flour, divided
1 package RED STAR® Active Dry Yeast or
    QUICK•RISE™ Yeast
1 tablespoon sugar
1/2 teaspoon salt
1 cup warm water (120° to 130°F)
2 tablespoons oil
2 quarts water
1/3 cup baking soda
1 egg white, slightly beaten
    Coarse salt

In large mixer bowl, combine 1-1/4 cups flour, yeast, sugar and salt; mix well. Add 1 cup warm water and oil to flour mixture. Blend at low speed until moistened; beat 3 minutes at medium speed. By hand, gradually stir in enough remaining flour to make a firm dough. Knead on floured surface until smooth and elastic, 5 to 8 minutes. Place in greased bowl, turning to grease top. Cover; let rise in warm place until light and doubled, about 1 hour (30 minutes for Quick•Rise™ Yeast).

Punch down dough. Divide into 4 parts. Divide each part into 3 pieces. On lightly floured surface, roll each piece into an 18-inch rope. Shape rope into a circle, overlapping about 4 inches from each end and leaving ends free. Take one end of dough in each hand and twist at the point where dough overlaps. Carefully lift ends across to the opposite edge of the circle. Tuck ends under edge to make a pretzel shape; moisten and press ends to seal. Place on greased cookie sheets. Let rise, uncovered, until puffy, about 20 minutes (10 minutes for Quick•Rise™ Yeast). In a 3-quart stainless or enameled saucepan, bring water and baking soda to a boil. Lower 1 or 2 pretzels into saucepan; simmer for 10 seconds on each side. Lift from water with slotted spoon or spatula; drain. Place on well greased cookie sheet. Let dry briefly. Brush with egg white; sprinkle with coarse salt. Bake at 425°F for 12 to 15 minutes until browned. Remove from cookie sheet. Serve warm with butter or mustard, if desired.

Makes 12 pretzels

Bacon Brunch Buns

Fruited Oat Scones

(Pictured at right)

1-1/2 cups all-purpose flour
1-1/4 cups QUAKER® Oats (quick or old fashioned, uncooked)
1/4 cup sugar
1 tablespoon baking powder
1/4 teaspoon salt (optional)
1/3 cup (5-1/3 tablespoons) margarine
1-1/3 cups (6-ounce package) diced dried mixed fruit
1/2 cup milk
1 egg, lightly beaten
1 teaspoon sugar
1/8 teaspoon ground cinnamon

Preheat oven to 375°F. Combine flour, oats, 1/4 cup sugar, baking powder and salt; mix well. Cut in margarine until mixture resembles coarse crumbs; stir in fruit. Add milk and egg, mixing just until moistened. Shape dough to form a ball. Turn out onto floured surface; knead gently 6 times. On lightly greased cookie sheet, pat out dough to form 8-inch circle. With sharp knife, score round into 12 wedges; sprinkle with combined 1 teaspoon sugar and cinnamon. Bake about 30 minutes or until golden brown. Break apart; serve warm.

Makes 1 dozen scones

Pumpernickel Raisin Bread

3 tablespoons plus 1 teaspoon GRANDMA'S® Gold Molasses, divided
2 packages (1/4 ounce each) active dry yeast
1-1/4 cups warm water (105° to 115°F), divided
2 cups all-purpose flour
1 cup rye flour
2 tablespoons unsweetened cocoa powder
2 teaspoons salt
2 teaspoons caraway seeds
1-1/2 cups golden raisins

GLAZE
1 tablespoon GRANDMA'S® Gold Molasses
1 tablespoon water
2 tablespoons caraway seeds

1. Dissolve 1 teaspoon Grandma's® Gold Molasses and yeast in 1/4 cup warm water in small bowl. Let stand until foamy, about 5 minutes.

2. Combine flours, cocoa, salt and 2 teaspoons caraway seeds in 12-cup food processor fitted with dough or steel blade. Add yeast mixture; mix well. Mix remaining 1 cup warm water and 3 tablespoons Grandma's® Gold Molasses in medium bowl.

3. With machine running, pour molasses mixture slowly through food tube. When dough forms a ball, process 1 minute. If dough sticks to side of bowl, add additional flour, 2 tablespoons at a time. If dough is too dry and does not stick together, add water, 1 tablespoon at a time.

4. Place dough in large greased bowl and turn to coat; cover with plastic wrap. Bring large shallow pot of water to a simmer. Remove from heat; place wire rack in pot. Place bowl with dough on rack; cover with towel. Let rise 1 to 1-1/4 hours or until doubled in bulk.

5. Punch dough down; flatten to 1/4-inch thickness. Sprinkle with raisins; roll up dough and knead several times. Shape into 8-inch round; place on greased baking sheet. Place on rack over hot water as directed above; cover with towel. Let rise 1 to 1-1/4 hours or until doubled.

6. For glaze, combine 1 tablespoon Grandma's® Gold Molasses and 1 tablespoon water. Brush over loaf; sprinkle with 2 tablespoons caraway seeds.

7. Bake in 350°F oven 25 to 30 minutes until bread sounds hollow when tapped. Cool on rack 30 minutes.

Makes 1 large loaf

> ### *Helpful Hint*
> *Before measuring molasses, lightly coat a measuring cup with nonstick cooking spray so the molasses will slide out easily instead of clinging to the cup.*

Broccoli & Cheddar Muffins

(Pictured at right)

3 cups buttermilk baking and pancake mix
2 eggs, lightly beaten
2/3 cup milk
1 teaspoon dried basil
1 cup shredded Cheddar cheese
1 box (10 ounces) BIRDS EYE® frozen Chopped
   Broccoli, thawed and drained

• Preheat oven to 350°F. Combine baking mix, eggs, milk and basil. Mix until moistened. (Do not overmix.)

• Add cheese and broccoli; stir just to combine. Add salt and pepper to taste.

• Spray 12 muffin cups with nonstick cooking spray. Pour batter into muffin cups. Bake 25 to 30 minutes or until golden brown.

• Cool 5 minutes in pan. Loosen sides of muffins with knife; remove from pan and serve warm.
Makes 1 dozen large muffins

Southwestern Corn Muffins: Prepare 1 box corn muffin mix according to package directions; add 2/3 cup BIRDS EYE® frozen Corn and 1 teaspoon chili powder to batter. Mix well; bake according to package directions.

Glazed Cocoa Batter Bread

2-3/4 cups all-purpose flour, divided
1 tablespoon plus 2 cups granulated sugar,
   divided
1 package active dry yeast
3/4 cup milk
1/4 cup water
3/4 cup (1-1/2 sticks) butter or margarine,
   softened
2/3 cup HERSHEY'S Cocoa
1/2 cup hot water
3 eggs, slightly beaten
1 teaspoon vanilla extract
1 teaspoon baking soda
1/4 teaspoon salt
1 cup chopped pecans or walnuts
   Powdered Sugar Frosting (recipe follows)
   Chopped pecans or walnuts

1. Grease 10-inch tube pan.

2. Combine 3/4 cup flour, 1 tablespoon sugar and yeast in large bowl. Heat milk and 1/4 cup water in saucepan until lukewarm. Add to flour mixture; beat on low speed of mixer 2 minutes, scraping sides and bottom of bowl often. Add 3/4 cup flour or enough flour to make soft dough; beat on medium speed 2 minutes. Cover; let rise in warm place (85°F), free from draft until mixture is light and spongy, about 45 minutes.

3. Meanwhile, beat butter with remaining 2 cups sugar; set aside. Stir together cocoa and hot water until smooth; let cool. Add butter and cocoa mixtures to yeast mixture. Beat in eggs, vanilla, remaining flour, baking soda, salt and nuts. Pour into prepared pan. Let rise, uncovered, in warm place free from draft until doubled, about 2 hours. Heat oven to 350°F.

4. Bake 45 minutes or until bread sounds hollow when tapped. Cool on wire rack 10 minutes; remove from pan. Cool completely. Drizzle with Powdered Sugar Frosting; sprinkle additional nuts over top. Let stand 2 to 3 hours before slicing.
Makes 12 to 16 servings

Powdered Sugar Frosting

1 cup sifted powdered sugar
1 tablespoon milk
1/4 teaspoon vanilla extract

Combine all ingredients in small bowl. Add additional milk, 1 teaspoon at a time, until frosting is smooth and of drizzling consistency.
Makes about 1/2 cup frosting

> ### *Helpful Hint*
>
> *For quick-batter breads, such as muffins and coffee cakes, add the combined liquid ingredients to the combined dry ingredients and stir just until the mixture is evenly moistened. The batter should look lumpy when it goes into the prepared pans. Too much stirring or beating will give the breads a tough texture with lots of holes and tunnels.*

*Broccoli & Cheddar Muffins and
Southwestern Corn Muffins*

State Fair Cracked Wheat Bread

(Pictured below)

1-1/3 cups water
2 tablespoons butter or margarine
1 teaspoon salt
1/4 cup cracked wheat
3 cups bread flour
1/2 cup whole wheat flour
3 tablespoons nonfat dry milk powder
2 tablespoons firmly packed brown sugar
2 teaspoons FLEISCHMANN'S® Bread Machine Yeast

Add ingredients to bread machine pan in the order suggested by manufacturer. (If dough is too dry or stiff or too soft or slack, adjust dough consistency.) Recommended cycle: Basic/white bread cycle; medium/normal crust color setting.

Makes 1 (2-pound) loaf

State Fair Cracked Wheat Bread

Pumpkin Maple Cream Cheese Muffins

CREAM CHEESE FILLING
4 ounces cream cheese, softened
2 tablespoons packed brown sugar
1-1/2 teaspoons maple flavoring

MUFFINS
2 cups all-purpose flour
3/4 cup packed brown sugar
1/2 cup chopped walnuts
2 teaspoons baking powder
1 teaspoon ground cinnamon
1/2 teaspoon baking soda
1/4 teaspoon salt
1 cup LIBBY'S® 100% Pure Pumpkin
3/4 cup NESTLÉ® CARNATION® Evaporated Milk
2 eggs
1/4 cup vegetable oil
2 teaspoons maple flavoring
Nut Topping (recipe follows)

FOR CREAM CHEESE FILLING
COMBINE cream cheese, 2 tablespoons brown sugar and 1-1/2 teaspoons maple flavoring in small bowl until blended.

FOR MUFFINS
COMBINE flour, 3/4 cup brown sugar, walnuts, baking powder, cinnamon, baking soda and salt in large bowl. Combine pumpkin, evaporated milk, eggs, oil and 2 teaspoons maple flavoring; mix well. Add pumpkin mixture to flour mixture, mixing just until blended.

SPOON into 12 greased or paper-lined muffin cups (cups will be very full). Dollop 1 heaping teaspoon of Cream Cheese Filling into center of each cup, pressing into batter slightly. Sprinkle Nut Topping over muffins.

BAKE in preheated 400°F. oven 20 to 25 minutes or until wooden pick inserted in center of muffin comes out clean. Cool in pan 5 minutes; remove to wire rack to cool completely.   *Makes 12 muffins*

Nut Topping: COMBINE 2 tablespoons packed brown sugar and 1/4 cup chopped walnuts in bowl.

Calico Bell Pepper Muffins

Calico Bell Pepper Muffins

(Pictured above)

1/4 cup *each* finely chopped red, yellow and green
    bell pepper
2 tablespoons margarine
2 cups all-purpose flour
4 tablespoons sugar
1 tablespoon baking powder
3/4 teaspoon salt
1/2 teaspoon dried basil leaves
1 cup low-fat milk
1 whole egg
2 egg whites

Preheat oven to 400°F. Paper-line 12 muffin cups
or spray with cooking spray. In small skillet, cook
peppers in margarine over medium-high heat until
color is bright and peppers are tender-crisp, about
3 minutes. Set aside.

In large bowl, combine flour, sugar, baking powder,
salt and basil. In small bowl, combine milk, whole
egg and egg whites until blended. Add milk mixture
and peppers with drippings to flour mixture and stir
until just moistened. Spoon into prepared muffin
cups. Bake 15 minutes or until golden brown and
wooden pick inserted in center comes out clean.
Cool briefly and remove from pan.

Makes 12 muffins

Favorite recipe from **The Sugar Association, Inc.**

Helpful Hint

*To easily fill muffin cups, place
the batter in a 4-cup glass
measure. Fill each cup 3/4 full.*

Pecan Sticky Buns

(Pictured at right)

DOUGH *
4-1/2 to 5-1/2 cups all-purpose flour, divided
1/2 cup granulated sugar
1-1/2 teaspoons salt
2 packages active dry yeast
3/4 cup warm milk (105° to 115°F)
1/2 cup warm water (105° to 115°F)
1/4 cup (1/2 stick) margarine or butter, softened
2 eggs

GLAZE
1/2 cup KARO® Light or Dark Corn Syrup
1/2 cup packed light brown sugar
1/4 cup (1/2 stick) margarine or butter
1 cup pecans, coarsely chopped

FILLING
1/2 cup firmly packed light brown sugar
1 teaspoon ground cinnamon
2 tablespoons margarine or butter, melted

1. For Dough: In large bowl combine 2 cups flour, granulated sugar, salt and yeast. Stir in milk, water and softened margarine until blended. Stir in eggs and enough additional flour (about 2 cups) to make a soft dough. Knead on floured surface until smooth and elastic, about 8 minutes. Cover dough and let rest on floured surface 10 minutes.*

2. For Glaze: Meanwhile, in small saucepan over low heat stir corn syrup, brown sugar and margarine until smooth. Pour into 13×9×2-inch baking pan. Sprinkle with pecans; set aside.

3. For Filling: Combine brown sugar and cinnamon; set aside. Roll dough to a 20×12-inch rectangle. Brush dough with 2 tablespoons melted margarine; sprinkle with brown sugar mixture. Starting from a long side, roll up jelly-roll fashion. Pinch seam to seal. Cut into 15 slices. Place cut side up in prepared pan. Cover tightly. Refrigerate 2 to 24 hours.

4. To bake, preheat oven to 375°F. Remove pan from refrigerator. Uncover pan and let stand at room temperature 10 minutes. Bake 28 to 30 minutes or until tops are browned. Invert onto serving tray. Serve warm or cool completely. *Makes 15 rolls*

To use frozen bread dough, omit ingredients for dough. Thaw two 1-pound loaves frozen bread dough in refrigerator overnight. In step 3, press loaves together and roll to a 20×12-inch rectangle; complete as recipe directs.

Freezer Rolls

(Pictured on page 108)

1-1/4 cups warm water (100° to 110°F)
2 envelopes FLEISCHMANN'S® Active Dry Yeast
1/2 cup warm milk (100° to 110°F)
1/3 cup butter or margarine, softened
1/2 cup sugar
1-1/2 teaspoons salt
5-1/2 to 6 cups all-purpose flour
2 large eggs

Place 1/2 cup warm water in large warm bowl. Sprinkle in yeast; stir until dissolved. Add remaining warm water, warm milk, butter, sugar, salt and 2 cups flour. Beat 2 minutes at medium speed of electric mixer. Add eggs and 1/2 cup flour. Beat at high speed for 2 minutes. Stir in enough remaining flour to make soft dough. Turn out onto lightly floured surface. Knead until smooth and elastic, about 8 to 10 minutes. Cover with plastic wrap; let rest for 20 minutes.

Punch dough down. Shape into desired shapes (see below) for dinner rolls. Place on greased baking sheets. Cover with plastic wrap and foil, sealing well. Freeze up to 1 week.* Once frozen, rolls may be placed in plastic freezer bags.

Remove rolls from freezer; place on greased baking sheets. Cover; let rise in warm, draft-free place until doubled in size, about 1-1/2 hours.

Bake at 350°F for 15 minutes or until done. Remove from baking sheets; cool on wire racks.
Makes about 2 dozen rolls

To bake without freezing: After shaping, let rise in warm, draft-free place, until doubled in size, about 1 hour. Bake according to above directions.

Shaping the Dough: Crescents: Divide dough in half. Roll each half to 14-inch circle. Cut each circle into 12 pie-shaped wedges. Roll up tightly from wide end. Curve ends slightly to form crescents.
Knots: Divide dough into 24 equal pieces; roll each piece into 9-inch rope. Tie once loosely.
Coils: Divide dough into 24 equal pieces; roll each piece into 9-inch rope. Coil each rope and tuck end under coil.
Twists: Divide dough into 24 equal pieces; roll each piece into 12-inch rope. Fold each rope in half and twist three to four times. Pinch ends to seal.

Main Dishes

Country Sausage Macaroni and Cheese

(Pictured at left)

1 pound BOB EVANS® Special Seasonings Roll Sausage
1-1/2 cups milk
12 ounces pasteurized processed Cheddar cheese, cut into cubes
1/2 cup Dijon mustard
1 cup diced fresh or drained canned tomatoes
1 cup sliced mushrooms
1/3 cup sliced green onions
1/8 teaspoon cayenne pepper
12 ounces uncooked elbow macaroni
2 tablespoons grated Parmesan cheese

Preheat oven to 350°F. Crumble and cook sausage in medium skillet until browned. Drain on paper towels. Combine milk, cheese and mustard in medium saucepan; cook and stir over low heat until cheese melts and mixture is smooth. Stir in sausage, tomatoes, mushrooms, green onions and cayenne pepper. Remove from heat.

Cook macaroni according to package directions; drain. Combine hot macaroni and cheese mixture in large bowl; toss until well coated. Spoon into greased 2-quart casserole dish. Cover and bake 15 to 20 minutes. Stir; sprinkle with Parmesan cheese. Bake, uncovered, 5 minutes more. Let stand 10 minutes before serving. Refrigerate leftovers.

Makes 6 to 8 servings

Clockwise from top left: *Hickory Pork Tenderloin with Apple Topping (p. 138), Country Sausage Macaroni and Cheese, Hearty Ground Beef Stew (p. 134) and California Chicken Pot Pies (p. 142)*

Hidden Valley® Fried Chicken

(Pictured at right)

> 1 broiler-fryer chicken, cut up (2 to
>   2-1/2 pounds)
> 1 cup prepared HIDDEN VALLEY® Original
>   Ranch® Salad Dressing
> 3/4 cup all-purpose flour
> 1 teaspoon salt
> 1/2 teaspoon freshly ground black pepper
>   Vegetable oil

Place chicken pieces in shallow baking dish; pour salad dressing over chicken. Cover; refrigerate at least 8 hours. Remove chicken. Shake off excess marinade; discard marinade. Preheat oven to 350°F. On plate, mix flour, salt and pepper; roll chicken in seasoned flour. Heat 1/2 inch oil in large skillet until small cube of bread dropped into oil browns in 60 seconds or until oil is 375°F. Fry chicken until golden, 5 to 7 minutes on each side; transfer to baking pan. Bake until chicken is tender and juices run clear, about 30 minutes. Serve with corn muffins, if desired.   *Makes 4 main-dish servings*

Tuscan Tuna Stuffed Pasta Salad

> 16 uncooked jumbo pasta shells
> 1/2 cup balsamic vinaigrette salad dressing
> 1/4 cup chopped fresh basil or parsley
> 1/2 teaspoon salt
> 1/8 teaspoon ground black pepper
>   1 can (15 ounces) white kidney beans, rinsed
>   and drained
>   1 can (6 ounces) white tuna packed in water,
>   drained and flaked
>   1 jar (4 ounces) chopped pimiento, rinsed and
>   drained
> 1-1/3 cups *French's® Taste Toppers*™ French Fried
>   Onions, divided

Cook pasta shells according to package directions using shortest cooking time. Drain; rinse under cold running water. Set aside.

Combine salad dressing, basil, salt and pepper in medium bowl; whisk until well blended. Stir in beans, tuna, pimiento and *2/3 cup Taste Toppers*. Spoon 3 tablespoons bean mixture into each pasta shell. Sprinkle with remaining *2/3 cup Taste Toppers*.

Makes 4 main course or 8 appetizer servings

Mushroom Cheese Burgers

> 3 tablespoons CRISCO® Oil,* divided
> 1/2 cup sliced fresh mushrooms
> 1/2 small onion, peeled and chopped (about
>   1/4 cup)
> 1 teaspoon jarred minced garlic *or* 1 small garlic
>   clove, peeled and minced
> 1 pound lean ground beef
> 1 cup (4 ounces) shredded Cheddar, Swiss or
>   Monterey Jack cheese (or your favorite
>   blend of cheeses)
> 3 tablespoons plain bread crumbs
> 2 tablespoons milk
> 1/2 teaspoon salt
> 1/4 teaspoon freshly ground black pepper
> 1/4 teaspoon dried thyme leaves
> 4 crusty French rolls, toasted if desired

*Use your favorite Crisco Oil product.

1. Heat 2 tablespoons oil in large skillet on medium-high heat. Add mushrooms, onion and garlic. Sauté 5 minutes, stirring often, or until onions are soft. Scrape mixture into mixing bowl. Wipe out skillet with paper towels.

2. Combine mushroom mixture with beef, cheese, bread crumbs, milk, salt, pepper and thyme. Mix well. Form 4 ovals in shape and size of rolls.

3. Heat remaining 1 tablespoon oil in wiped-out skillet on medium-high heat. Add burgers. Cook 4 to 5 minutes. Turn with spatula. Cook 4 to 5 minutes, or to desired doneness. Serve on rolls with favorite burger fixings.   *Makes 4 servings*

> ### Helpful Hint
>
> *Ground beef is a fairly meaningless term. Most people want to know what kind of beef has been ground. To meet USDA standards, all ground beef must be at least 70 percent lean. Ground sirloin and ground round are the leanest. Ground chuck contains more fat and therefore produces juicier hamburgers and meat loaf.*

Sweet 'n' Sour Country Ribs

(Pictured at right)

    3 pounds country-style pork ribs, fat trimmed
    3 large sweet potatoes, peeled and cut into
        2-inch chunks
    2 cups apple juice
1/4 cup cider vinegar
1/4 cup *French's®* Worcestershire Sauce
1/4 cup packed brown sugar
    2 tablespoons *French's®* Hearty Deli Brown
        Mustard
    2 tart green apples, cored and cut into 1-inch
        chunks
    1 tablespoon cornstarch

1. Heat *1 tablespoon oil* in 6-quart saucepot or Dutch oven over high heat. Cook ribs 10 minutes or until well-browned on all sides; drain fat.

2. Add potatoes to ribs. Whisk together apple juice, vinegar, Worcestershire, sugar and mustard. Pour over rib mixture; stir well. Heat to boiling. Reduce heat to low. Cook, covered, 40 minutes or until pork is tender and no longer pink in center, stirring occasionally.

3. Stir in apples; cook 5 minutes or until tender. Transfer ribs, potatoes and apples to platter; keep warm. Combine cornstarch with *2 tablespoons water.* Stir into pot. Heat to boiling, whisking constantly. Cook 1 to 2 minutes or until liquid thickens, stirring often. Serve with corn and crusty bread, if desired.

Makes 6 servings (with 2 cups gravy)

Cheesy Broccoli Bake

    1 (10-ounce) package frozen chopped broccoli
    1 (10-3/4-ounce) can condensed Cheddar
        cheese soup
1/2 cup sour cream
    2 cups (12 ounces) chopped CURE 81® ham
    2 cups cooked rice
1/2 cup soft, torn bread crumbs
    1 tablespoon butter or margarine, melted

Heat oven to 350°F. Cook broccoli according to package directions; drain. Combine soup and sour cream. Stir in broccoli, ham and rice. Spoon into 1-1/2-quart casserole. Mix bread crumbs and butter; sprinkle over casserole. Bake 30 to 35 minutes or until thoroughly heated.   *Makes 4 to 6 servings*

Peppered Steaks with Blackberry Sauce

STEAKS
1/3 cup lemon juice
1/3 cup oil
1/4 cup chopped onion
    2 cloves garlic, crushed
    4 (4- to 6-ounce) beef tenderloin or eye of round
        steaks, trimmed of fat
    1 tablespoon coarsely ground pepper
BLACKBERRY SAUCE
1/2 cup SMUCKER'S® Seedless Blackberry Jam
1/4 cup red wine vinegar
1/4 teaspoon onion powder
1/4 cup fresh or frozen blackberries, thawed

Combine lemon juice, oil, onion and garlic in large resealable plastic bag; mix well. Place steaks in bag, seal and refrigerate 6 to 24 hours, turning bag occasionally. When ready to cook, remove steaks from marinade; discard marinade and bag. Rub pepper around edges of each steak.

Heat grill. In small saucepan, combine jam, vinegar and onion powder. Cook over medium heat until jam is melted, stirring constantly. Remove from heat.

Oil grill rack. Place steaks on gas grill over medium heat or on charcoal grill 4 to 6 inches from medium-hot coals. Cook 8 to 12 minutes or until desired doneness, turning once halfway through cooking. To serve, spread steaks with blackberry sauce; top with fresh berries.   *Makes 4 servings*

Note: Steaks can be cooked in the broiler. Place on oiled broiler pan. Broil 4 to 6 inches from heat for 7 to 10 minutes or until desired doneness, turning once halfway through cooking.

> ### *Helpful Hint*
>
> *To prevent meat from sticking to the grill grid and to make cleanup easier, coat the grid with oil or cooking spray. However, spraying the grill over an open fire could cause a flare-up. The best approach is to spray or wipe down the grid before using.*

Sweet 'n' Sour Country Ribs

Peachy Pork Roast

(Pictured at right)

1 (3- to 4-pound) rolled boneless pork loin roast
1 cup (12-ounce jar) SMUCKER'S® Currant Jelly
1/2 cup SMUCKER'S® Peach Preserves
    Fresh peach slices and currants for garnish, if desired

Place pork in roasting pan; insert ovenproof meat thermometer into one end of roast. Bake at 325°F 30 to 40 minutes or until browned. Turn roast and bake an additional 30 minutes to brown the bottom. Turn roast again and drain off drippings.

In saucepan over medium heat, melt currant jelly and peach preserves. Brush roast generously with sauce.

Continue baking until meat thermometer reads 160°F, about 15 minutes, basting occasionally with sauce.

Remove roast from oven. Garnish with peach slices and currants. Serve with remaining sauce.
Makes 8 to 10 servings

Note: Canned, sliced peaches can be substituted for fresh peaches.

Country Meat Loaf

1 tablespoon vegetable oil
2 stalks celery, minced
1 medium onion, minced
1 large clove garlic, crushed
1 jar (16 ounces) TABASCO® 7 Spice Chili Recipe
1 pound lean ground beef
1 pound ground turkey
1 large egg
1/2 cup fresh bread crumbs
1 tablespoon TABASCO® brand Pepper Sauce
1-1/2 teaspoons salt
1-1/2 teaspoons dried thyme leaves
1 teaspoon ground cumin

In 10-inch skillet over medium heat in hot oil, cook celery, onion and garlic until tender, about 5 minutes, stirring occasionally.

Set aside 1/2 cup TABASCO® 7 Spice Chili Recipe. In large bowl combine remaining chili recipe, ground beef, ground turkey, egg, bread crumbs, TABASCO® Sauce, salt, thyme, cumin and cooked celery mixture until well mixed.

Preheat oven to 350°F. In 12×8-inch baking dish shape mixture into 10×4-inch oval loaf. Brush top with reserved 1/2 cup TABASCO® 7 Spice Chili Recipe. Bake 1 hour.
Makes 8 servings

Serving Suggestion: Serve meat loaf with roasted new potatoes and vegetables, such as baby carrots, broccoli, cauliflower and green beans.

Crispy Catfish

4 catfish fillets (about 6 to 8 ounces each)
1/3 cup cornmeal
1/3 cup all-purpose flour
1 teaspoon salt
1/2 teaspoon paprika
1/4 teaspoon onion powder
1/8 teaspoon freshly ground black pepper
1 egg, lightly beaten
1 tablespoon water
1/2 cup CRISCO® Oil*
    Tartar sauce (optional)

*Use your favorite Crisco Oil product.

1. Rinse fish. Pat dry. Combine cornmeal, flour, salt, paprika, onion powder and pepper on sheet of plastic wrap or waxed paper.

2. Combine egg and water in shallow dish or pie plate. Dip fish in egg mixture. Coat with cornmeal mixture.

3. Heat oil to 365°F in electric skillet or on medium-high heat in large heavy skillet. Fry fish for 5 to 7 minutes on each side or until crisp and browned. Drain on paper towels. Serve with tartar sauce, if desired.
Makes 4 servings

Note: Any firm, white-fleshed fish fillet such as flounder, sole or cod can be cooked in the same way. The coating also works well on turkey cutlets or boneless, skinless chicken breasts.

Tip: To keep fried fish warm, place fish on baking sheet lined with paper towels in a 200°F oven.

Peachy Pork Roast

Hearty Ground Beef Stew

(Pictured on page 126)

1 pound ground beef
3 cloves garlic, minced
1 package (16 ounces) Italian-style frozen
    vegetables
2 cups southern-style hash brown potatoes
1 jar (15 ounces) marinara sauce
1 can (10-1/2 ounces) condensed beef broth
3 tablespoons *French's®* Worcestershire Sauce

1. Brown beef with garlic in large saucepan; drain. Add remaining ingredients. Heat to boiling. Cover. Reduce heat to medium-low. Cook 10 minutes or until vegetables are crisp-tender.

2. Serve in warm bowls with garlic bread, if desired.
Makes 6 servings

Spinach Lasagna Roll-Ups

Spinach Lasagna Roll-Ups

(Pictured bottom left)

8 ounces uncooked 2-1/2-inch-wide lasagna
    noodles (12 noodles)
1 package (8 ounces) cream cheese, softened
1 packet (1 ounce) HIDDEN VALLEY® Original
    Ranch® Salad Dressing & Recipe Mix
1 package (10 ounces) frozen chopped spinach,
    thawed and squeezed dry
1 can (8 ounces) tomato sauce
3/4 cup milk
3/4 cup (3 ounces) shredded mozzarella cheese

Cook lasagna according to package directions. Rinse with cold water; drain well. Lay noodles on oiled baking sheets. Meanwhile, beat cream cheese and salad dressing & recipe mix until smooth. Remove 1/2 cup cream cheese mixture and combine with spinach in a small mixing bowl. Spread about 2 tablespoons spinach mixture evenly on each noodle. Starting from narrow ends, roll up noodles and place, seam side down, in a 13×9-inch baking dish. Whisk tomato sauce and milk into remaining cream cheese mixture until smooth; pour sauce evenly over roll-ups. Cover with foil. Bake at 325°F for 25 minutes. Sprinkle roll-ups with mozzarella cheese, cover loosely and continue baking 10 minutes longer or until hot and bubbly.
Makes 6 servings

Barbecue Chicken Pizza

2 boneless skinless chicken breast halves (about
    3/4 pound), cut into thin strips
1 green pepper, cut into strips
1/4 cup thinly sliced red onion
1 prepared pizza crust (12 inch)
1/3 cup BULL'S-EYE® Original Barbecue Sauce
1 package (8 ounces) VELVEETA® Mild Cheddar
    Shredded Pasteurized Prepared Cheese Food

1. Spray large skillet with no stick cooking spray. Add chicken, green pepper and onion; cook and stir on medium-high heat 4 to 5 minutes or until chicken is cooked through.

2. Place crust on cookie sheet. Spread with barbecue sauce. Top with chicken mixture and Velveeta.

3. Bake at 375°F for 12 to 15 minutes or until Velveeta is melted and crust is golden brown.
Makes 4 to 6 servings

Homestyle Tuna Pot Pie

Homestyle Tuna Pot Pie

(Pictured above)

1 package (15 ounces) refrigerated pie crusts
1 can (12 ounces) STARKIST® Solid White or
   Chunk Light Tuna, drained and chunked
1 package (10 ounces) frozen peas and carrots,
   thawed and drained
1/2 cup chopped onion
1 can (10-3/4 ounces) condensed cream of
   potato or cream of mushroom soup
1/3 cup milk
1/2 teaspoon poultry seasoning or dried thyme
   Salt and pepper to taste

Line 9-inch pie pan with one crust; set aside.
Reserve second crust. In medium bowl, combine
remaining ingredients; mix well. Pour tuna mixture
into pie shell; top with second crust. Crimp edges
to seal. Cut slits in top crust to vent. Bake in 375°F
oven 45 to 50 minutes or until golden brown.

Makes 6 servings

Savory Pork Roast

2 tablespoons lemon juice
1 tablespoon olive oil
2 teaspoons LAWRY'S® Seasoned Salt
1 teaspoon LAWRY'S® Garlic Salt
1 teaspoon dried thyme, crushed
1 (about 5 pounds) boneless pork roast
1 to 2 tablespoons all-purpose flour
1/2 cup water

In small bowl, combine lemon juice, oil, Seasoned
Salt, Garlic Salt and thyme. In shallow roasting pan,
place meat; brush with seasoning mixture. Bake,
uncovered, in 350°F oven 2 hours or until internal
meat temperature reaches 160°F. Remove meat to
serving platter, reserving drippings in pan; keep
meat warm. Combine flour and water; add to
drippings in pan. Cook over medium heat until
thickened, stirring constantly.

Makes 6 to 8 servings

Serving Suggestion: Serve gravy over slices of
roast—great with mashed potatoes.

Garlic 'n Lemon Roast Chicken

(Pictured at right and on front cover)

1 small onion, finely chopped
1 envelope LIPTON® RECIPE SECRETS® Savory
    Herb with Garlic Soup Mix
2 tablespoons olive or vegetable oil
2 tablespoons lemon juice
1 (3-1/2-pound) roasting chicken

1. In large plastic bag or bowl, combine onion and soup mix blended with oil and lemon juice; add chicken. Close bag and shake, or toss in bowl, until chicken is evenly coated. Cover and marinate in refrigerator, turning occasionally, 2 hours.

2. Preheat oven to 350°F. Place chicken and marinade in 13×9-inch baking or roasting pan. Arrange chicken, breast side up; discard bag.

3. Bake uncovered, basting occasionally, 1 hour and 20 minutes or until meat thermometer reaches 180°F. (Insert meat thermometer into thickest part of thigh between breast and thigh; make sure tip does not touch bone.) *Makes 4 servings*

Pepper & Pineapple Pork Stew

4 top loin pork chops, cut into 1-inch cubes
4 carrots, sliced
1/2 cup chicken broth
3 tablespoons teriyaki sauce
1 tablespoon cornstarch
1 (8-ounce) can pineapple chunks in juice,
    drained and juice reserved
1 green bell pepper, seeded and cut into 1-inch
    pieces

SLOW COOKER DIRECTIONS
Brown pork cubes in hot skillet, if desired (optional). Mix pork, carrots, broth and teriyaki in 3-1/2-quart slow cooker; cover and cook on low for 7 to 8 hours. Mix cornstarch with reserved pineapple juice; stir into pork mixture. Stir in pineapple and green pepper. Cover and cook on high 15 minutes or until thickened and bubbly.
Makes 4 servings

Favorite recipe from **National Pork Board**

Creamy Alfredo Seafood Newburg

2 tablespoons margarine or butter
1/4 cup finely chopped onion
1 pound uncooked medium shrimp, peeled,
    deveined and coarsely chopped
1 jar (16 ounces) RAGÚ® Cheese Creations!®
    Classic Alfredo Sauce
1/4 teaspoon ground white pepper
4 croissants or crescent rolls

1. In 12-inch nonstick skillet, melt margarine over medium-high heat and cook onion, stirring occasionally, 2 minutes or until tender.

2. Stir in shrimp and cook, stirring constantly, 2 minutes or until shrimp are almost pink. Stir in Ragú Cheese Creations! Sauce and pepper. Bring to a boil over high heat.

3. Reduce heat to low and simmer uncovered, stirring occasionally, 5 minutes or until shrimp turn pink. To serve, spoon shrimp mixture onto bottom of croissants and sprinkle, if desired, with chopped fresh parsley. Top with remaining croissant halves.
Makes 4 servings

Baked Ham with Apple-Raspberry Sauce

1 (3-pound) canned ham
1 cup chopped apples
1/2 cup SMUCKER'S® Red Raspberry Preserves
1/2 cup SMUCKER'S® Apple Jelly
3/4 cup apple cider
1 tablespoon cider vinegar
2 tablespoons cornstarch
    Endive or parsley sprigs
    Whole crabapples

Bake ham according to package directions.

Mix chopped apples, preserves and jelly in medium saucepan. Combine cider, vinegar and cornstarch; stir into saucepan. Heat to boiling; boil, stirring constantly, until thickened, about 1 minute.

Slice ham and arrange on platter; garnish with endive and crabapples. Serve with sauce.
Makes 8 to 10 servings

Garlic 'n Lemon Roast Chicken

Layered Mexican Casserole

(Pictured at right)

8 ounces ground beef
1 (11-ounce) can whole kernel corn, drained
1 (15-ounce) jar chunky salsa
1 (2-1/4-ounce) can sliced pitted ripe olives, drained, divided
1 cup cream-style cottage cheese
1 (8-ounce) carton sour cream
5 cups tortilla chips (7 to 8 ounces)
2 cups (8 ounces) shredded Wisconsin Cheddar cheese, divided
1/2 cup chopped tomato

Brown ground beef in large skillet; drain. Add corn and salsa; cook until thoroughly heated. Reserve 2 tablespoons olives; stir remaining olives into beef mixture. Combine cottage cheese and sour cream in bowl.

In 2-quart casserole, layer 2 cups chips, half of meat mixture, 3/4 cup Cheddar cheese and half of cottage cheese mixture. Repeat layers; cover. Bake in preheated 350°F oven, 35 minutes. Line edge of casserole with remaining 1 cup chips; top with tomato, reserved 2 tablespoons olives and remaining 1/2 cup Cheddar cheese. Bake 10 minutes or until cheese is melted and chips are hot.

Makes 4 to 6 servings

Favorite recipe from **Wisconsin Milk Marketing Board**

Hickory Pork Tenderloin with Apple Topping

(Pictured on page 126)

1-1/4 cups plus 2 tablespoons LAWRY'S® Hickory Marinade with Apple Cider, divided
1 pork tenderloin (2-1/2 to 3 pounds)
1 can (1 pound 5 ounces) apple pie filling or topping

In large resealable plastic food storage bag, combine 1 cup Hickory Marinade and tenderloin; seal bag. Marinate in refrigerator at least 30 minutes. Remove tenderloin from marinade; discard used marinade. Grill tenderloin, using indirect heat method, until no longer pink, about 35 minutes, turning once and basting often with additional 1/4 cup Hickory Marinade. Let stand 10 minutes before slicing. In medium saucepan, combine additional 2 tablespoons Hickory Marinade and apple pie filling. Cook over low heat until heated through. Spoon over tenderloin slices. *Makes 6 to 8 servings*

Serving Suggestion: Serve with brussels sprouts and cornbread. Garnish with cranberries, if desired.

Hint: Various flavored applesauces can be substituted for the apple pie filling. Try chunky applesauce with brown sugar and cinnamon.

Vegetable Stuffed Peppers

1 small zucchini, quartered lengthwise and cut into 1/4-inch slices
1 cup quartered fresh mushrooms
1/2 cup chopped onion
1 clove garlic, minced
1 teaspoon olive oil
1 can (15 ounces) cannellini or navy beans, drained
1 fresh tomato, chopped
1 cup cooked rice
3/4 cup HEINZ® Tomato Ketchup
1/2 cup tomato sauce
1/4 cup plus 2 tablespoons grated Parmesan cheese, divided
1 teaspoon dried basil leaves
1/2 teaspoon salt
1/4 teaspoon dried oregano leaves
3 medium red, yellow or green bell peppers, cut in half lengthwise and seeded

Spray 2-quart oblong baking dish with nonstick cooking spray. In large skillet, sauté zucchini, mushrooms, onion and garlic in oil until vegetables are crisp-tender, stirring frequently. Add beans, tomato, rice, ketchup, tomato sauce, 1/4 cup Parmesan cheese, basil, salt and oregano; mix well. Spoon vegetable mixture into pepper halves; place in prepared baking dish. Cover; bake in 375°F oven 35 minutes. Uncover; baste with pan juices. Sprinkle each pepper with 1 teaspoon Parmesan cheese. Bake an additional 20 minutes or until filling is hot.

Makes 6 servings

Layered Mexican Casserole

In small bowl, combine bread crumbs, thyme, rosemary, 1/2 teaspoon salt, 1/4 teaspoon pepper and remaining 1/4 cup olive oil.

Carefully remove roast from oven. Place potatoes around roast. Press bread crumb mixture onto top of roast to form crust. Sprinkle any remaining bread crumb mixture over potatoes. Roast an additional 40 to 45 minutes or until meat thermometer registers 145°F for medium-rare or until desired doneness is reached. Transfer roast to carving board; tent with foil. Let stand 5 to 10 minutes before carving. Cut into 1/4-inch-thick slices. Serve immediately with potatoes, spooning any bread crumb mixture from roasting pan onto meat.

Makes 8 servings

Campbell's® Chicken Florentine Lasagna

2 cans (10-3/4 ounces each) CAMPBELL'S® Condensed Cream of Chicken with Herbs Soup
2 cups milk
1 egg
1 container (15 ounces) ricotta cheese
6 *uncooked* lasagna noodles
1 package (about 10 ounces) frozen chopped spinach, thawed and well drained
2 cups cubed cooked chicken *or* turkey
2 cups shredded Cheddar cheese (8 ounces)

1. Mix soup and milk until smooth. Set aside.

2. Mix egg and ricotta. Set aside.

3. In 3-quart shallow baking dish, spread *1 cup* soup mixture. Top with *3 uncooked* lasagna noodles, ricotta mixture, spinach, chicken, *1 cup* Cheddar cheese and *1 cup* soup mixture. Top with remaining *3 uncooked* lasagna noodles and remaining soup mixture. **Cover.**

4. Bake at 375°F. for 1 hour. Uncover and top with remaining Cheddar cheese. Let stand 5 minutes.

Makes 6 servings

Tip: To thaw spinach, microwave on HIGH 3 minutes, breaking apart with a fork halfway through heating.

Herb-Crusted Roast Beef and Potatoes

Herb-Crusted Roast Beef and Potatoes

(Pictured above)

1 (4-1/2-pound) eye of round or sirloin tip beef roast
3/4 cup plus 2 tablespoons FILIPPO BERIO® Olive Oil, divided
Salt and freshly ground black pepper
2 tablespoons paprika
2 pounds small red skin potatoes, cut into halves
1 cup dry bread crumbs
1 teaspoon dried thyme leaves
1 teaspoon dried rosemary
1/2 teaspoon salt
1/4 teaspoon freshly ground black pepper

Preheat oven to 325°F. Brush roast with 2 tablespoons olive oil. Season to taste with salt and pepper. Place in large roasting pan; insert ovenproof meat thermometer into center of thickest part of roast. Roast 45 minutes.

Meanwhile, in large bowl, combine 1/2 cup olive oil and paprika. Add potatoes; toss until lightly coated.

Shrimp Scampi

(Pictured below)

2 tablespoons olive or vegetable oil
1/2 cup diced onion
1 large clove garlic, minced
1 small green bell pepper, cut into strips
1 small yellow bell pepper, cut into strips
8 ounces medium shrimp, peeled, deveined
1 can (14.5 ounces) CONTADINA® Recipe Ready Diced Tomatoes with Italian Herbs, undrained
2 tablespoons chopped fresh parsley *or* 2 teaspoons dried parsley flakes
1 tablespoon lemon juice
1/2 teaspoon salt

1. Heat oil in large skillet over medium-high heat. Add onion and garlic; sauté 1 minute.

2. Add bell peppers; sauté 2 minutes. Add shrimp; cook 2 minutes or until shrimp turn pink.

3. Add undrained tomatoes, parsley, lemon juice and salt; cook 2 to 3 minutes or until heated through. Serve over hot cooked pasta, if desired.

Makes 4 servings

15-Minute Beef Stew

1 tablespoon olive or vegetable oil
1 pound boneless sirloin steak, cut into 1-inch cubes
1 envelope LIPTON® RECIPE SECRETS® Onion Soup Mix*
1 cup water
2 tablespoons tomato paste
1 can (14-1/2 ounces) new potatoes, drained and cut into chunks
1 package (10 ounces) frozen peas and carrots, thawed

Also terrific with Lipton® Recipe Secrets® Onion Mushroom, Beefy Onion or Beefy Mushroom Soup Mix.

1. In 12-inch nonstick skillet, heat oil over medium-high heat and brown steak.

2. Stir in remaining ingredients. Bring to a boil over high heat.

3. Reduce heat to low and simmer uncovered 10 minutes or until steak is tender.

Makes 4 servings

Shrimp Scampi

French Bistro Ham

(Pictured at right and on back cover)

2 pounds sliced HILLSHIRE FARM® Ham

DIJON GLAZE
1/4 cup juices from cooked HILLSHIRE FARM® Ham
2 tablespoons Dijon mustard
2 tablespoons butter or margarine

PARSLEY POTATOES
1 pound small new potatoes
3 tablespoons butter
1/4 cup chopped parsley
1 teaspoon salt
1/4 teaspoon black pepper

SAUERKRAUT
1 pound sauerkraut
8 juniper berries, crushed (optional)

Prepare Ham according to directions on package. Reserve juices from cooked ham; set aside for Dijon Glaze.

For Dijon Glaze, mix reserved cooking juices and mustard in small bowl. Stir in butter and allow to melt.

For Parsley Potatoes, bring 4 quarts water to a boil in large saucepan over high heat. Boil potatoes until tender, about 20 minutes; drain. Melt butter in large skillet; add potatoes, parsley, salt and pepper, shaking skillet to coat potatoes.

For Sauerkraut, drain sauerkraut of most of its juices. Place in small saucepan with juniper berries, if desired. Heat gently over low heat about 7 minutes or until warmed through.

Serve Dijon Glaze over ham. Serve Parsley Potatoes and Sauerkraut alongside ham.

Makes 6 servings

Helpful Hint

New potatoes are freshly dug young potatoes. They may be any variety, but most often are round reds. New potatoes can be as small as marbles or almost as large as full-size potatoes, but they should have a very thin, wispy skin.

California Chicken Pot Pies

(Pictured on page 126)

1 (9-inch) folded refrigerated unbaked pie crust
1 can (10-3/4 ounces) condensed cream of chicken soup
1 cup half 'n' half or milk
2 cups (10 ounces) cooked chicken, cut into 1/2-inch cubes
1 bag (16 ounces) California-style frozen vegetable combination, such as cauliflower, carrots and asparagus, thawed and drained*
1-1/3 cups *French's® Taste Toppers™* French Fried Onions, divided
1/4 teaspoon dried thyme leaves
1/2 cup (2 ounces) shredded Swiss cheese

*Or, substitute any package of combination vegetables for California-style vegetables.

Preheat oven to 400°F. Roll out pie crust onto lightly floured board. Invert 10-ounce custard cup on top of crust. With sharp knife, trace around cup and cut out circle; prick several times with fork. Repeat 5 more times, rerolling scraps of pie crust as necessary. Cover; set crusts aside.

Combine soup and half 'n' half in large bowl. Stir in chicken, vegetables, *2/3 cup Taste Toppers* and thyme. Spoon mixture evenly into 6 (10-ounce) custard cups. Place filled cups on baking sheet. Place 1 crust over each cup. Bake, uncovered, 30 minutes or until crust is browned.

Sprinkle crusts with cheese; top with remaining *2/3 cup Taste Toppers*. Bake 1 minute or until *Taste Toppers* are golden.   *Makes 6 servings*

Note: Filling may be baked in 9-inch pie plate. Top with uncut 9-inch pie crust. Bake at 400°F for 35 minutes or until crust is golden. Top with cheese and remaining 2/3 cup onions. Bake 1 minute or until onions are golden.

Prepare-Ahead Tips: Pot pies may be prepared ahead, baked and frozen. Do not top with cheese and remaining onions before freezing. To reheat: Microwave individual pies in microwavable dishes on HIGH 5 minutes or until heated through. Top with remaining cheese and 2/3 cup onions. Microwave 1 minute or until onions are golden. OR prepare pies as directed. Do not bake. Cover; freeze. Bake at 400°F 40 minutes or until heated through and crust is golden. Top with cheese and remaining 2/3 cup onions. Bake 1 minute.

French Bistro Ham

Easy Chicken and Potato Dinner

(Pictured at right)

1 package (2 pounds) bone-in chicken breasts or thighs
1 pound potatoes, cut into wedges
1/2 cup KRAFT® Zesty Italian Dressing
1 tablespoon Italian seasoning
1/2 cup KRAFT® 100% Grated Parmesan Cheese

• **PLACE** chicken and potatoes in 13×9-inch baking pan.

• **POUR** dressing over chicken and potatoes. Sprinkle evenly with Italian seasoning and cheese.

• **BAKE** at 400°F for 1 hour or until chicken is cooked through. *Makes 4 servings*

Campbell's® Ham & Broccoli Shortcut Stromboli

1 package (10 ounces) refrigerated pizza dough
1 can (10-3/4 ounces) CAMPBELL'S® Condensed Cream of Celery Soup
1 cup cooked chopped broccoli
2 cups cubed cooked ham
1 cup shredded Cheddar cheese (4 ounces)

1. Preheat oven to 400°F. Unroll dough onto greased baking sheet. Set aside.

2. Mix soup, broccoli and ham. Spread soup mixture down center of dough. Top with cheese. Fold long sides of dough over filling and pinch to seal. Pinch short sides to seal.

3. Bake 20 minutes or until golden brown. Slice and serve. *Makes 4 servings*

Campbell's® Roast Beef & Bean Shortcut Stromboli: Substitute 1 can CAMPBELL'S® Condensed Cream of Mushroom Soup, 1 cup cut green beans and 2 cups cubed cooked roast beef for Cream of Celery Soup, broccoli and ham.

Campbell's® Chicken & Vegetable Shortcut Stromboli: Substitute 1 can CAMPBELL'S® Condensed Cream of Chicken Soup, 1 cup mixed vegetables and 2 cups cubed cooked chicken *or* turkey for Cream of Celery Soup, broccoli and ham.

Hungarian Goulash Stew

3/4 pound lean ground beef (80% lean)
1/2 cup chopped onion
1 clove garlic, minced
1 package (4.8 ounces) PASTA RONI® Angel Hair Pasta with Herbs
1 can (14.5 ounces) diced tomatoes, undrained
1 cup frozen corn *or* 1 can (8.75 ounces) whole kernel corn, drained
1-1/2 teaspoons paprika
1/8 teaspoon black pepper
Sour cream (optional)

1. In 3-quart saucepan, brown ground beef, onion and garlic; drain.

2. Add 1-1/3 cups water, pasta, Special Seasonings, tomatoes, corn and seasonings. Bring just to a boil.

3. Reduce heat to medium.

4. Boil, uncovered, stirring frequently, 5 to 6 minutes or until pasta is tender.

5. Let stand 3 minutes or until desired consistency. Stir before serving. Serve with sour cream, if desired. *Makes 4 servings*

Ranch-Style Chicken and Pasta

2 BUTTERBALL® Boneless Skinless Chicken Breasts
1/2 cup prepared ranch salad dressing, divided
1 cup uncooked rotini pasta
2 cups broccoli florets
1/4 cup diced red bell pepper
2 tablespoons chopped green onion

Combine chicken breasts and 1/4 cup ranch salad dressing in large bowl; marinate in refrigerator 15 minutes. Cook pasta 8 minutes; add broccoli during last 3 minutes of cooking. Drain pasta and broccoli; set aside. Remove chicken from marinade; discard marinade. Grill chicken 4 to 5 minutes on each side or until no longer pink in center. Combine cooked pasta, broccoli, bell pepper and onion in large bowl. Toss with remaining 1/4 cup ranch salad dressing. Serve chicken breasts with ranch-style pasta. *Makes 2 servings*

Easy Chicken and Potato Dinner

Stromboli

(Pictured at right)

1/4 cup *French's®* Hearty Deli Brown Mustard
2 tablespoons chopped fresh basil *or* 2 teaspoons dried basil leaves
1 tablespoon chopped green olives
1 pound frozen bread dough, thawed at room temperature
1/4 pound sliced salami
1/4 pound sliced provolone cheese
1/4 pound sliced ham
1/8 pound thinly sliced pepperoni (2-inch diameter)
1 egg, beaten
1 teaspoon poppy or sesame seeds

1. Grease baking sheet. Stir mustard, basil and olives in small bowl; set aside.

2. Roll dough on floured surface to 16×10-inch rectangle.*Arrange salami on dough, overlapping slices, leaving 1-inch border around edges. Spread half of the mustard mixture thinly over salami. Arrange provolone and ham over salami. Spread with remaining mustard mixture. Top with pepperoni.

3. Fold one-third of dough toward center from long edge of rectangle. Fold second side toward center enclosing filling. Pinch long edge to seal. Pinch ends together and tuck under dough. Place on prepared baking sheet. Cover; let rise in warm place 15 minutes.

4. Preheat oven to 375°F. Cut shallow crosswise slits 3 inches apart, on top of dough. Brush Stromboli lightly with beaten egg; sprinkle with poppy seeds. Bake 25 minutes or until browned. Remove to rack; cool slightly. Serve warm.   *Makes 12 servings*

If dough is too hard to roll, allow to rest on floured surface for 5 to 10 minutes.

Helpful Hint

Chopped fresh basil tends to bruise and discolor easily. To avoid this, stack the leaves together and roll them up cigar style. With a sharp knife, cut the leaves crosswise into strips and then make several cross cuts.

Campbell's® Lemon Chicken

2 cans (10-3/4 ounces each) CAMPBELL'S® Condensed Cream of Chicken Soup *or* 98% Fat Free Cream of Chicken Soup
1/2 cup water
1/4 cup lemon juice
2 teaspoons Dijon-style mustard
1-1/2 teaspoons garlic powder
8 large carrots, thickly sliced (about 6 cups)
8 skinless, boneless chicken breast halves (about 2 pounds)
8 cups hot cooked egg noodles
Grated Parmesan cheese

1. In slow cooker mix soup, water, lemon juice, mustard, garlic powder and carrots. Add chicken and turn to coat. Cover and cook on *low* 7 to 8 hours or until chicken is done.

2. Serve over noodles. Sprinkle with cheese.
Makes 8 servings

Vegetable Pork Stir-Fry

3/4 pound pork tenderloin
1 tablespoon vegetable oil
1-1/2 cups (about 6 ounces) sliced fresh mushrooms
1 large green pepper, cut into strips
1 zucchini, thinly sliced
2 ribs celery, cut into diagonal slices
1 cup thinly sliced carrots
1 clove garlic, minced
1 cup chicken broth
2 tablespoons reduced sodium soy sauce
1-1/2 tablespoons cornstarch
3 cups hot cooked rice

Slice pork across the grain into 1/8-inch strips. Brown pork strips in oil in large skillet over medium-high heat. Push meat to side of skillet. Add mushrooms, pepper, zucchini, celery, carrots and garlic; stir-fry about 3 minutes. Combine broth, soy sauce and cornstarch. Add to skillet and cook, stirring, until thickened; cook 1 minute longer. Serve over rice.   *Makes 6 servings*

Favorite recipe from **USA Rice Federation**

Chicken Gumbo

(Pictured at right)

4 TYSON® Fresh Skinless Chicken Thighs
4 TYSON® Fresh Skinless Chicken Drumsticks
1/4 cup all-purpose flour
2 teaspoons Cajun or Creole seasoning blend
2 tablespoons vegetable oil
1 large onion, chopped
1 cup thinly sliced celery
3 cloves garlic, minced
1 can (14-1/2 ounces) stewed tomatoes, undrained
1 can (14-1/2 ounces) chicken broth
1 large green bell pepper, cut into 1/2-inch pieces
1/2 to 1 teaspoon hot pepper sauce or to taste

PREP: CLEAN: Wash hands. Combine flour and Cajun seasonings in reclosable plastic bag. Add chicken, 2 pieces at a time; shake to coat. Reserve excess flour mixture. CLEAN: Wash hands.

COOK: In large saucepan, heat oil over medium heat. Add chicken and brown on all sides; remove and set aside. Sauté onion, celery and garlic 5 minutes. Add reserved flour mixture; cook 1 minute, stirring frequently. Add tomatoes, chicken broth, bell pepper and hot sauce. Bring to a boil. Return chicken to saucepan, cover and simmer over low heat, stirring occasionally, 30 minutes or until internal juices of chicken run clear. (Or insert instant-read meat thermometer in thickest part of chicken. Temperature should read 180°F.)

SERVE: Serve in shallow bowls, topped with hot cooked rice, if desired.

CHILL: Refrigerate leftovers immediately.
Makes 6 to 8 servings

Beef 'n' Broccoli

1/2 cup A.1.® Steak Sauce
1/4 cup soy sauce
2 cloves garlic, crushed
1 pound top round steak, thinly sliced
1 (16-ounce) bag frozen broccoli, red bell peppers, bamboo shoots and mushrooms, thawed*
Hot cooked rice (optional)

*1 (16-ounce) bag frozen broccoli cuts, thawed, may be substituted.

In small bowl, combine steak sauce, soy sauce and garlic. Pour marinade over steak in nonmetal dish. Cover; refrigerate 1 hour, stirring occasionally.

Remove steak from marinade; reserve marinade. In large lightly oiled skillet, over medium-high heat, stir-fry steak 3 to 4 minutes or until steak is no longer pink. Remove steak with slotted spoon; keep warm.

In same skillet, heat vegetables and reserved marinade to a boil; reduce heat to low. Cover; simmer for 2 to 3 minutes. Stir in steak. Serve over rice, if desired.
Makes 4 servings

Crab Cakes

1 egg
2 tablespoons mayonnaise
1 teaspoon dry mustard
1 teaspoon LAWRY'S® Seasoned Pepper
1/2 teaspoon LAWRY'S® Seasoned Salt
1/4 teaspoon cayenne pepper
4 cans (6 ounces each) crabmeat, drained, rinsed and cartilage removed
3 tablespoons finely chopped fresh parsley
2 tablespoons soda cracker crumbs
Vegetable oil for frying (about 1/2 cup)

In medium, deep bowl, beat egg. Blend in mayonnaise, mustard, Seasoned Pepper, Seasoned Salt and cayenne pepper. Add crabmeat, parsley and cracker crumbs; mix lightly. Divide mixture into eight equal portions; shape each into a ball, about 2 inches in diameter. Flatten each ball slightly; wrap in waxed paper. Refrigerate 30 minutes. In large, deep skillet, heat oil. Carefully add crab cakes, four at a time, to skillet and fry over medium-high heat 8 minutes or until golden brown on all sides, turning frequently. With slotted spoon, remove cakes from oil; drain on paper towels. Serve immediately.
Makes 8 cakes

Serving Suggestion: Serve with tartar sauce and lemon wedges.

Chicken Gumbo

Herbed Roast

(Pictured below)

1 beef top round roast (about 3 pounds)
1/3 cup Dijon-style mustard
1-1/2 teaspoons dried thyme, crushed
1 teaspoon dried rosemary, crushed
1 teaspoon LAWRY'S® Seasoned Pepper
1 teaspoon LAWRY'S® Garlic Powder with
   Parsley
1/2 teaspoon LAWRY'S® Seasoned Salt

Brush all sides of roast with mustard. In small bowl, combine remaining ingredients; mix well. Sprinkle on top and sides of roast, pressing into meat. Place roast, fat side up, on rack in roasting pan. Roast in 325°F oven, 50 minutes to 1 hour or until internal temperature reaches 160°F. Remove roast from oven. Let stand, covered, 15 minutes.

Makes 6 to 8 servings

Serving Suggestion: Slice thinly and serve with roasted potato wedges and steamed vegetables.

Herbed Roast

Baked Pork Chops with Yams and Apples

1/2 cup maple syrup
1 teaspoon jarred minced garlic *or* 1 small garlic
   clove, peeled and minced
1/2 teaspoon ground ginger
1/2 teaspoon salt
1/2 teaspoon freshly ground black pepper
1/4 teaspoon ground cinnamon
1 cup chicken stock or broth
3 tablespoons CRISCO® Oil*
4 boneless loin pork chops, 1-1/2 inches thick
3 medium yams or sweet potatoes, peeled and
   cut into 1-inch cubes
2 Granny Smith apples, quartered, cored, and
   cut into 1-inch slices

*Use your favorite Crisco Oil product.

1. Heat oven to 375°F. Combine maple syrup, garlic, ginger, salt, pepper, cinnamon and stock in small bowl. Mix well. Line roasting pan with heavy duty aluminum foil.

2. Heat oil in large skillet on medium-high heat. Brown pork chops on both sides. Remove from pan.

3. Place chops in roasting pan. Add yams and apples. Pour maple syrup mixture over all. Bake uncovered at 375°F for 25 minutes. Remove pan from oven. Turn chops, yams and apples gently with spatula. Return to oven. Bake 15 minutes, or until apples and potatoes are soft and pork is no longer pink in center.

Makes 4 servings

Country Stew

2 bags SUCCESS® Brown Rice
1 pound ground turkey
1 small onion, chopped
2 cans (14-1/2 ounces each) tomatoes, cut-up,
   undrained
1 teaspoon pepper
1/2 teaspoon dried basil leaves, crushed
1/2 teaspoon garlic powder
1 can (about 15 ounces) whole kernel corn,
   drained

Prepare rice according to package directions. Brown ground turkey with onion in large skillet, stirring occasionally to separate turkey. Add tomatoes, pepper, basil and garlic powder; simmer 20 minutes, stirring occasionally. Stir in rice and corn; heat thoroughly, stirring occasionally.

Makes 8 servings

Pizza Primavera

Pizza Primavera

(Pictured above)

3/4 cup RAGÚ® Pizza Quick® Sauce
1 (10-inch) prebaked pizza crust
1 medium red bell pepper, thinly sliced
1 cup sliced zucchini
1/2 cup chopped red onion
1 cup shredded mozzarella cheese (about 4 ounces)

Preheat oven to 450°F. Evenly spread Ragú® Pizza Quick® Sauce on pizza crust, then top with remaining ingredients. Bake 12 minutes or until cheese is melted.   *Makes 4 servings*

Campbell's® Asian Tomato Beef

2 cans (10-3/4 ounces each) CAMPBELL'S® Condensed Tomato Soup
1/3 cup soy sauce
1/3 cup vinegar
1-1/2 teaspoons garlic powder
1/4 teaspoon pepper
1 (3- to 3-1/2-pound) boneless beef round steak, 3/4 inch thick, cut into strips
6 cups broccoli flowerets
8 cups hot cooked rice

1. In slow cooker mix soup, soy sauce, vinegar, garlic powder, pepper and beef. Cover and cook on *low* 7 to 8 hours or until beef is done.

2. Stir. Arrange broccoli over beef. Cover and cook on *high* 15 minutes more or until tender-crisp. Serve over rice.   *Makes 8 servings*

Tip: No time to chop fresh produce? Buy bags of precut vegetables—they work great in many recipes!

Herb-Baked Fish & Rice

(Pictured at right)

1-1/2 cups hot chicken bouillon
1/2 cup uncooked regular rice
1/4 teaspoon Italian seasoning
1/4 teaspoon garlic powder
1 package (10 ounces) frozen chopped broccoli, thawed and drained
1-1/3 cups *French's*® *Taste Toppers*™ French Fried Onions, divided
1 tablespoon grated Parmesan cheese
1 pound unbreaded fish fillets, thawed if frozen Paprika (optional)
1/2 cup (2 ounces) shredded Cheddar cheese

Preheat oven to 375°F. In 12×8-inch baking dish, combine hot bouillon, uncooked rice and seasonings. Bake, covered, at 375°F for 10 minutes. Top with broccoli, *2/3 cup* **Taste Toppers** and the Parmesan cheese. Place fish fillets diagonally down center of dish; sprinkle fish lightly with paprika. Bake, covered, at 375°F for 20 to 25 minutes or until fish flakes easily with fork. Stir rice. Top fish with Cheddar cheese and remaining *2/3 cup* **Taste Toppers;** bake, uncovered, 3 minutes or until **Taste Toppers** are golden brown.

Makes 3 to 4 servings

Microwave Directions: In 12×8-inch microwave-safe dish, prepare rice mixture as above, except reduce bouillon to 1-1/4 cups. Cook, covered, on HIGH 5 minutes, stirring halfway through cooking time. Stir in broccoli, *2/3 cup* **Taste Toppers** and the Parmesan cheese. Arrange fish fillets in single layer on top of rice mixture; sprinkle fish lightly with paprika. Cook, covered, on MEDIUM (50-60%) 18 to 20 minutes or until fish flakes easily with fork and rice is done. Rotate dish halfway through cooking time. Top fish with Cheddar cheese and remaining *2/3 cup* **Taste Toppers;** cook, uncovered, on HIGH 1 minute or until cheese melts. Let stand 5 minutes.

Helpful Hint

When purchasing fresh fish fillets look for fillets that have moist flesh that is free from discoloration and skin that is shiny and resilient. Also, if the fillet has a strong fishy odor, it is not fresh.

Grilled Lemon Chicken

4 skinless boneless chicken breast halves (about 1 pound)
1/4 cup HEINZ® Worcestershire Sauce
2 tablespoons lemon juice
1 tablespoon olive or vegetable oil
1 clove garlic, minced
1/2 teaspoon basil leaves
1/2 teaspoon grated lemon peel
1/2 teaspoon salt
1/4 teaspoon pepper

Lightly flatten chicken breasts to uniform thickness. For marinade, combine Worcestershire sauce and remaining ingredients. Brush chicken generously with marinade. Grill or broil 4 minutes. Turn; brush with marinade. Grill an additional 3 to 4 minutes or until chicken is cooked.

Makes 4 servings

Special Stuffed Hamburgers

1-1/2 pounds ground beef
1 tablespoon Dijon mustard
1 teaspoon dill weed
1/4 pound (4 ounces) VELVEETA® Pasteurized Prepared Cheese Product, cut into four slices
1 medium onion, sliced
1 tablespoon butter or margarine
4 Kaiser rolls or hamburger buns, split, toasted KRAFT® Thousand Island Dressing

Preheat electric broiler (not necessary to preheat gas broiler).

Mix together meat, mustard and dill; shape into eight 5-inch patties.

Place one prepared cheese product slice on each of four patties; top with remaining patties. Pinch edges of patties together to seal.

Place patties on rack of broiler pan so tops are 3 to 4 inches from heat. Broil 5 to 7 minutes on each side or to desired doneness.

Sauté onion in butter. Fill rolls with patties; top with onion and dressing.

Makes 4 sandwiches

Hearty Hot Dish

(Pictured at right)

    1/3 cup honey
    1/4 cup spicy brown mustard
    1/4 cup vegetable oil
      1 tablespoon soy sauce
      2 cloves garlic, minced
      1 teaspoon ground ginger
      1 pound HILLSHIRE FARM® Beef Smoked
          Sausage,* sliced
      2 onions, cut into quarters
      1 cup chopped carrots
      1 cup chopped celery
      1 cup sliced mushrooms

Or use any variety Hillshire Farm® Smoked Sausage.

Combine honey, mustard, oil, soy sauce, garlic and ginger in large bowl; blend thoroughly. Add Smoked Sausage, onions, carrots, celery and mushrooms. Sauté sausage mixture in large skillet over medium-high heat until sausage is lightly browned.

Makes 4 to 6 servings

Sour Cream Chicken Quiche

CRUST
        Classic Crisco® Single Crust (recipe follows)
FILLING
      2 tablespoons CRISCO® Stick or 2 tablespoons
          CRISCO® all-vegetable shortening
      2 tablespoons chopped green bell pepper
      2 tablespoons chopped onion
      1 cup cubed cooked chicken
      1 tablespoon all-purpose flour
    1/4 teaspoon salt
        Dash nutmeg
        Dash pepper
    1/2 cup shredded sharp Cheddar cheese
    1/4 cup shredded Swiss cheese
      2 eggs, lightly beaten
    3/4 cup milk
    3/4 cup dairy sour cream

1. For crust, prepare as directed. Press into 9-inch pie pan. Do not bake. Heat oven to 400°F.

2. For filling, melt Crisco in small skillet. Add green pepper and onion. Cook on medium-high heat 3 minutes, stirring frequently. Add chicken and flour. Cook and stir 2 minutes. Spread in bottom of

unbaked pie crust. Sprinkle with salt, nutmeg and pepper. Top with Cheddar cheese and Swiss cheese.

3. Combine eggs, milk and sour cream in medium bowl. Stir until smooth. Pour carefully over cheese.

4. Bake at 400°F for 20 minutes. Reduce oven temperature to 350°F. Bake 30 to 35 minutes or until knife inserted near center comes out clean. *Do not overbake.* Cool 10 minutes before cutting and serving. Refrigerate leftover pie.

Makes 1 (9-inch) pie

Classic Crisco® Single Crust

    1-1/3 cups all-purpose flour
      1/2 teaspoon salt
      1/2 CRISCO® Stick or 1/2 cup CRISCO®
          all-vegetable shortening
        3 tablespoons cold water

1. Spoon flour into measuring cup and level. Combine flour and salt in medium bowl.

2. Cut in shortening using pastry blender or 2 knives until all flour is blended to form pea-size chunks.

3. Sprinkle with water, 1 tablespoon at a time. Toss lightly with fork until dough forms a ball.

4. Press dough between hands to form 5- to 6-inch "pancake." Flour rolling surface and rolling pin lightly. Roll dough into circle. Trim circle 1 inch larger than upside-down pie plate. Carefully remove trimmed dough. Set aside to reroll and use for pastry cutout garnish, if desired.

5. Fold dough into quarters. Unfold and press into pie plate. Fold edge under. Flute.

6. **For recipes using a baked pie crust,** heat oven to 425°F. Prick bottom and side thoroughly with fork (50 times) to prevent shrinkage. Bake at 425°F for 10 to 15 minutes or until lightly browned.

7. **For recipes using an unbaked pie crust,** follow directions given for that recipe.

Makes 1 (9-inch) single crust

> ### *Helpful Hint*
> *For tender, flaky pie crusts, it is important to keep the ingredients cold and handle the dough as little as possible.*

Herb Roasted Turkey

(Pictured at right)

1 (12-pound) turkey, thawed if frozen
1/2 cup FLEISCHMANN'S® Original Margarine,
softened, divided
1 tablespoon Italian seasoning

1. Remove neck and giblets from turkey cavities. Rinse turkey; drain well and pat dry. Free legs from tucked position; do not cut band of skin. Using rubber spatula or hand, loosen skin over breast, starting at body cavity opening by legs.

2. Blend 6 tablespoons margarine and Italian seasoning. Spread 2 tablespoons herb mixture inside body cavity; spread remaining herb mixture on meat under skin. Hold skin in place at opening with wooden picks. Return legs to tucked position; turn wings back to hold neck skin in place.

3. Place turkey, breast-side up, on flat rack in shallow open pan. Insert ovenproof meat thermometer deep into thickest part of thigh next to body, not touching bone. Melt remaining 2 tablespoons margarine; brush over skin.

4. Roast at 325°F for 3-1/2 to 3-3/4 hours. When skin is golden brown, shield breast loosely with foil to prevent overbrowning. Check for doneness; thigh temperature should be 180°F to 185°F. Transfer turkey to cutting board; let stand 15 to 20 minutes before carving. Remove wooden toothpicks just before carving. *Makes 12 servings*

Beach Grill

1 cup vegetable oil
2 teaspoons LAWRY'S® Seasoned Salt
1 teaspoon LAWRY'S® Garlic Powder with
Parsley
1/2 teaspoon hot pepper sauce (optional)
12 raw medium shrimp, peeled and deveined
12 sea scallops
1 small red onion, cut into 12 wedges
Skewers

In large resealable plastic food storage bag, combine oil, Seasoned Salt, Garlic Powder with Parsley and hot pepper sauce, if desired; mix well. Add shrimp, scallops and onion; seal bag. Marinate in refrigerator at least 1 hour. Remove shrimp, scallops and onion from marinade; discard used marinade. Alternately thread shrimp, scallops and onion onto skewers. Grill or broil skewers 4 to 6 minutes or until shrimp are pink and scallops are opaque, turning halfway through grilling time. *Makes 6 servings*

Serving Suggestion: Serve with lime wedges and crusty French bread.

Hint: If using wooden skewers, soak them in water overnight before using to prevent scorching.

Country-Style Pot Roast

1 (3- to 3-1/2-pound) boneless beef pot roast
(rump, chuck or round)
1 envelope LIPTON® RECIPE SECRETS® Onion
Soup Mix*
2-1/2 cups water, divided
4 medium all-purpose potatoes, cut into 1-inch
pieces (about 2 pounds)
4 carrots, sliced
2 to 4 tablespoons all-purpose flour

Also terrific with Lipton® Recipe Secrets® Onion Mushroom, Beefy Onion or Beefy Mushroom Soup Mix.

1. In Dutch oven or 6-quart saucepot, brown roast over medium-high heat. Add soup mix blended with 2 cups water. Bring to a boil over high heat. Reduce heat to low and simmer covered, turning roast occasionally, 2 hours.

2. Add vegetables and cook an additional 30 minutes or until vegetables and roast are tender; remove roast and vegetables.

3. For gravy, blend remaining 1/2 cup water with flour; add to Dutch oven. Bring to a boil over high heat. Reduce heat to low and simmer uncovered, stirring constantly, until thickened, about 5 minutes. *Makes 8 servings*

Slow Cooker Method: Place vegetables then beef in slow cooker. Combine 2 cups water with soup mix. Pour over beef. Cover. Cook on LOW 8 to 10 hours or until beef is tender. Remove beef and vegetables to serving platter. Stir remaining water with flour into juices in slow cooker. Cook on HIGH 15 minutes or until thickened.

Herb Roasted Turkey

Mexican Lasagna

Mexican Lasagna

(Pictured above)

1 package (16 sheets) BARILLA® Oven Ready
    Lasagna Noodles (do not boil)
1 pound ground beef
1 package (1.5 ounces) taco seasoning
1 jar (26 ounces) BARILLA® Lasagna & Casserole
    Sauce or Marinara Pasta Sauce
2 eggs
1 container (15 ounces) ricotta cheese
4 cups (16 ounces) shredded Mexican-style
    cheese, divided

1. Preheat oven to 375°F. Spray 13×9×2-inch baking pan with nonstick cooking spray. Remove 12 lasagna noodles from package. Do not boil.

2. Cook ground beef and taco seasoning in large skillet, following directions on seasoning package. Remove from heat; stir in lasagna sauce.

3. Beat eggs in medium bowl. Stir in ricotta cheese and 2 cups Mexican-style cheese.

4. To assemble lasagna, spread 1 cup meat mixture over bottom of pan. Arrange 4 uncooked lasagna noodles over meat mixture, overlapping edges if necessary to fit pan. Top with half of ricotta mixture and 1 cup meat mixture. Repeat layers (4 uncooked lasagna noodles, remaining half of ricotta mixture and 1 cup meat mixture); top with remaining 4 uncooked lasagna noodles, remaining meat mixture and remaining 2 cups Mexican-style cheese.

5. Cover with foil and bake 45 to 55 minutes or until bubbly. Uncover and continue cooking about 5 minutes or until cheese is melted. Let stand 15 minutes before cutting.   *Makes 12 servings*

Hearty Sausage Stew

1/4 cup olive oil
  4 carrots, chopped
  1 onion, cut into quarters
  1 cup chopped celery
  2 cloves garlic, finely chopped
  1 teaspoon finely chopped fennel
    Salt and black pepper to taste
12 small new potatoes
  1 pound mushrooms, cut into halves
  2 cans (14-1/2 ounces each) diced tomatoes,
    undrained
  1 can (8 ounces) tomato sauce
  1 tablespoon dried oregano leaves
  1 pound HILLSHIRE FARM® Polska Kielbasa,*
    sliced

Or use any variety Hillshire Farm® Smoked Sausage.

Heat oil in heavy skillet over medium-high heat; add carrots, onion, celery, garlic, fennel, salt and pepper. Sauté until vegetables are soft. Add potatoes, mushrooms, tomatoes with liquid, tomato sauce and oregano; cook 20 minutes over low heat. Add Polska Kielbasa; simmer 15 minutes or until heated through.   *Makes 6 servings*

Farm Fresh Tip: Did you know?—If you don't have 2 cups of tomato sauce, you can substitute with 3/4 cup of tomato paste mixed into 1 cup of water.

Country Chicken Stew with Dumplings

(Pictured below)

- 1 tablespoon olive or vegetable oil
- 1 chicken (3 to 3-1/2 pounds), cut into serving pieces (with or without skin)
- 4 large carrots, cut into 2-inch pieces
- 3 ribs celery, cut into 1-inch pieces
- 1 large onion, cut into 1-inch wedges
- 1 envelope LIPTON® RECIPE SECRETS® Savory Herb with Garlic Soup Mix*
- 1-1/2 cups water
- 1/2 cup apple juice
  Parsley Dumplings, optional (recipe follows)

Also terrific with Lipton® Recipe Secrets® Golden Onion Soup Mix.

In 6-quart Dutch oven or heavy saucepot, heat oil over medium-high heat and brown 1/2 of the chicken; remove and set aside. Repeat with remaining chicken. Return chicken to Dutch oven. Stir in carrots, celery, onion and soup mix blended with water and apple juice. Bring to a boil over high heat. Reduce heat to low and simmer covered 25 minutes or until chicken is done and vegetables are tender.

Meanwhile, prepare Parsley Dumplings. Drop 12 rounded tablespoonfuls of batter into simmering broth around chicken. Continue simmering covered 10 minutes or until toothpick inserted in center of dumpling comes out clean. Season stew, if desired, with salt and pepper. *Makes about 6 servings*

Parsley Dumplings: In medium bowl, combine 1-1/3 cups all-purpose flour, 2 teaspoons baking powder, 1 tablespoon chopped fresh parsley and 1/2 teaspoon salt; set aside. In measuring cup, blend 2/3 cup milk, 2 tablespoons melted butter or margarine and 1 egg. Stir milk mixture into flour mixture just until blended.

Variation: Add 1 pound quartered red potatoes to stew with carrots; eliminate dumplings.

Country Chicken Stew with Dumplings

Roasted Garlic Swedish Meatballs

(Pictured at right)

1 pound ground beef
1/2 cup plain dry bread crumbs
1 egg
1 jar (16 ounces) RAGÚ® Cheese Creations!®
    Roasted Garlic Parmesan Sauce
1-1/4 cups beef broth
2 teaspoons Worcestershire sauce
1 teaspoon ground allspice (optional)

In large bowl, combine ground beef, bread crumbs and egg; shape into 20 (1-1/2-inch) meatballs.

In 12-inch nonstick skillet, brown meatballs over medium-high heat.

Meanwhile, in medium bowl, combine Ragú Cheese Creations! Sauce, beef broth, Worcestershire sauce and allspice; stir into skillet. Bring to a boil over high heat. Reduce heat to low and simmer uncovered, stirring occasionally, 10 minutes or until meatballs are done and sauce is slightly thickened. Serve, if desired, over hot cooked noodles or rice.

Makes 4 servings

Fillets Stuffed with Crabmeat

1 envelope LIPTON® RECIPE SECRETS® Savory
    Herb with Garlic Soup Mix*
1/2 cup fresh bread crumbs
6 ounces frozen crabmeat, thawed and well-
    drained
1/2 cup water
2 teaspoons lemon juice
4 fish fillets (about 1 pound)
1 tablespoon margarine or butter, melted

Also terrific with Lipton® Recipe Secrets® Golden Onion Soup Mix.

Preheat oven to 350°F.

In medium bowl, combine soup mix, bread crumbs, crabmeat, water and lemon juice.

Top fillets evenly with crabmeat mixture; roll up and secure with wooden toothpicks. Place in lightly greased 2-quart oblong baking dish. Brush fish with margarine and bake 25 minutes or until fish flakes. Remove toothpicks before serving.

Makes 4 servings

Bacon-Wrapped Pork and Apple Patties

1 pound lean ground pork
3/4 cup quick-cooking rolled oats
    Salt
1/2 teaspoon ground sage
1/4 teaspoon each pepper and dried thyme leaves
1/3 cup applesauce
1 egg, slightly beaten
2 tablespoons chopped green onion
4 slices bacon
1 large tart green apple, cut into thin wedges
1/2 medium onion, cut into small wedges
1 tablespoon olive oil

In bowl mix oats, 1/2 teaspoon salt, sage, pepper and thyme. Stir in applesauce, egg and green onion. Stir in ground pork until well blended. Form into 4 patties about 3/4 to 1 inch thick. Wrap 1 bacon strip around each patty; secure with toothpick. Grill or broil patties 4 to 5 minutes on each side until no longer pink in center. Meanwhile in skillet, cook and stir apple and onion in hot oil until tender. Sprinkle with salt. Serve with patties. *Makes 4 servings*

Favorite recipe from **National Pork Producers Council**

Barbecued Ribs

1 cup ketchup
1/2 cup GRANDMA'S® Molasses
1/4 cup each cider vinegar and Dijon mustard
2 tablespoons Worcestershire sauce
1 teaspoon garlic powder
1 teaspoon hickory flavor liquid smoke (optional)
1/4 teaspoon ground red pepper
1/4 teaspoon hot pepper sauce
4 to 6 pounds baby back ribs

1. Prepare grill for direct cooking. Mix all ingredients except ribs in large bowl. Place ribs on grid over medium hot coals. Cook ribs 40 to 45 minutes or just until they begin to brown; turning occasionally.

2. Cook and baste ribs with sauce an additional 1 to 1-1/2 hours or until tender and cooked through.*

Makes 4 to 6 servings

Do not baste during last 5 minutes of grilling.

Roasted Garlic Swedish Meatballs

Tex-Mex Chops

(Pictured at right)

4 boneless pork loin chops, about 1 pound
1 teaspoon vegetable oil
1-1/2 cups bottled salsa, chunky style
1 can (4 ounces) diced green chilies
1/2 teaspoon ground cumin
1/4 cup shredded Cheddar cheese

Heat oil in nonstick pan over medium-high heat.
Brown chops on one side, about 2 minutes. Turn
chops over. Add salsa, chilies and cumin to skillet;
mix well. Lower heat, cover and barely simmer
for 8 minutes. Uncover; top each chop with
1 tablespoon cheese. Cover and simmer an
additional 2 to 3 minutes or until cheese melts.
Serve immediately. *Makes 4 servings*

Favorite recipe from **National Pork Producers Council**

Stuffed Cabbage Rolls

3/4 pound lean ground beef
1/2 cup chopped onion
1 cup cooked long grain white rice
1/4 teaspoon ground cinnamon
    Salt-free herb seasoning (optional)
1 egg white
6 large cabbage leaves
1 can (14-1/2 ounces) DEL MONTE® Original
    Recipe Stewed Tomatoes (No Salt Added)
1 can (15 ounces) DEL MONTE® Tomato Sauce
    (No Salt Added)

1. Brown meat and onion in large skillet over
medium-high heat; drain. Add rice and cinnamon.
Season with salt-free herb seasoning, if desired.

2. Remove from heat; stir in egg white. Pre-cook
cabbage leaves 3 minutes in small amount of boiling
water; drain. Divide meat mixture among cabbage
leaves. Roll cabbage leaves loosely around meat
mixture, allowing room for rice to swell. Secure with
toothpicks.

3. Combine undrained tomatoes and tomato sauce
in a 4-quart saucepan; bring to boil. Reduce heat;
add cabbage rolls. Simmer, uncovered, 30 minutes.
Makes 6 servings

Campbell's® Jambalaya One Dish

1 tablespoon vegetable oil
1/2 pound skinless, boneless chicken breasts, cut
    up
1/2 pound hot Italian pork sausage, sliced
1/4 teaspoon garlic powder *or* 2 cloves garlic,
    minced
1 can (10-1/2 ounces) CAMPBELL'S® Condensed
    French Onion Soup
1/3 cup PACE® Picante Sauce *or* Thick & Chunky
    Salsa
1 cup *uncooked* Minute® Original Rice
1/2 cup frozen peas
1/2 pound frozen cooked large shrimp

1. In medium skillet over medium-high heat, heat oil.
Add chicken, sausage and garlic powder and cook
and stir 5 minutes or until browned. Pour off fat.

2. Add soup and picante sauce. Heat to a boil. Stir
in rice, peas and shrimp. Reduce heat to low. Cover
and cook 5 minutes or until chicken and sausage are
no longer pink and most of liquid is absorbed.
Makes 4 servings

Honey-Mustard Glazed Chicken

2 tablespoons Dijon-style mustard
2 tablespoons honey
1 tablespoon butter or margarine, melted
1 teaspoon McCORMICK® Basil Leaves
1/2 teaspoon McCORMICK® California Style Garlic
    Powder
1 pound boneless, skinless chicken breasts
    (4 half breasts)

1. Preheat broiler or grill.

2. Combine mustard, honey, butter, basil and garlic
powder in small bowl and beat until well mixed.

3. Arrange chicken on lightly greased broiler pan or
grill and broil 3 to 4 minutes. Brush half of mustard
mixture on chicken and broil 2 minutes.

4. Turn chicken over and broil 3 to 4 minutes. Brush
with remaining mustard mixture. Broil 2 minutes or
until chicken is no longer pink in center.
Makes 4 servings

Manhattan Turkey à la King

(Pictured at right)

> 8 ounces wide egg noodles
> 1 pound boneless turkey or chicken, cut into
>   strips
> 1 tablespoon vegetable oil
> 1 can (14-1/2 ounces) DEL MONTE® Diced
>   Tomatoes with Garlic and Onions
> 1 can (10-3/4 ounces) condensed cream of
>   celery soup
> 1 medium onion, chopped
> 2 stalks celery, sliced
> 1 cup sliced mushrooms

1. Cook noodles according to package directions; drain. In large skillet, brown turkey in oil over medium-high heat. Season with salt and pepper, if desired.

2. Add remaining ingredients, except noodles. Cover and cook over medium heat 5 minutes.

3. Remove cover; cook 5 minutes or until thickened, stirring occasionally. Serve over hot noodles. Garnish with chopped parsley, if desired.

Makes 6 servings

Hint: Cook pasta ahead; rinse and drain. Cover and refrigerate. Just before serving, heat in microwave or dip in boiling water.

Crown Roast of Pork with Peach Stuffing

> 1 (7- to 8-pound) crown roast of pork (12 to
>   16 ribs)
> 1-1/2 cups water
> 1 cup FLEISCHMANN'S® Original Margarine,
>   divided
> 1 (16-ounce) package seasoned bread cubes
> 1 cup chopped celery
> 2 medium onions, chopped
> 1 (15-1/4-ounce) can sliced peaches, drained
>   and chopped, reserve liquid
> 1/2 cup seedless raisins

1. Place crown roast, bone tips up, on rack in shallow roasting pan. Make a ball of foil and press into cavity to hold open. Wrap bone tips in foil. Roast at 325°F, uncovered, for 2 hours; baste with pan drippings occasionally.

2. Heat water and 3/4 cup margarine in large heavy pot to a boil; remove from heat. Add bread cubes, tossing lightly with a fork; set aside.

3. Cook and stir celery and onions in remaining margarine in large skillet over medium-high heat until tender, about 5 minutes.

4. Add celery mixture, peaches with liquid and raisins to bread cube mixture, tossing to mix well.

5. Remove foil from center of roast. Spoon stuffing lightly into cavity. Roast 30 to 45 minutes more or until meat thermometer registers 155°F (internal temperature will rise to 160°F upon standing). Cover stuffing with foil, if necessary, to prevent overbrowning. Bake any remaining stuffing in greased, covered casserole during last 30 minutes of roasting.

Makes 12 to 16 servings

Reuben Casserole

> 1 cup FRANK'S® or SNOWFLOSS® Kraut, drained
> 1/2 cup chopped onion
> 2 tablespoons butter
> 1 apple, peeled and chopped
> 1/2 teaspoon caraway seeds
> 1 cup cubed corned beef
> 1/4 cup Thousand Island dressing
> 1 cup cubed Swiss cheese
> 2 slices rye bread, toasted and cubed
> 2 tablespoons melted butter
> 1 small jar red pimiento
> 1 green bell pepper, sliced

1. Preheat oven to 400°F. Sauté the onion in 2 tablespoons butter until soft.

2. Add apple and sauté until soft.

3. Add caraway seeds, kraut and corned beef; sauté 1 minute to blend flavors. Place mixture in medium casserole dish.

4. Drizzle kraut mixture with Thousand Island dressing, top with Swiss cheese and with toasted bread cubes.

5. Pour remaining 2 tablespoons melted butter over top, dot with pimiento and decorate with bell pepper.

6. Bake at 400°F for 20 minutes.

Makes 4 servings

Manhattan Turkey à la King

Cowboy Kabobs

(Pictured at right)

1/2 cup A.1.® Original or A.1.® BOLD & SPICY
   Steak Sauce
1/2 cup barbecue sauce
2-1/2 teaspoons prepared horseradish
   1 (1-1/2-pound) beef top round steak, cut into
      1/2-inch strips
   4 medium-size red skin potatoes, cut into
      wedges, blanched
   1 medium onion, cut into wedges
1/3 cup red bell pepper strips
1/3 cup green bell pepper strips
1/3 cup yellow bell pepper strips

Soak 8 (10-inch) wooden skewers in water at least
30 minutes.

Blend steak sauce, barbecue sauce and horseradish;
set aside.

Thread steak strips (accordion style) and vegetables
onto skewers. Place kabobs in nonmetal dish; coat
with 2/3 cup reserved steak sauce mixture. Cover;
refrigerate 1 hour, turning occasionally.

Remove kabobs from marinade; discard marinade.
Grill kabobs over medium heat or broil 6 inches
from heat source 6 to 10 minutes or until steak is
desired doneness, turning occasionally and basting
with remaining steak sauce mixture. Serve
immediately.   *Makes 4 servings*

Maple Barbecued Chicken

1/2 cup bottled chili sauce
1/2 cup pure maple syrup
   3 tablespoons cider vinegar
   3 tablespoons CRISCO® Oil*
   1 tablespoon prepared mustard
1/2 teaspoon salt
1/4 teaspoon hot red pepper sauce
   3 pounds bone-in chicken pieces (with or
      without skin) *or* 1-1/2 pounds boneless,
      skinless chicken breasts flattened to even
      thickness

*Use your favorite Crisco Oil product.

1. Heat oven to 375°F. Line 13×9×2-inch pan with
heavy duty aluminum foil.

2. Combine chili sauce, maple syrup, vinegar, oil,
mustard, salt and hot red pepper sauce in small
saucepan. Heat on medium heat until mixture
comes to a boil. Reduce heat to low. Simmer
6 minutes, or until slightly thickened.

3. Rinse chicken. Pat dry. Arrange in pan. (If using
bone-in pieces, arrange with underside up.) Brush
generously with sauce. Bake at 375°F for 20 minutes
for bone-in pieces and 15 minutes for boneless
pieces. Remove from oven. Turn chicken with tongs.
Brush generously with sauce. Return to oven. Bake
30 minutes for bone-in pieces or 15 minutes for
boneless pieces, or until chicken is no longer pink in
center. Serve immediately.   *Makes 4 servings*

Campbell's® Cornbread Chicken Pot Pie

   1 can (10-3/4 ounces) CAMPBELL'S® Condensed
      Cream of Chicken Soup *or* 98% Fat Free
      Cream of Chicken Soup
   1 can (about 8-1/2 ounces) whole kernel corn,
      drained
   2 cups cubed cooked chicken or turkey
   1 package (8-1/2 ounces) corn muffin mix
3/4 cup milk
   1 egg
1/2 cup shredded Cheddar cheese (2 ounces)

1. Preheat oven to 400°F. In 9-inch pie plate mix
soup, corn and chicken.

2. Mix muffin mix, milk and egg. Pour over chicken
mixture. Bake for 30 minutes or until golden.
Sprinkle with cheese.   *Makes 4 servings*

Campbell's® Cornbread Chicken Chili Pot Pie: In
Step 1 add 1 can (about 4 ounces) chopped green
chilies, drained, with the corn.

Oven Jambalaya

Oven Jambalaya

(Pictured at left)

1 pound sweet Italian sausages
2 stalks celery, sliced
1 green bell pepper, diced
1 medium onion, diced
2 cloves garlic, minced
1 (28-ounce) can crushed tomatoes
2 cups chicken broth
1 cup long-grain rice
2 teaspoons TABASCO® brand Pepper Sauce
1 teaspoon salt
1 pound large shrimp, peeled and deveined

Preheat oven to 400°F. Cook sausages in 12-inch skillet over medium-high heat until well browned on all sides, turning frequently. Remove sausages to plate; reserve drippings in skillet. When cool enough to handle, cut sausages into 1/2-inch slices. Add celery, green bell pepper, onion and garlic to same skillet; cook 3 minutes over medium heat, stirring occasionally.

Combine tomatoes, chicken broth, rice, TABASCO® Sauce, salt, sausages and vegetable mixture in 3-quart casserole. Bake 40 minutes. Stir in shrimp; cook 5 minutes or until rice is tender and shrimp are cooked. *Makes 8 servings*

Speedy Stroganoff

1 pound beef sirloin, cut into narrow strips
1 tablespoon CRISCO® Stick or 1 tablespoon
    CRISCO® all-vegetable shortening
1 medium onion, sliced
1 clove garlic, minced
1 can (10-3/4 ounces) condensed cream of
    mushroom soup
1 cup sour cream
1 can (4 ounces) mushrooms, stems and pieces,
    undrained
2 tablespoons ketchup
2 teaspoons Worcestershire sauce
    Poppy Noodles (recipe follows)

In large skillet, brown beef strips in hot 1 tablespoon shortening. Add onion and garlic; cook until onion is crisp-tender. Combine soup, sour cream, mushrooms with liquid, ketchup and Worcestershire; pour over beef mixture. Cook and stir over low heat until hot. Serve over Poppy Noodles. *Makes 4 servings*

Poppy Noodles: Toss 4 cups hot cooked noodles with 1 tablespoon butter and 1 teaspoon poppy seeds.

Springtime Pasta with Lemon Cream Sauce

2 (9-ounce) packages frozen ravioli
1 pound asparagus, cut into 1-1/2-inch pieces
1/2 cup milk
1 (3-ounce) package cream cheese, softened
1/4 cup butter or margarine
1 tablespoon freshly grated lemon peel
1 cup (6 ounces) diced CURE 81® ham
1/2 cup grated Parmesan cheese
1/8 teaspoon white pepper

In large saucepan, cook ravioli and asparagus in boiling water 7 minutes or until ravioli is tender. Drain. Meanwhile, in saucepan, combine milk, cream cheese, butter and lemon peel. Cook over medium heat 5 minutes. Stir in ham, Parmesan cheese and white pepper. Toss cream mixture with ravioli and asparagus. Serve immediately. *Makes 4 servings*

Roast Turkey with Honey Cranberry Relish

(Pictured below)

1 medium orange
12 ounces fresh or frozen whole cranberries
3/4 cup honey
2 pounds sliced roasted turkey breast

Quarter and slice unpeeled orange, removing seeds. Coarsely chop orange and cranberries. Place in medium saucepan and stir in honey. Bring to a boil over medium-high heat. Cook 3 to 4 minutes; cool. Serve over turkey. *Makes 8 servings*

Favorite recipe from **National Honey Board**

Helpful Hint

Fresh unwashed cranberries can be kept in an unopened plastic bag for up to one month in the refrigerator.

Hunt's® Linguine with Red Clam Sauce

1 tablespoon olive oil
3/4 cup finely chopped onion
1/2 teaspoon minced fresh garlic
1 (15-ounce) can HUNT'S® Tomato Sauce
1 (10-ounce) can whole baby clams, reserve 1/4 cup clam juice
1 tablespoon chopped fresh parsley
1 teaspoon dried basil leaves
1/2 teaspoon dried oregano leaves
1/8 teaspoon pepper
Hot cooked linguine
Grated Parmesan cheese

In large saucepan, heat oil; sauté onion and garlic until tender. Stir in tomato sauce, clams, 1/4 cup clam juice, parsley, basil, oregano and pepper. Simmer, uncovered, 10 to 15 minutes; stir occasionally. Serve over linguine and top with Parmesan cheese. *Makes 4 servings*

Roast Turkey with Honey Cranberry Relish

Sweet and Sour Pork

(Pictured at right)

3/4 pound boneless pork
1 teaspoon vegetable oil
1 bag (16 ounces) BIRDS EYE® frozen Farm Fresh
    Mixtures Pepper Stir Fry vegetables
1 tablespoon water
1 jar (11.5 ounces) sweet and sour sauce
1 can (8 ounces) pineapple chunks, drained

• Cut pork into thin strips.

• In large skillet, heat oil over medium-high heat.

• Add pork; stir-fry until pork is browned.

• Add vegetables and water; cover and cook over medium heat 5 to 7 minutes or until vegetables are crisp-tender.

• Uncover; stir in sweet and sour sauce and pineapple. Cook until heated through.

Makes 4 servings

Birds Eye® Idea: For a quick sweet and sour sauce for chicken nuggets or egg rolls, add sugar and vinegar to taste to jarred strained apricots or peaches.

Noodles Stroganoff

1 package (12 ounces) BARILLA® Wide or Extra
    Wide Egg Noodles
2 tablespoons butter or margarine
2 packages (8 ounces each) sliced mushrooms
1 medium onion, chopped
1 clove garlic, minced *or* 1/2 teaspoon bottled
    minced garlic
1-1/2 teaspoons salt
1/2 teaspoon pepper
1 pound ground beef
1 jar (12 ounces) beef gravy
1 container (8 ounces) sour cream
1/8 teaspoon paprika

1. Cook noodles according to package directions; drain.

2. Meanwhile, melt butter in large skillet. Add mushrooms, onion, garlic, salt and pepper. Cook over medium heat, stirring occasionally, until mushrooms are lightly browned. Add ground beef and cook until no longer pink, stirring to break up meat.

3. Add gravy and heat to boiling. Remove from heat; stir in sour cream. Serve beef mixture over noodles; sprinkle with paprika. *Makes 8 to 10 servings*

Turkey and Rice Quiche

3 cups cooked rice, cooled to room temperature
1-1/2 cups chopped cooked turkey
1 medium tomato, seeded and finely diced
1/4 cup sliced green onions
1/4 cup finely diced green bell pepper
1 tablespoon chopped fresh basil *or* 1 teaspoon
    dried basil leaves
1/2 teaspoon seasoned salt
1/8 to 1/4 teaspoon ground red pepper
1/2 cup skim milk
3 eggs, beaten
    Vegetable cooking spray
1/2 cup (2 ounces) shredded Cheddar cheese
1/2 cup (2 ounces) shredded mozzarella cheese

Combine rice, turkey, tomato, onions, bell pepper, basil, salt, red pepper, milk and eggs in 13×9×2-inch pan coated with cooking spray. Top with cheeses. Bake at 375°F for 20 minutes or until knife inserted near center comes out clean. To serve, cut quiche into 8 squares; cut each square diagonally into 2 triangles. *Makes 8 servings (2 triangles each)*

Favorite recipe from **USA Rice Federation**

Helpful Hint

Tomatoes should never be refrigerated before cutting because cold temperatures cause their flesh to become mealy and lose flavor. Store them at room temperature. To seed a tomato, cut it in half crosswise. Holding each tomato half over a bowl, cut side down, gently squeeze the tomato to remove the seeds.

Sweet and Sour Pork

Grilled Meat Loaves and Potatoes

(Pictured at right)

    1 pound ground beef
1/2 cup A.1.® Original or A.1.® BOLD & SPICY
        Steak Sauce, divided
1/2 cup plain dry bread crumbs
    1 egg, beaten
1/4 cup finely chopped green bell pepper
1/4 cup finely chopped onion
    2 tablespoons margarine or butter, melted
    4 (6-ounce) red skin potatoes, blanched, sliced
        into 1/4-inch-thick rounds
        Grated Parmesan cheese
        Additional A.1.® Original or A.1.® BOLD &
        SPICY Steak Sauce (optional)

Mix ground beef, 1/4 cup steak sauce, bread crumbs, egg, pepper and onion. Shape into 4 (4-inch) oval loaves; set aside.

Blend remaining 1/4 cup steak sauce and margarine; set aside.

Grill meat loaves over medium heat 20 to 25 minutes and potato slices 10 to 12 minutes or until beef is no longer pink in center and potatoes are tender, turning and basting both occasionally with reserved steak sauce mixture. Sprinkle potatoes with cheese. Serve immediately with additional steak sauce if desired.   *Makes 4 servings*

Hearty Chicken Bake

    3 cups hot mashed potatoes
    1 cup (4 ounces) shredded Cheddar cheese,
        divided
1-1/3 cups *French's® Taste Toppers*™ French Fried
        Onions, divided
1-1/2 cups (7 ounces) cubed cooked chicken
    1 package (10 ounces) frozen mixed vegetables,
        thawed and drained
    1 can (10-3/4 ounces) condensed cream of
        chicken soup
1/4 cup milk
1/2 teaspoon ground mustard
1/4 teaspoon garlic powder
1/4 teaspoon pepper

Preheat oven to 375°F. In medium bowl, combine mashed potatoes, 1/2 cup cheese and *2/3 cup Taste Toppers;* mix thoroughly. Spoon potato mixture into greased 1-1/2-quart casserole. Using back of spoon, spread potatoes across bottom and up sides of dish to form a shell. In large bowl, combine chicken, mixed vegetables, soup, milk and seasonings; pour into potato shell. Bake, uncovered, at 375°F for 30 minutes or until heated through. Top with remaining cheese and *2/3 cup Taste Toppers;* bake, uncovered, 3 minutes or until *Taste Toppers* are golden brown. Let stand 5 minutes before serving.
Makes 4 to 6 servings

Old-Fashioned Tuna Noodle Casserole

1/4 cup plain dry bread crumbs
    3 tablespoons margarine or butter, melted and
        divided
    1 tablespoon finely chopped parsley
1/2 cup chopped onion
1/2 cup chopped celery
    1 cup water
    1 cup milk
    1 package LIPTON® Noodles & Sauce—Butter
    2 cans (6 ounces each) tuna, drained and flaked

In small bowl, thoroughly combine bread crumbs, 1 tablespoon margarine and parsley; set aside.

In medium saucepan, melt remaining 2 tablespoons margarine over medium heat and cook onion and celery, stirring occasionally, 2 minutes or until onion is tender. Add water and milk; bring to the boiling point. Stir in Noodles & Sauce—Butter. Continue boiling over medium heat, stirring occasionally, 8 minutes or until noodles are tender. Stir in tuna. Turn into greased 1-quart casserole, then top with bread crumb mixture. Broil until bread crumbs are golden.   *Makes about 4 servings*

Grilled Meat Loaf and Potatoes

Polynesian Chicken and Rice

(Pictured at right)

> 1 can (20 ounces) DOLE® Pineapple Tidbits or Pineapple Chunks
> 1/2 cup DOLE® Seedless or Golden Raisins
> 1/2 cup sliced green onions
> 2 teaspoons finely chopped fresh ginger *or* 1/2 teaspoon ground ginger
> 1 clove garlic, finely chopped
> 3 cups cooked white or brown rice
> 2 cups chopped cooked chicken breast or turkey breast
> 2 tablespoons low-sodium soy sauce

• Drain pineapple; reserve 4 tablespoons juice.

• Heat 2 tablespoons reserved juice over medium heat in large, nonstick skillet. Add raisins, green onions, ginger and garlic; cook and stir 3 minutes.

• Stir in pineapple, rice, chicken, soy sauce and remaining 2 tablespoons juice. Cover; reduce heat to low and cook 5 minutes more or until heated through. Garnish with cherry tomatoes and green onions, if desired. *Makes 4 servings*

Spanish Rice and Meatballs

> 6 slices bacon
> 1 pound lean ground beef
> 1/2 cup soft bread crumbs
> 1 egg, slightly beaten
> 1/2 teaspoon salt
> 1/8 teaspoon pepper
> 1/2 cup chopped onion
> 1/2 cup sliced celery
> 2/3 cup uncooked white rice
> 1-1/2 cups water
> 1 can (14-1/2 ounces) whole peeled tomatoes, cut into bite-size pieces
> 1/3 cup HEINZ® 57 Sauce
> 1/4 teaspoon pepper
> 1/8 teaspoon hot pepper sauce
> 1 green bell pepper, cut into 3/4-inch chunks

In large skillet, cook bacon until crisp; remove, coarsely crumble and set aside. Drain drippings, reserving 1 tablespoon. In large bowl, combine beef, bread crumbs, egg, salt and 1/8 teaspoon pepper. Form into 20 meatballs, using a rounded tablespoon for each. In same skillet, brown meatballs in reserved drippings; remove. In same skillet, sauté onion and celery until tender-crisp; drain excess fat. Add rice, water, tomatoes, 57 Sauce, 1/4 teaspoon pepper and hot pepper sauce. Cover; simmer 20 minutes. Stir in bacon, meatballs and green pepper. Cover; simmer an additional 10 minutes or until rice is tender and liquid is absorbed, stirring occasionally.

Makes 4 servings (4 cups rice mixture)

Grilled Apple-Stuffed Pork Chops

> 5 tablespoons *French's*® Hearty Deli Brown Mustard, divided
> 3 tablespoons honey, divided
> 1 cup corn bread stuffing mix
> 1 small McIntosh apple, peeled, cored and chopped
> 1/4 cup minced onion
> 1/4 cup chopped fresh parsley
> 4 rib pork chops, cut 1-1/4 inches thick (about 2 pounds)

1. Combine 1/4 cup water, 2 tablespoons mustard and 1 tablespoon honey in medium bowl. Add stuffing mix, apple, onion and parsley; toss until crumbs are moistened. Combine remaining 3 tablespoons mustard and 2 tablespoons honey in small bowl; set aside for glaze.

2. Cut horizontal slits in pork chops, using sharp knife, to make pockets for stuffing. Spoon stuffing evenly into pockets. Secure openings with toothpicks.

3. Place pork chops on oiled grid. Grill over medium heat 40 to 45 minutes until no longer pink near bone, turning often. Baste chops with reserved glaze during last 10 minutes of cooking.

Makes 4 servings

Polynesian Chicken and Rice

20-Minute White Bean Chili

(Pictured at right)

1 cup chopped onion
1 clove garlic, minced
1 tablespoon vegetable oil
1 pound ground turkey
1 cup chicken broth
1 (14-1/2-ounce) can stewed tomatoes
1/3 cup GREY POUPON® Dijon Mustard
1 tablespoon chili powder
1/8 to 1/4 teaspoon ground red pepper
1 (15-ounce) can cannellini beans, drained and rinsed
1 (8-ounce) can corn, drained
   Tortilla chips, shredded Cheddar cheese and cilantro, optional

Sauté onion and garlic in oil in 3-quart saucepan until tender. Add turkey; cook until done, stirring occasionally to break up meat. Drain. Stir in chicken broth, tomatoes, mustard, chili powder and pepper. Heat to a boil; reduce heat. Simmer for 10 minutes. Stir in beans and corn; cook for 5 minutes. Top with tortilla chips, shredded cheese and cilantro, if desired.   *Makes 6 servings*

Home-Style Beef Brisket

1 envelope LIPTON® RECIPE SECRETS® Onion Soup Mix*
3/4 cup water
1/2 cup ketchup
1 teaspoon garlic powder
1/2 teaspoon ground black pepper
1 (3-pound) boneless brisket of beef

Also terrific with Lipton® Recipe Secrets® Onion-Mushroom, Beefy Mushroom, Beefy Onion or Savory Herb with Garlic Soup Mix.

1. Preheat oven to 325°F. In 13×9-inch baking or roasting pan, add soup mix blended with water, ketchup, garlic powder and pepper.

2. Add brisket; turn to coat.

3. Loosely cover with aluminum foil and bake 3 hours or until brisket is tender. If desired, thicken gravy.   *Makes 8 servings*

Recipe Tip: For a quick one-dish dinner, during last hour of baking, add 1/2 pound carrots, cut into 2-inch pieces and 1 pound potatoes, peeled, if desired, and cut into 2-inch chunks.

Southwest Pork and Dressing

1 pound boneless pork, cut into 1-inch strips
2 teaspoons chili powder
1/4 cup margarine or butter
1/2 cup diagonally sliced green onions
1-1/2 cups water
1 cup frozen sweet corn, thawed
1 can (4 ounces) chopped green chilies, drained
3 cups STOVE TOP® Cornbread Stuffing Mix in the Canister
1-1/4 cups (5 ounces) shredded Monterey Jack cheese, divided

TOSS meat with chili powder. Melt margarine in large skillet on medium-high heat. Add meat and onions; cook and stir until meat is browned.

STIR in water, corn and chilies. Bring to boil. Stir in stuffing mix and 3/4 cup of the cheese. Remove from heat. Sprinkle with remaining 1/2 cup cheese. Cover. Let stand 5 minutes.   *Makes 4 to 6 servings*

Chicken Parmesan

1/4 cup seasoned dry bread crumbs
2 tablespoons KRAFT® 100% Grated Parmesan Cheese
4 boneless skinless chicken breast halves (about 1-1/4 pounds)
1 egg, beaten
2 tablespoons oil
1 can (14-1/2 ounces) stewed tomatoes
1 can (8 ounces) tomato sauce
1/4 teaspoon dried oregano leaves
1-1/2 cups MINUTE® White Rice, uncooked
1/2 cup KRAFT® Shredded Mozzarella Cheese

MIX bread crumbs and Parmesan cheese. Dip chicken in egg, shaking off excess. Coat with crumb mixture.

HEAT oil in large skillet on medium-high heat. Add chicken; brown on both sides until cooked through. Remove from skillet. Drain on paper towels.

STIR tomatoes, tomato sauce and oregano into skillet. Bring to boil. Stir in rice. Top with chicken. Sprinkle with mozzarella cheese; cover. Remove from heat. Let stand 5 minutes.

Makes 4 servings

20-Minute White Bean Chili

Country Skillet Hash

Sweet and Sour Fish

1/3 cup GRANDMA'S® Molasses
1/4 cup cider vinegar
1/4 cup plus 2 tablespoons cornstarch, divided
  2 tablespoons pineapple juice, reserved from chunks
  2 tablespoons ketchup
  2 tablespoons soy sauce
  1 pound swordfish or red snapper, cut into 1-inch cubes
  3 tablespoons vegetable oil, divided
  1 green, red or yellow bell pepper, cut into strips
  2 green onions, chopped
  1 (8-ounce) can pineapple chunks in its own juice, drained, reserving 2 tablespoons juice for sauce
    Cherry tomatoes, cut into halves
    Hot cooked rice or noodles

In medium bowl, combine molasses, vinegar, 2 tablespoons cornstarch, pineapple juice, ketchup and soy sauce; blend well. Set aside. Coat swordfish with remaining 1/4 cup cornstarch. In large skillet, heat 2 tablespoons oil. Stir-fry 5 minutes or until fish flakes easily with fork. Remove from skillet. Heat remaining 1 tablespoon oil in skillet. Stir-fry bell pepper and onions 2 minutes or until crisp-tender. Add molasses mixture; cook until thickened. Add fish, pineapple and tomatoes; cook until heated through. Serve with rice. *Makes 4 servings*

Teriyaki Turkey Burgers

  1 pound ground turkey
1/3 cup LAWRY'S® Teriyaki Marinade with Pineapple Juice
  3 tablespoons thinly sliced green onions
1/4 cup crushed pineapple, drained
1/2 teaspoon LAWRY'S® Garlic Powder with Parsley

In medium bowl, combine all ingredients; mix well. Form into 4 patties (mixture will be moist). Grill or broil 5 inches from heat source 3 to 5 minutes on each side or until cooked through.

Makes 4 servings

Serving Suggestion: Excellent on onion buns with lettuce, red onion and pineapple slices.

Country Skillet Hash

(Pictured above)

  2 tablespoons butter or margarine
  4 pork chops (3/4 inch thick), diced
1/4 teaspoon black pepper
1/4 teaspoon cayenne pepper (optional)
  1 medium onion, chopped
  2 cloves garlic, minced
  1 can (14-1/2 ounces) DEL MONTE® Whole New Potatoes, drained and diced
  1 can (14-1/2 ounces) DEL MONTE® Diced Tomatoes, undrained
  1 medium green bell pepper, chopped
1/2 teaspoon thyme, crushed

1. Melt butter in large skillet over medium heat. Add meat; cook, stirring occasionally, until no longer pink in center. Season with black pepper and cayenne pepper, if desired.

2. Add onion and garlic; cook until tender. Stir in potatoes, tomatoes, green pepper and thyme. Cook 5 minutes, stirring frequently. Season with salt, if desired. *Makes 4 servings*

Chicken Gone Garlic

(Pictured below)

1 BUTTERBALL® Fresh Young Roaster, giblets
   removed
3 tablespoons butter or margarine, softened
2 tablespoons minced fresh parsley
1/2 teaspoon poultry seasoning
1/2 teaspoon salt
1/4 teaspoon cracked black pepper
   Juice of 1/2 lemon
4 heads garlic, cloves separated and peeled
4 large potatoes, cut into wedges
1 cup water

Combine butter, parsley, poultry seasoning, salt
and pepper in small bowl. Pour lemon juice into
cavity of chicken. Rub butter mixture on skin. Place
chicken in roasting pan. Arrange garlic cloves and
potatoes around chicken. Pour water into pan; cover.
Roast 1 hour in preheated 375°F oven. Uncover and
continue roasting 45 minutes to 1 hour or until
internal temperature reaches 180°F in thigh and skin
is golden brown. Serve with brussels sprouts, if
desired.   *Makes 8 servings*

"All the Fixings" Turkey
Pot Roast

1 large oven bag
1 (2- to 2-1/2-pound) turkey breast half
1/3 cup WESSON® Canola Oil
   Seasoned salt
   Seasoned pepper
1 large sweet onion, sliced 1/4 inch thick
8 carrots, peeled and cut in half
4 small russet potatoes, sliced in half lengthwise
   Garlic salt

Preheat oven to 350°F. Place oven bag in a
13×9×2-inch baking dish. Loosen and fold back
skin from turkey breast but do not detach. Brush
breast with Wesson® Oil and place in oven bag.
Generously sprinkle turkey with seasoned salt and
seasoned pepper. Top turkey with 4 to 5 onion
slices. Brush onions with oil; cover onions with skin.
Brush turkey with oil and sprinkle with seasoned
salt and pepper. Brush carrots, potatoes and
remaining onion slices with oil; sprinkle with garlic
salt and seasoned pepper. Place vegetables around
turkey breast and close bag; cut four 1/2-inch slits in
top of bag. Bake for 1-1/2 to 2 hours or until turkey
juices run clear.   *Makes 4 to 6 servings*

Chicken Gone Garlic

Campbell's® Country Skillet Supper

(Pictured at right)

1 pound ground beef
1 medium onion, chopped (about 1/2 cup)
1/8 teaspoon garlic powder *or* 1 clove garlic, minced
1 can (10-3/4 ounces) CAMPBELL'S® Condensed Golden Mushroom Soup
1 can (10-1/2 ounces) CAMPBELL'S® Condensed Beef Broth
1 can (14-1/2 ounces) diced tomatoes
1 small zucchini, sliced (about 1 cup)
1/2 teaspoon dried thyme leaves, crushed
1-1/2 cups *uncooked* corkscrew pasta

1. In medium skillet over medium-high heat, cook beef, onion and garlic powder until beef is browned, stirring to separate meat. Pour off fat.

2. Add soup, broth, tomatoes, zucchini and thyme. Heat to a boil. Stir in pasta. Reduce heat to low. Cook 15 minutes or until pasta is done, stirring often.

Makes 4 servings

Campbell's® Country Skillet Supper Provençal: Top with sliced pitted ripe olives.

Holiday Pork Roast

1 tablespoon minced fresh ginger
2 cloves garlic, minced
1 teaspoon dried sage leaves, crushed
1/4 teaspoon salt
1 (5- to 7-pound) pork loin roast
1/3 cup apple jelly
1/2 teaspoon TABASCO® brand Pepper Sauce
2 medium carrots, sliced
2 medium onions, sliced
1-3/4 cups water, divided
1 teaspoon browning and seasoning sauce

Preheat oven to 325°F. Combine ginger, garlic, sage and salt; rub over pork. Place in shallow roasting pan. Roast pork 1-1/2 hours. Remove from oven; score meat in diamond pattern.

Combine jelly and TABASCO® Sauce; spread generously over roast. Arrange carrots and onions around meat; add 1 cup water. Roast 1 hour until meat thermometer registers 160°F. Remove roast to serving platter; keep warm.

Skim fat from drippings in pan; discard fat. Place vegetables and drippings in food processor or blender; process until puréed. Return purée to roasting pan. Stir in remaining 3/4 cup water and browning sauce; heat. Serve sauce with roast.

Makes 6 to 8 servings

Turkey Cutlets with Tex-Mex Salsa

1 package BUTTERBALL® Fresh Boneless Turkey Breast Cutlets
1 can (15 ounces) black beans, rinsed and drained
1 can (11 ounces) Mexican-style corn, drained
1 cup salsa
2 tablespoons chopped fresh cilantro
1 tablespoon Mexican seasoning blend*
1 teaspoon salt
1 tablespoon vegetable oil
Lime wedges (optional)

To make your own Mexican seasoning, combine 1-1/2 teaspoons chili powder, 3/4 teaspoon oregano and 3/4 teaspoon cumin.

Combine black beans, corn, salsa and cilantro in large bowl; stir to blend. Chill until served. Combine seasoning blend and salt. Dip cutlets into seasoning mixture. Heat oil in large skillet over medium heat until hot. Cook cutlets 2 to 2-1/2 minutes on each side until lightly browned and no longer pink. Place bean salsa on serving platter; arrange cutlets on top of salsa. Serve with a squeeze of fresh lime.

Makes 7 servings

Helpful Hint

When storing raw meat or poultry, be sure to keep the package away from other food items, especially produce and unwrapped items. The juices can drip and contaminate other foods.

Desserts

"Make Your Own Sundae" Pie

(Pictured at left)

1 cup hot fudge ice cream topping, warmed and divided
1 prepared (9-inch) vanilla cookie crumb pie crust
6 cups vanilla ice cream, softened
1 cup caramel ice cream topping, warmed and divided
1/4 cup marshmallow cream
1 tablespoon milk
2/3 cup "M&M's"® Chocolate Mini Baking Bits
1/4 cup chopped nuts
    Aerosol whipped topping and maraschino cherry for
      garnish

Spread 1/2 cup hot fudge topping on bottom of crust; freeze
10 minutes. Spread 1 cup ice cream over fudge layer; freeze
10 minutes. Spread 1/2 cup caramel topping over ice cream
layer; freeze for 10 minutes. Mound scoops of ice cream over
caramel layer. Cover and freeze until ready to serve. Just
before serving, in small bowl combine marshmallow cream
and milk. Microwave at HIGH 10 seconds; stir until well
combined. Drizzle pie with remaining 1/2 cup hot fudge
topping, remaining 1/2 cup caramel topping and marshmallow
sauce. Sprinkle with 1/3 cup "M&M's"® Chocolate Mini Baking
Bits and nuts. Garnish with whipped topping, remaining
1/3 cup "M&M's"® Chocolate Mini Baking Bits and maraschino
cherry. Serve immediately. *Makes 8 servings*

Clockwise from top left: *"Make Your Own
Sundae" Pie, Ultimate Sugar Cookies (p. 186),
Peach Blueberry Cheesecake (p. 188) and
Two Great Tastes Pudding Parfaits (p. 184)*

Sumptuous Strawberry Rhubarb Pie

(Pictured at right)

CRUST

    9-inch Classic Crisco® Double Crust (recipe follows)

FILLING

    4 cups fresh cut rhubarb (1/2-inch pieces)
    3 cups sliced strawberries
  1-1/3 cups sugar
    1/3 cup plus 1/4 cup all-purpose flour
    2 tablespoons plus 1-1/2 teaspoons quick-cooking tapioca
    1/2 teaspoon grated orange peel
    1/2 teaspoon ground cinnamon
    1/4 teaspoon ground nutmeg
    2 tablespoons butter or margarine

GLAZE

    1 egg, beaten
    1 tablespoon sugar

1. Prepare 9-inch Classic Crisco® Double Crust; roll and press bottom crust into 9-inch pie plate. *Do not bake.* Heat oven to 425°F.

2. For Filling, combine rhubarb and strawberries in large bowl. Combine 1-1/3 cups sugar, flour, tapioca, orange peel, cinnamon and nutmeg in medium bowl; stir well. Add to fruit. Toss to coat. Spoon filling into unbaked pie crust. Dot with butter. Moisten pastry edge with water.

3. Roll out top crust. Lift onto filled pie. Trim 1/2 inch beyond edge of pie plate. Fold top edge under bottom crust; flute. Cut desired shapes into top crust to allow steam to escape.

4. For Glaze, brush top crust with egg. Sprinkle with 1 tablespoon sugar.

5. Bake at 425°F for 40 to 50 minutes or until filling in center is bubbly and crust is golden brown. *Do not overbake.* Cover edge with foil, if necessary, to prevent overbrowning. Cool until barely warm or at room temperature before serving.

Makes 1 (9-inch) pie

9-inch Classic Crisco® Double Crust

    2 cups all-purpose flour
    1 teaspoon salt
    3/4 CRISCO® Stick or 3/4 cup CRISCO® all-vegetable shortening
    5 tablespoons cold water

1. Spoon flour into measuring cup and level. Combine flour and salt in medium bowl.

2. Cut in shortening using pastry blender or 2 knives until flour is blended to form pea-size chunks.

3. Sprinkle with water, 1 tablespoon at a time. Toss lightly with fork until dough forms a ball.

4. Divide dough in half. Press half of dough between hands to form a 5- to 6-inch "pancake." Flour rolling surface and rolling pin lightly. Roll dough into circle. Trim circle 1 inch larger than upside-down pie plate. Carefully remove trimmed dough. Set aside to reroll and use for pastry cutout garnish, if desired. Repeat with remaining half of dough.

Makes 2 (9-inch) crusts

Two Great Tastes Pudding Parfaits

(Pictured on page 182)

    1 package (6-serving size, 4.6 ounces) vanilla cook & serve pudding and pie filling mix*
  3-1/2 cups milk
    1 cup REESE'S® Peanut Butter Chips
    1 cup HERSHEY'S Semi-Sweet or Milk Chocolate MINI KISSES™ Baking Pieces
    Whipped topping (optional)
    Additional MINI KISSES™ or grated chocolate

Do not use instant pudding mix.

1. Combine pudding mix and 3-1/2 cups milk in large heavy saucepan (rather than amount listed in package directions). Cook over medium heat, stirring constantly, until mixture comes to a full boil. Remove from heat; divide hot mixture between 2 heat-proof medium bowls.

2. Immediately stir peanut butter chips into mixture in one bowl and Mini Kisses™ into second bowl. Stir both mixtures until chips are melted and mixture is smooth. Cool slightly, stirring occasionally.

3. Alternately layer peanut butter and chocolate mixtures in parfait dishes, wine glasses or dessert dishes. Place plastic wrap directly onto surface of each dessert; refrigerate about 6 hours. Garnish with whipped topping, if desired, and Mini Kisses™.

Makes 4 to 6 servings

Sumptuous Strawberry Rhubarb Pie

Cheesecake-Topped Brownies

(Pictured at right)

1 (19.8-ounce) package fudge brownie mix
1 (8-ounce) package cream cheese, softened
2 tablespoons butter or margarine, softened
1 tablespoon cornstarch
1 (14-ounce) can EAGLE® BRAND Sweetened
    Condensed Milk (NOT evaporated milk)
1 egg
2 teaspoons vanilla extract
    Ready-to-spread chocolate frosting (optional)
    Orange peel (optional)

1. Preheat oven to 350°F. Prepare brownie mix as package directs. Spread into well-greased 13×9-inch baking pan.

2. In large mixing bowl, beat cream cheese, butter and cornstarch until fluffy.

3. Gradually beat in Eagle Brand. Add egg and vanilla; beat until smooth. Pour cheesecake mixture evenly over brownie batter.

4. Bake 40 to 45 minutes or until top is lightly browned. Cool. Spread with frosting or sprinkle with orange peel, if desired. Cut into bars. Store covered in refrigerator. *Makes 36 to 40 brownies*

Ultimate Sugar Cookies

(Pictured on page 182)

1-1/4 cups granulated sugar
    1 Butter Flavor CRISCO® Stick or 1 cup Butter
        Flavor CRISCO® all-vegetable shortening
    2 eggs
    1/4 cup light corn syrup or regular pancake syrup
    1 tablespoon vanilla
    3 cups all-purpose flour plus 4 tablespoons,
        divided
    3/4 teaspoon baking powder
    1/2 teaspoon baking soda
    1/2 teaspoon salt
        Decorations of your choice: granulated sugar,
            colored sugar crystals, frosting, decors,
            candies, chips, nuts, raisins, decorating gel

1. Combine sugar and 1 cup shortening in large bowl. Beat at medium speed of electric mixer until well blended. Add eggs, syrup and vanilla. Beat until well blended and fluffy.

2. Combine 3 cups flour, baking powder, baking soda and salt. Add gradually to creamed mixture at low speed. Mix until well blended. Divide dough into 4 quarters. (If dough is too sticky or too soft to roll, wrap each quarter of dough with plastic wrap and refrigerate 1 hour.)

3. Heat oven to 375°F. Place sheets of foil on countertop for cooling cookies.

4. Spread 1 tablespoon flour on large sheet of waxed paper. Place 1/4 of dough on floured paper. Flatten slightly. Turn dough over and cover with another large sheet of waxed paper. Roll dough to 1/4-inch thickness. Remove top sheet of waxed paper.

5. Cut out cookies with floured cutter. Transfer to ungreased baking sheet. Place 2 inches apart. Roll out remaining dough. Sprinkle with granulated sugar, colored sugar crystals, decors or leave plain to frost or decorate when cooled.

6. Bake one baking sheet at a time at 375°F for 5 to 9 minutes, depending on the size of your cookies (bake smaller, thinner cookies closer to 5 minutes: larger cookies closer to 9 minutes). *Do not overbake.* Cool 2 minutes on baking sheet. Remove cookies to foil to cool completely, then frost if desired.
Makes about 3 to 4 dozen cookies

Baked Custard Fruit Tart

2 teaspoons sugar
1-1/2 cups milk
    2 eggs
    2 tablespoons flour
    1 package (4-serving size) JELL-O® Vanilla Flavor
        Cook & Serve Pudding & Pie Filling (not
        instant)
    1 can (15 ounces) sliced peaches, drained

HEAT oven to 350°F. Grease 9-inch pie plate; sprinkle with sugar.

BEAT milk, eggs, flour and pudding mix until well mixed. Pour into prepared pie plate. Arrange peaches in pudding mixture.

BAKE 40 to 45 minutes or until filling is set and surface is golden brown. Cool on wire rack. Serve warm or cold, with whipped topping, if desired.
Makes 8 servings

Cheesecake-Topped Brownies

Layer After Layer Lemon Pie

Layer After Layer Lemon Pie

(Pictured above and on back cover)

1/3 cup strawberry jam
1 prepared graham cracker or shortbread crumb
  crust (6 ounces or 9 inches)
4 ounces PHILADELPHIA® Cream Cheese,
  softened
1 tablespoon sugar
1 tub (8 ounces) COOL WHIP® Whipped
  Topping, thawed, divided
1-1/2 cups cold milk or half-and-half
2 packages (4-serving size each) JELL-O® Lemon
  Flavor Instant Pudding & Pie Filling
2 teaspoons grated lemon peel

SPREAD jam gently onto bottom of pie crust. Mix
cream cheese and sugar in large bowl with wire
whisk until smooth. Gently stir in 1/2 of the whipped
topping. Spread on top of jam.

POUR milk into large bowl. Add pudding mixes and
lemon peel. Beat with wire whisk 1 minute. (Mixture
will be thick.) Gently stir in remaining whipped
topping. Spread over cream cheese layer.

REFRIGERATE 4 hours or until set. Garnish with
additional whipped topping, if desired.
Makes 8 servings

Best of the Season: For an extra-special fruity flavor,
place 1 cup strawberries into jam on bottom of
crust; proceed as directed.

Take a Shortcut: Soften cream cheese in microwave
on HIGH 15 to 20 seconds.

Peach Blueberry Cheesecake

(Pictured on page 182)

CRUST
1-1/2 cups crushed graham cracker crumbs
  1/2 cup crushed gingersnap cookies
    5 tablespoons butter, melted

FILLING
    2 packages (8 ounces each) cream cheese,
      softened
  3/4 cup sugar
  1/2 cup GRANDMA'S® Molasses
    7 egg yolks
    2 tablespoons lemon juice
1-1/2 teaspoons vanilla extract
  1/2 teaspoon salt
    3 cups sour cream

TOPPING
    1 can (15 ounces) peach slices, drained
      Fresh blueberries
    2 tablespoons peach or apricot preserves, melted

1. Heat oven to 350°F. Grease 9-inch springform pan.
In small bowl, combine crust ingredients; press over
bottom and half way up side of pan. Refrigerate.
Place large roasting pan filled with 1 inch hot water
on middle rack of oven. In large bowl, beat cream
cheese and sugar until very smooth, about 3 minutes.
Beat in molasses. Add egg yolks, beating until batter
is smooth. Add lemon juice, vanilla and salt; beat
until well incorporated. Beat in sour cream just until
blended. Pour batter into prepared crust.

2. Place cheesecake in large roasting pan. Bake
45 minutes. Turn oven off without opening door and
let cake cool 1 hour. Transfer cheesecake to wire
rack (center will be jiggly) and cool to room
temperature, about 1 hour. Cover pan with plastic
wrap and refrigerate overnight. Remove side of pan.
Top with peach slices and blueberries. Brush fruit
with preserves. *Makes 12 to 16 servings*

Cranberry Cobbler

(Pictured below)

2 (15-ounce) cans sliced peaches in light syrup,
    drained
1 (16-ounce) can whole berry cranberry sauce
1 package DUNCAN HINES® Cinnamon Swirl
    Muffin Mix
1/2 cup chopped pecans
1/3 cup butter or margarine, melted
    Whipped topping or ice cream

Preheat oven to 350°F.

Cut peach slices in half lengthwise. Combine peach
slices and cranberry sauce in *ungreased* 9-inch
square pan. Knead swirl packet from Mix for
10 seconds. Squeeze contents evenly over fruit.

Combine muffin mix, contents of topping packet
from mix and pecans in large bowl. Add melted
butter. Stir until thoroughly blended (mixture will
be crumbly). Sprinkle crumbs over fruit. Bake 40 to
45 minutes or until lightly browned and bubbly.
Serve warm with whipped topping.

Makes 9 servings

Tip: Store leftovers in the refrigerator. Reheat in
microwave oven to serve warm.

Almond Cream Cheese Cookies

1 (3-ounce) package cream cheese, softened
1 cup butter, softened
1 cup sugar
1 egg yolk
1 tablespoon milk
1/8 teaspoon almond extract
2-1/2 cups sifted cake flour
1 cup BLUE DIAMOND® Sliced Natural
    Almonds, toasted

Beat cream cheese with butter and sugar until
fluffy. Blend in egg yolk, milk and almond extract.
Gradually mix in flour. Gently stir in almonds.
(Dough will be sticky.) Divide dough in half; place
each half on large sheet of waxed paper. Working
through waxed paper, shape each dough half into
12×1-1/2-inch roll. Chill until very firm.

Preheat oven to 325°F. Cut rolls into 1/4-inch slices.
Bake on ungreased cookie sheets 10 to 15 minutes
or until edges are golden. (Cookies will not brown.)
Cool on wire racks.

Makes about 4 dozen cookies

Cranberry Cobbler

Double Almond Ice Cream

(Pictured at right)

      3 cups whipping cream
      1 cup milk
      3/4 cup plus 2 tablespoons sugar, divided
      4 egg yolks, beaten
      1 tablespoon vanilla extract
      2 teaspoons almond extract
      2 tablespoons butter
  1-1/2 cups BLUE DIAMOND® Chopped Natural
         Almonds

Combine cream, milk and 3/4 cup sugar in medium saucepan. Cook and stir over medium heat until sugar is dissolved and mixture is hot. Gradually add 1 cup cream mixture to beaten egg yolks, whisking constantly. When mixture is smooth, strain into double boiler. Gradually pour in remaining cream mixture, whisking constantly. Cook over simmering water until mixture thickens slightly and coats back of spoon, about 8 minutes, stirring constantly. Do not boil. Stir in extracts. Cool.

Meanwhile, melt butter and stir in remaining 2 tablespoons sugar in small saucepan. Cook and stir over medium heat until sugar begins to bubble, about 30 seconds. Add almonds; cook and stir over medium heat until golden and well coated. Cool. Stir almonds into ice cream mixture. Pour into ice cream maker container. Freeze according to manufacturer's instructions.   *Makes 1 quart ice cream*

Strawberry Chiffon Pie

      Chocolate Pastry (recipe follows)
      1 package (3 ounces) strawberry-flavored gelatin
      3/4 cup boiling water
  1-1/2 cups chopped fresh strawberries
      2 cups frozen non-dairy whipped topping,
         thawed
      1/2 cup HERSHEY'S Semi-Sweet Chocolate Chips
      1 teaspoon shortening (do *not* use butter,
         margarine, spread or oil)
      8 whole strawberries

1. Prepare Chocolate Pastry.

2. Dissolve gelatin in boiling water in medium bowl; cool slightly. Crush strawberries or purée to equal 3/4 cup. Stir strawberry purée into gelatin mixture; refrigerate until partially set (consistency of unbeaten egg whites). Fold whipped topping into strawberry mixture. Spoon into prepared crust. Refrigerate 2 to 3 hours or until set.

3. Line tray with wax paper. Place chocolate chips and shortening in small microwave-safe bowl. Microwave at HIGH (100%) 1 minute; stir. If necessary, microwave at HIGH an additional 15 seconds at a time, stirring after each heating, just until chips are melted when stirred. Dip whole strawberries into melted chocolate; place on prepared tray. Refrigerate, uncovered, about 30 minutes or until chocolate is firm. Just before serving, garnish pie with chocolate-covered strawberries. Cover; refrigerate leftover pie.
                              Makes 8 servings

Chocolate Pastry

  1-1/4 cups all-purpose flour
      1/4 cup sugar
         3 tablespoons HERSHEY'S Cocoa
      1/4 teaspoon salt
      1/3 cup vegetable oil
         3 tablespoons cold water

1. Stir together flour, sugar, cocoa and salt in medium bowl. Place oil in measuring cup; add water. Do not stir. Pour liquid over flour mixture; stir lightly with fork until well blended. (If mixture is too dry, add 1 to 2 teaspoons additional cold water.)

2. With hands, shape mixture into ball. Place between two pieces of wax paper; roll into 12-inch circle. Peel off top sheet of paper. Gently invert pastry over 9-inch pie plate; peel off paper. Fit pastry into pie plate. Fold under extra pastry around edge; flute edge. With fork, prick bottom and side of crust thoroughly. Refrigerate about 30 minutes.

3. Meanwhile, heat oven to 450°F. Bake 10 minutes. Cool completely.

Helpful Hint

When cutting chiffon pies, the slices will cut better if the knife is wiped with a damp cloth or paper towel between cuts.

Double Almond Ice Cream

Coconut Jam Cake

(Pictured at right)

    1 package (2-layer size) yellow cake mix
    1 package (7 ounces) BAKER'S® ANGEL FLAKE®
        Coconut, divided
  1/2 cup strawberry jam
    1 tub (8 ounces) COOL WHIP® Whipped
        Topping, thawed
  1/2 cup apricot jam
        Sliced fresh strawberries
        Canned apricot halves, drained
        Fresh mint leaves

HEAT oven to 350°F.

PREPARE and bake cake mix as directed on package
for 2 (9-inch) round cake layers, gently stirring
1 cup coconut into batter just before pouring into
pans. Cool 10 minutes; remove from pans. Cool
completely on wire racks.

PLACE 1 cake layer on serving plate; spread top
with strawberry jam. Spread 3/4 cup whipped
topping over jam; top with second cake layer.
Spread top of cake with apricot jam. Frost top and
side of cake with remaining whipped topping. Pat
remaining coconut onto side of cake.

REFRIGERATE until ready to serve. Garnish with
fruit and mint just before serving.

Makes 12 servings

Lemon Mousse with Raspberry Sauce

1-1/2 cups boiling water
    1 package (8-serving size) *or* 2 packages
        (4-serving size) JELL-O® Brand Lemon Flavor
        Gelatin Dessert
    2 teaspoons grated lemon peel
    1 cup cold water
  3/4 cup cold orange juice
    1 tub (8 ounces) COOL WHIP® Whipped
        Topping, thawed
    1 package (10 ounces) frozen raspberries or
        strawberries in syrup, thawed, puréed in
        blender

STIR boiling water into gelatin and lemon peel
in large bowl at least 2 minutes until gelatin is
completely dissolved. Stir in cold water and orange
juice. Refrigerate about 1-1/4 hours or until slightly
thickened (consistency of unbeaten egg whites).

STIR in whipped topping with wire whisk until
smooth. Pour into 12 (6-ounce) custard cups, filling
each about 3/4 full. (Or, pour into 6-cup mold.)

REFRIGERATE 3 hours or until firm. Unmold. Serve
with strawberry sauce.   *Makes 12 servings*

Tip: To unmold, dip mold in warm water for about
15 seconds. Gently pull gelatin from around edges
with moist fingers. Place moistened serving plate on
top of mold. Invert mold and plate; holding mold
and plate together, shake slightly to loosen. Gently
remove mold and center gelatin on plate.

Variation: Apple juice may be substituted for the
orange juice.

Chocolate Drop Sugar Cookies

  2/3 cup butter or margarine, softened
    1 cup sugar
    1 egg
1-1/2 teaspoons vanilla extract
1-1/2 cups all-purpose flour
  1/2 cup HERSHEY'S Cocoa
  1/2 teaspoon baking soda
  1/4 teaspoon salt
  1/3 cup buttermilk or sour milk*
        Additional sugar

*To sour milk: Use 1 teaspoon white vinegar plus milk to equal
1/3 cup.*

1. Heat oven to 350°F. Lightly grease cookie sheet.

2. Beat butter and sugar in large bowl until well
blended. Add egg and vanilla; beat until fluffy. Stir
together flour, cocoa, baking soda and salt; add
alternately with buttermilk to butter mixture. Using
ice cream scoop or 1/4-cup measuring cup, drop
dough about 2 inches apart onto prepared cookie
sheet.

3. Bake 13 to 15 minutes or until cookie springs back
when touched lightly in center. While cookies are on
cookie sheet, sprinkle lightly with additional sugar.
Cool slightly; remove from cookie sheet to wire
rack. Cool completely.

Makes about 1 dozen cookies

Oatmeal Butterscotch Cookies

(Pictured at right)

3/4 cup (1-1/2 sticks) butter or margarine, softened
3/4 cup granulated sugar
3/4 cup packed light brown sugar
2 eggs
1 teaspoon vanilla extract
1-1/4 cups all-purpose flour
1 teaspoon baking soda
1/2 teaspoon salt
1/2 teaspoon ground cinnamon
3 cups quick-cooking or regular rolled oats, uncooked
1-2/3 cups (10-ounce package) HERSHEY'S Butterscotch Chips

1. Heat oven to 375°F.

2. Beat butter, granulated sugar and brown sugar in large bowl until well blended. Add eggs and vanilla; blend thoroughly. Stir together flour, baking soda, salt and cinnamon; gradually add to butter mixture, beating until well blended. Stir in oats and butterscotch chips; mix well. Drop by teaspoons onto ungreased cookie sheet.

3. Bake 8 to 10 minutes or until golden brown. Cool slightly; remove from cookie sheet to wire rack. Cool completely. *Makes about 4 dozen cookies*

Chocolate Chip Ice Cream Sandwiches

1-1/4 cups firmly packed light brown sugar
3/4 Butter Flavor CRISCO® Stick or 3/4 cup Butter Flavor CRISCO® all-vegetable shortening
2 tablespoons milk
1 tablespoon vanilla
1 egg
1-3/4 cups all-purpose flour
1 teaspoon salt
3/4 teaspoon baking soda
1 cup semisweet chocolate chips
1 cup chopped pecans
2 pints ice cream, any flavor

1. Heat oven to 375°F. Place sheets of foil on countertop for cooling cookies.

2. Place brown sugar, shortening, milk and vanilla in large bowl. Beat at medium speed of electric mixer until well blended. Add egg; beat well.

3. Combine flour, salt and baking soda. Add to shortening mixture; beat at low speed just until blended. Stir in chocolate chips and pecans.

4. Measure 1/4 cup dough; shape into ball. Repeat with remaining dough. Place balls 4 inches apart on ungreased baking sheets. Flatten balls into 3-inch circles.

5. Bake one baking sheet at a time at 375°F for 10 to 12 minutes or until cookies are lightly browned. *Do not overbake.* Cool 2 minutes on baking sheet. Remove cookies to foil to cool completely.

6. Remove ice cream from freezer to soften slightly. Measure 1/2 cup ice cream; spread onto bottom of one cookie. Cover with flat side of second cookie. Wrap sandwich in plastic wrap. Place in freezer. Repeat with remaining cookies and ice cream.
Makes about 10 ice cream sandwiches

Note: Chocolate Chip Ice Cream Sandwiches should be eaten within two days. After two days, cookies will absorb moisture and become soggy. If longer storage is needed, make and freeze cookies, but assemble ice cream sandwiches within two days of serving.

Citrus Parfaits

2 cups boiling water
1 package (4-serving size) JELL-O® Brand Lime Flavor Gelatin
1 package (4-serving size) JELL-O® Brand Lemon Flavor Gelatin
2 cups cold apple juice, divided
1 tub (8 ounces) COOL WHIP® Whipped Topping, thawed

STIR 1 cup boiling water into each flavor of gelatin in separate bowls at least 2 minutes until completely dissolved. Stir 1 cup cold juice into each bowl. Pour into separate 9×9-inch pans.

REFRIGERATE 4 hours or until firm. Cut each pan of gelatin into 1/2-inch cubes. Layer, alternating with flavors of gelatin cubes and whipped topping, into 8 dessert glasses. Garnish with additional whipped topping and berries, if desired. Store leftover dessert in refrigerator. *Makes 8 servings*

Oatmeal Butterscotch Cookies

Orange Dream Cake

      3/4 cup MIRACLE WHIP® Salad Dressing
        1 (two-layer) yellow cake mix
        1 envelope DREAM WHIP® Whipped Topping
           Mix
      3/4 cup orange juice
        3 eggs
        2 teaspoons grated orange peel
    1-1/2 cups powdered sugar
        2 tablespoons milk
        1 tablespoon multicolored sprinkles

• BEAT salad dressing, cake mix, whipped topping mix, juice, eggs and peel at medium speed with electric mixer for 2 minutes. Pour into greased and floured 10-inch fluted tube pan.

• BAKE at 350°F for 35 to 40 minutes or until wooden toothpick inserted near center comes out clean. Let stand 10 minutes; remove from pan. Cool.

• STIR together powdered sugar and milk until smooth. Drizzle over cake. Decorate with sprinkles.

Makes 8 to 10 servings

*Banana Pecan Torte with
Chocolate Ganache Filling*

Banana Pecan Torte with Chocolate Ganache Filling

(Pictured bottom left)

CAKE
        3 medium bananas, mashed
        2 eggs
        1 cup sugar
        1 teaspoon vanilla extract
    1-1/2 cups all-purpose flour
        1 teaspoon baking soda
        1 teaspoon ground cinnamon
      1/4 teaspoon salt
      1/2 cup (1 stick) I CAN'T BELIEVE IT'S NOT
           BUTTER!® Spread
      1/2 cup finely chopped toasted pecans
      1/2 cup coarsely grated chocolate from dark
           chocolate candy bar

FILLING
      1/2 cup whipping or heavy cream
        1 cup (6 ounces) semi-sweet chocolate chips

TOPPING
        1 cup (1/2 pint) whipping or heavy cream
        2 tablespoons confectioners' sugar
      1/4 teaspoon vanilla extract

For Cake, preheat oven to 350°F. Line bottoms of two 9-inch round cake pans with parchment or waxed paper, then grease and flour bottoms and sides of pans; set aside. In large bowl, with wire whisk, beat bananas, eggs, sugar and vanilla until blended; set aside.

In medium bowl, combine flour, baking soda, cinnamon and salt. With pastry blender or two knives, cut in I Can't Believe It's Not Butter! Spread until mixture is size of small peas. Stir flour mixture into banana mixture just until blended. Stir in pecans and chocolate. Evenly spread into prepared pans. Bake 20 minutes or until toothpick inserted in center of cakes comes out clean. On wire rack, cool 10 minutes; remove from pans and cool completely.

For Filling, in medium microwave-safe bowl, microwave cream and chocolate at HIGH (Full Power) 1 minute or until chocolate is melted; stir until smooth. Chill, stirring occasionally, until frosting consistency. Spread top of one cake layer with chocolate mixture, then top with second cake layer.

For Topping, in large bowl, with electric mixer, beat cream, sugar and vanilla just until stiff peaks form. Spread on top cake layer, leaving 1-inch border around edge. Garnish as desired.

Makes 12 servings

Cherry Glazed Chocolate Torte

Cherry Glazed Chocolate Torte

(Pictured above and on front cover)

1/2 cup (1 stick) butter or margarine, melted
1 cup granulated sugar
1 teaspoon vanilla extract
2 eggs
1/2 cup all-purpose flour
1/3 cup HERSHEY'S Cocoa
1/4 teaspoon baking powder
1/4 teaspoon salt
1 package (8 ounces) cream cheese, softened
1 cup powdered sugar
1 cup frozen non-dairy whipped topping, thawed
1 can (21 ounces) cherry pie filling, divided

1. Heat oven to 350°F. Grease bottom of 9-inch springform pan.

2. Stir together butter, sugar and vanilla in large bowl. Add eggs; using spoon, beat well. Stir together flour, cocoa, baking powder and salt; gradually add to egg mixture, beating until well blended. Spread batter into prepared pan.

3. Bake 25 to 30 minutes or until cake is set. (Cake will be fudgey and will not test done.) Remove from oven; cool completely in pan on wire rack.

4. Beat cream cheese and powdered sugar in medium bowl until well blended; gradually fold in whipped topping, blending well. Spread over top of cake. Spread 1 cup cherry pie filling over cream layer; refrigerate several hours. With knife, loosen cake from side of pan; remove side of pan. Cut into wedges; garnish with remaining pie filling. Cover; refrigerate leftover dessert.

Makes 10 to 12 servings

Helpful Hint

At home, butter should be stored in the coldest part of the refrigerator or frozen. Either way, wrap it tightly so that it can't pick up other flavors.

Very Beary Peanut Brittle

(Pictured at right)

2 cups sugar
1 cup water
1/2 cup light corn syrup
1 tablespoon margarine or butter
1/2 cup PLANTERS® COCKTAIL Peanuts
1 teaspoon vanilla extract
1/2 teaspoon baking soda
1 cup TEDDY GRAHAMS® Graham Snacks, any flavor

1. Heat sugar, water, corn syrup and margarine or butter in medium saucepan over medium-low heat, stirring occasionally, until mixture reaches 290°F on candy thermometer.

2. Stir in peanuts; continue to heat to 300°F. Remove from heat; stir in vanilla and baking soda.

3. Thinly spread mixture onto greased baking sheet. Press bear-shaped graham snacks into mixture while still hot.

4. Cool completely; break into bite-size pieces. Store in airtight container for up to 2 weeks.

Makes about 1-1/2 pounds

Cream Cheese Cutout Cookies

1 cup butter, softened
1 (8-ounce) package cream cheese, softened
1-1/2 cups sugar
1 egg
1 teaspoon vanilla
1/2 teaspoon almond extract
3-1/2 cups all-purpose flour
1 teaspoon baking powder
Almond Frosting (recipe follows)

In large mixer bowl combine butter and cream cheese. Beat until well combined. Add sugar; beat until fluffy. Add egg, vanilla and almond extract; beat well.

In medium bowl stir together flour and baking powder. Add flour mixture to cream cheese mixture; beat until well mixed. Divide dough in half. Cover and chill in refrigerator about 1-1/2 hours or until dough is easy to handle.

On lightly floured surface roll dough to 1/8-inch thickness. Cut with desired cookie cutters. Place on ungreased cookie sheets. Bake in 375°F oven for

8 to 10 minutes or until done. Remove to wire racks; cool. Pipe or spread Almond Frosting on cooled cookies.

Makes about 90 cookies

Almond Frosting: In small mixer bowl beat 2 cups sifted powdered sugar, 2 tablespoons softened butter and 1/4 teaspoon almond extract until smooth. Beat in enough milk (4 to 5 teaspoons) until frosting is of piping consistency. For spreadable frosting, add a little more milk. Stir in a few drops of food coloring, if desired.

Favorite recipe from **Wisconsin Milk Marketing Board**

Baker's® One Bowl Brownies

4 squares BAKER'S® Unsweetened Baking Chocolate
3/4 cup (1-1/2 sticks) butter *or* margarine
2 cups sugar
3 eggs
1 teaspoon vanilla
1 cup flour
1 cup coarsely chopped nuts (optional)

HEAT oven to 350°F. Line 13×9-inch baking pan with foil; grease foil.

MICROWAVE chocolate and butter in large microwavable bowl on HIGH 2 minutes or until butter is melted. Stir until chocolate is completely melted.

STIR sugar into chocolate mixture until well blended. Mix in eggs and vanilla. Stir in flour and nuts until well blended. Spread in prepared pan.

BAKE 30 to 35 minutes or until toothpick inserted into center comes out with fudgy crumbs. DO NOT OVERBAKE. Cool in pan on wire rack. Lift out of pan onto cutting board. *Makes 2 dozen brownies*

Tips: For cakelike brownies, stir in 1/2 cup milk with eggs and vanilla and increase flour to 1-1/2 cups. For extra fudgy brownies, use 4 eggs. For extra thick brownies, bake in 9-inch square baking pan 50 minutes. For 13×9-inch glass baking dish, bake at 325°F.

Very Beary Peanut Brittle

Blueberry Streusel Cobbler

(Pictured at right)

1 pint fresh or frozen blueberries
1 (14-ounce) can EAGLE® BRAND Sweetened
    Condensed Milk (NOT evaporated milk)
2 teaspoons grated lemon peel
3/4 cup plus 2 tablespoons cold butter or
    margarine, divided
2 cups biscuit baking mix, divided
1/2 cup firmly packed brown sugar
1/2 cup chopped nuts
    Vanilla Ice Cream
    Blueberry Sauce (recipe follows)

1. Preheat oven to 325°F. In bowl, combine blueberries, Eagle Brand and peel.

2. In large bowl, cut 3/4 cup butter into 1-1/2 cups biscuit mix until crumbly; add blueberry mixture. Spread in greased 9-inch square baking pan.

3. In small bowl, combine remaining 1/2 cup biscuit mix and sugar; cut in remaining 2 tablespoons butter until crumbly. Add nuts. Sprinkle over cobbler.

4. Bake 1 hour and 10 minutes or until golden. Serve warm with vanilla ice cream and Blueberry Sauce. Refrigerate leftovers. *Makes 8 to 12 servings*

Blueberry Sauce: In saucepan, combine 1/2 cup sugar, 1 tablespoon cornstarch, 1/2 teaspoon ground cinnamon and 1/4 teaspoon ground nutmeg. Gradually add 1/2 cup water. Cook and stir until thickened. Stir in 1 pint blueberries; cook and stir until hot.

White Chocolate Raspberry Cake

1 package (6 squares) BAKER'S® Premium White
    Baking Chocolate, chopped
1/2 cup (1 stick) butter *or* margarine
1 package (2-layer size) white cake mix
1 cup milk
3 eggs
1 teaspoon vanilla
    White Chocolate Cream Cheese Frosting
    (recipe follows)
2 tablespoons seedless raspberry jam
1 cup raspberries

HEAT oven to 350°F. Grease and flour 2 (9-inch) round cake pans; set aside.

MICROWAVE chocolate and butter in medium microwavable bowl on HIGH 2 minutes or until butter is melted. Stir until chocolate is completely melted; cool slightly.

BEAT cake mix, milk, eggs, vanilla and chocolate mixture in large bowl with electric mixer on low speed just until moistened, scraping side of bowl often. Beat on medium speed 2 minutes or until well blended. Pour into prepared pans.

BAKE 25 to 28 minutes or until toothpick inserted in center comes out clean. Cool cakes in pans 10 minutes; remove from pans. Cool completely on wire rack.

PLACE 1 cake layer on serving plate. Spread with 2/3 cup of the frosting, then jam. Place second cake layer on top. Frost top and side with remaining frosting. Garnish with raspberries.
Makes 12 to 16 servings

White Chocolate Cream Cheese Frosting

1 package (8 ounces) PHILADELPHIA® Cream
    Cheese, softened
4 tablespoons (1/2 stick) butter *or* margarine,
    softened
1 package (6 ounces) BAKER'S® Premium White
    Baking Chocolate, melted, cooled slightly
1 teaspoon vanilla
2 cups powdered sugar

BEAT cream cheese and butter in large bowl with electric mixer on medium speed until well blended. Add melted chocolate and vanilla; beat until blended.

BEAT in sugar until light and fluffy.
Makes 3 cups

Marbled White Chocolate Raspberry Cake:
Prepare batter as directed. Remove 1 cup batter to small bowl. Stir in 2 tablespoons seedless raspberry jam and 2 drops red food coloring. Spoon remaining batter into prepared pans. Place spoonfuls of pink batter into each pan. Swirl with small knife to marbleize. Bake as directed.

Raspberry Summer Sensation

1 pint (2 cups) raspberry sorbet *or* sherbet, softened
1 cup cold milk
1 package (4-serving size) JELL-O® Vanilla Flavor Instant Pudding & Pie Filling
1 tub (8 ounces) COOL WHIP® Whipped Topping, thawed
Raspberries, strawberries and blueberries for garnish (optional)

LINE 8×4-inch loaf pan with foil. Spoon sorbet into pan; freeze 10 minutes.

POUR milk into large bowl. Add pudding mix. Beat with wire whisk 2 minutes. Stir in 3 cups whipped topping. Spread over sorbet in pan.

FREEZE 3 hours or overnight. Unmold onto plate; remove foil. Top with remaining whipped topping; garnish as desired. *Makes 10 servings*

Helpful Hint: Soften sorbet in microwave on MEDIUM 10 to 15 seconds.

Butterscotch Blondies

Butterscotch Blondies

(Pictured bottom left)

3/4 cup (1-1/2 sticks) butter or margarine, softened
3/4 cup packed light brown sugar
1/2 cup granulated sugar
2 eggs
2 cups all-purpose flour
1 teaspoon baking soda
1/2 teaspoon salt
1-2/3 cups (10-ounce package) HERSHEY'S Butterscotch Chips
1 cup chopped nuts (optional)

1. Heat oven to 350°F. Lightly grease 13×9×2-inch baking pan.

2. Beat butter, brown sugar and granulated sugar in large bowl until creamy. Add eggs; beat well. Stir together flour, baking soda and salt; gradually add to butter mixture, blending well. Stir in butterscotch chips and nuts, if desired. Spread into prepared pan.

3. Bake 30 to 35 minutes or until top is golden brown and center is set. Cool completely in pan on wire rack. Cut into bars. *Makes about 36 bars*

Lemon Nut Bars

1-1/3 cups all-purpose flour
1/2 cup firmly packed brown sugar
1/4 cup granulated sugar
3/4 cup butter or margarine
1 cup old-fashioned or quick oats, uncooked
1/2 cup chopped nuts
1 package (8 ounces) PHILADELPHIA® Cream Cheese, softened
1 egg
1 tablespoon grated lemon peel
3 tablespoons lemon juice

PREHEAT oven to 350°F.

STIR together flour and sugars in medium bowl. Cut in butter until mixture resembles coarse crumbs. Stir in oats and nuts. Reserve 1 cup crumb mixture; press remaining crumb mixture onto bottom of greased 13×9-inch baking pan. Bake 15 minutes.

BEAT cream cheese, egg, lemon peel and juice in small mixing bowl until well blended. Pour over crust; sprinkle with reserved crumb mixture.

BAKE 25 minutes. Cool in pan on wire rack. Cut into bars. *Makes about 3 dozen bars*

Orange Pecan Pie

Orange Pecan Pie

(Pictured above)

    3 eggs
1/2 cup GRANDMA'S® Molasses
1/2 cup light corn syrup
1/4 cup orange juice
    1 teaspoon grated orange peel
    1 teaspoon vanilla
1-1/2 cups whole pecan halves
    1 (9-inch) unbaked pie shell
    Whipping cream (optional)

Heat oven to 350°F. In large bowl, beat eggs. Add molasses, corn syrup, orange juice, orange peel, and vanilla; beat until well blended. Stir in pecans. Pour into unbaked pie shell. Bake 30 to 45 minutes or until filling sets. Cool on wire rack. Serve with whipping cream, if desired. *Makes 8 servings*

Easy Rocky Road

    2 cups (12-ounce package) HERSHEY'S
        Semi-Sweet Chocolate Chips
1/4 cup butter or margarine
    2 tablespoons shortening
    3 cups miniature marshmallows
1/2 cup coarsely chopped nuts

1. Butter 8-inch square pan.

2. Place chocolate chips, butter and shortening in large microwave-safe bowl. Microwave at HIGH (100%) 1 to 1-1/2 minutes or just until chocolate chips are melted and mixture is smooth when stirred. Add marshmallows and nuts; blend well.

3. Spread evenly in prepared pan. Cover; refrigerate until firm. Cut into 2-inch squares. Cover; store in refrigerator. *Makes 16 squares*

Cherry Crisp

(Pictured at right)

1 (21-ounce) can cherry pie filling
1/2 teaspoon almond extract
1/2 cup all-purpose flour
1/2 cup firmly packed brown sugar
1 teaspoon ground cinnamon
3 tablespoons butter or margarine, softened
1/2 cup chopped walnuts
1/4 cup flaked coconut
Ice cream or whipped cream (optional)

Pour cherry pie filling into ungreased 8×8×2-inch baking pan. Stir in almond extract.

Place flour, brown sugar and cinnamon in medium mixing bowl; mix well. Add butter; stir with fork until mixture is crumbly. Stir in walnuts and coconut. Sprinkle mixture over cherry pie filling.

Bake in preheated 350°F oven 25 minutes or until golden brown on top and filling is bubbly. Serve warm or at room temperature. If desired, top with ice cream or whipped cream.   *Makes 6 servings*

Note: This recipe can be doubled. Bake in two 8×8×2-inch baking pans or one 13×9×2-inch pan.

Favorite recipe from **Cherry Marketing Institute**

Oatmeal Toffee Bars

1 cup (2 sticks) butter or margarine, softened
1/2 cup packed light brown sugar
1/2 cup granulated sugar
2 eggs
1 teaspoon vanilla extract
1-1/2 cups all-purpose flour
1 teaspoon baking soda
1/2 teaspoon ground cinnamon
1/2 teaspoon salt
3 cups quick-cooking or regular rolled oats
1-3/4 cups (10-ounce package) SKOR® English
    Toffee Bits *or* 1-3/4 cups HEATH® BITS
    'O BRICKLE™, divided

1. Heat oven to 350°F. Lightly grease 13×9×2-inch baking pan.

2. Beat butter, brown sugar and granulated sugar in large bowl until well blended. Add eggs and vanilla; beat well. Stir together flour, baking soda, cinnamon and salt; gradually add to butter mixture, beating

until well blended. Stir in oats and 1-1/3 cups toffee bits (mixture will be stiff). Spread mixture into prepared pan.

3. Bake 25 minutes or until wooden pick inserted in center comes out clean. Immediately sprinkle remaining toffee bits over surface. Cool completely in pan on wire rack. Cut into bars.
Makes about 36 bars

Tip: Bar cookies can be cut into different shapes for variety. To cut into triangles, cut cookie bars into 2- to 3-inch squares, then diagonally cut each square in half. To make diamond shapes, cut parallel lines 2 inches apart across the length of the pan, then cut diagonal lines 2 inches apart.

Creamy Cranberry Fruit Freeze

2 packages (3 ounces each) cream cheese,
    softened
1/2 cup KARO® Light Corn Syrup
1 can (16 ounces) whole berry cranberry sauce
1 can (11 ounces) mandarin orange sections,
    well drained
1 can (8 ounces) crushed pineapple, well
    drained
1 container (8 ounces) non-dairy whipped
    topping
Fresh fruit and mint leaves (optional)

1. In large bowl with mixer at medium speed, beat cream cheese until fluffy. Gradually beat in corn syrup until smooth. Reduce speed to low; beat in cranberry sauce until combined.

2. Stir in oranges and pineapple. Gently fold in whipped topping just until combined. Spoon into 8- or 9-inch square pan.

3. Cover and freeze 6 hours or overnight.

4. To serve, cut into bars. Let stand 10 minutes at room temperature before serving. If desired, garnish with fresh fruit and mint leaves.
Makes 9 to 12 servings

Cherry Crisp

Chocolate Chiffon Pie

(Pictured at right)

2 (1-ounce) squares unsweetened chocolate, chopped
1 (14-ounce) can EAGLE® BRAND Sweetened Condensed Milk (NOT evaporated milk)
1 envelope unflavored gelatin
1/3 cup water
1/2 teaspoon vanilla extract
1 cup (1/2 pint) whipping cream, whipped
1 (6-ounce) ready-made chocolate or graham cracker crumb pie crust
Additional whipped cream

1. In heavy saucepan over low heat, melt chocolate with Eagle Brand. Remove from heat.

2. Meanwhile, in small saucepan, sprinkle gelatin over water; let stand 1 minute. Over low heat, stir until gelatin dissolves.

3. Stir gelatin into chocolate mixture. Add vanilla. Cool to room temperature. Fold in whipped cream. Spread into crust.

4. Chill 3 hours or until set. Garnish with additional whipped cream. Store covered in refrigerator.
Makes 1 pie

Pineapple Fruit Tart

1/4 cup ground almonds (about 2 tablespoons whole almonds)
1/4 cup butter or margarine, softened
1/4 cup sugar
2 tablespoons milk
1/2 teaspoon almond extract
3/4 cup all-purpose flour
2 packages (3 ounces each) cream cheese, softened
2 tablespoons sour cream
1/4 cup apricot preserves, divided
1 teaspoon vanilla extract
1 can (15-1/4 ounces) DEL MONTE® Sliced Pineapple In Its Own Juice, drained and cut in halves
2 kiwifruits, peeled, sliced and cut into halves
1 cup sliced strawberries

1. Combine almonds, butter, sugar, milk and almond extract; mix well. Blend in flour. Chill dough 1 hour.

2. Press dough evenly onto bottom and up sides of tart pan with removable bottom.

3. Bake at 350°F, 15 to 18 minutes or until golden brown. Cool.

4. Combine cream cheese, sour cream, 1 tablespoon apricot preserves and vanilla. Spread onto crust. Arrange pineapple, kiwi and strawberries over cream cheese mixture.

5. Heat remaining 3 tablespoons apricot preserves in small saucepan over low heat. Spoon over fruit.
Makes 8 servings

New York Cheesecake

1 cup graham cracker crumbs
3 tablespoons sugar
3 tablespoons butter or margarine, melted
5 packages (8 ounces each) PHILADELPHIA® Cream Cheese, softened
1 cup sugar
3 tablespoons flour
1 tablespoon vanilla
3 eggs
1 cup BREAKSTONE'S® or KNUDSEN® Sour Cream

MIX crumbs, 3 tablespoons sugar and butter; press onto bottom of 9-inch springform pan. Bake at 350°F for 10 minutes.

MIX cream cheese, 1 cup sugar, flour and vanilla with electric mixer on medium speed until well blended. Add eggs, 1 at a time, mixing on low speed after each addition, just until blended. Blend in sour cream.

BAKE 1 hour or until center is almost set. Run knife or metal spatula around rim of pan to loosen cake; cool before removing rim of pan. Refrigerate 4 hours or overnight.
Makes 12 servings

Chocolate New York Cheesecake: Substitute 1 cup chocolate wafer cookie crumbs for graham cracker crumbs. Blend 8 squares BAKER'S® Semi-Sweet Chocolate, melted and slightly cooled, into batter. Continue as directed.

Chocolate Chiffon Pie

Black Forest Torte

Black Forest Torte

(Pictured above)

1 package DUNCAN HINES® Moist Deluxe®
Dark Chocolate Fudge Cake Mix
2-1/2 cups whipping cream, chilled
2-1/2 tablespoons confectioners' sugar
1 (21-ounce) can cherry pie filling

Preheat oven to 350°F. Grease and flour two 9-inch round cake pans.

Prepare, bake and cool cake as directed on package.

Beat whipping cream in large bowl until soft peaks form. Add sugar gradually. Beat until stiff peaks form.

To assemble, place one cake layer on serving plate. Spread two-thirds cherry pie filling on cake to within 1/2 inch of edge. Spread 1-1/2 cups whipped cream mixture over cherry pie filling. Top with second cake layer. Frost sides and top with remaining whipped cream mixture. Spread remaining cherry pie filling on top to within 1 inch of edge. Refrigerate until ready to serve.   *Makes 12 to 16 servings*

Butterscotch Thins

2-2/3 cups all-purpose flour
1-1/2 teaspoons baking soda
1-2/3 cups (11-ounce package) NESTLÉ® TOLL
HOUSE® Butterscotch Flavored Morsels
1 cup (2 sticks) butter or margarine, cut into pieces
1-1/3 cups packed brown sugar
2 eggs
1-1/2 teaspoons vanilla extract
2/3 cup finely chopped nuts

COMBINE flour and baking soda in medium bowl.

MICROWAVE morsels and butter in large, microwave-safe mixer bowl on MEDIUM-HIGH (70% power) for 1 minute; stir. Microwave at additional 10- to 20-second intervals, stirring until smooth. Beat in sugar, eggs and vanilla extract. Gradually beat in flour mixture; stir in nuts. Cover; refrigerate for about 1 hour or until firm. Shape into two 14×1-1/2-inch logs; wrap in plastic wrap. Refrigerate for 2 hours or until firm.

PREHEAT oven to 350°F.

UNWRAP logs; slice into 1/4-inch-thick slices. Place slices on ungreased baking sheets. Bake for 5 to 6 minutes or until edges are set. Cool on baking sheets for 2 minutes; remove to wire racks to cool completely.   *Makes about 6 dozen cookies*

Berry Good Sorbet

1 pint blueberries
1 package (10 ounces) frozen raspberries in syrup, thawed
1-1/2 cups ginger ale
3/4 cup KARO® Light Corn Syrup
1/4 cup sugar
2 tablespoons lemon juice

1. In blender or food processor purée blueberries and raspberries until smooth. Press through a fine mesh strainer into a large bowl. Discard seeds.

2. Stir in ginger ale, corn syrup, sugar and lemon juice.

3. Pour into container of ice cream maker and freeze according to manufacturer's directions.
Makes about 1-1/2 quarts

Fast 'n' Fabulous Dark Chocolate Fudge

(Pictured below)

MAZOLA NO STICK® Cooking Spray
1/2 cup **KARO®** Light or Dark Corn Syrup
1/3 cup evaporated milk
3 cups (18 ounces) semisweet chocolate chips
3/4 cup confectioners' sugar, sifted
2 teaspoons vanilla
1 cup coarsely chopped nuts (optional)

1. Spray 8-inch square baking pan with cooking spray.

2. In 3-quart microwavable bowl, combine corn syrup and evaporated milk; stir until well blended. Microwave on HIGH (100%), 3 minutes.

3. Stir in chocolate chips until melted. Stir in confectioners' sugar, vanilla and nuts. With wooden spoon beat until thick and glossy.

4. Spread in prepared pan. Refrigerate 2 hours or until firm.   *Makes 25 squares*

Marvelous Marble Fudge: Omit nuts. Prepare fudge as directed in recipe; spread into prepared pan. Drop 1/3 cup SKIPPY® Creamy Peanut Butter over fudge in small dollops. With small spatula, swirl fudge to marbleize. Chill as directed.

Double Peanut Butter Chocolate Fudge: Prepare fudge as directed in recipe. Stir in 1/3 cup SKIPPY® SUPER CHUNK® Peanut Butter. Spread in prepared pan. Drop additional 1/3 cup peanut butter over fudge in small dollops. With small spatula, swirl fudge to marbleize. Chill as directed.

> ### *Helpful Hint*
> *If fudge is difficult to cut into neat squares, place it in the refrigerator or freezer until firm. This will make it easier to cut.*

Fast 'n' Fabulous Dark Chocolate Fudge

Della Robbia Cake

(Pictured at right)

1 package DUNCAN HINES® Angel Food Cake Mix
1-1/2 teaspoons grated lemon peel
1 cup water
6 tablespoons granulated sugar
1-1/2 tablespoons cornstarch
1 tablespoon lemon juice
1/2 teaspoon vanilla extract
   Few drops red food coloring
6 cling peach slices
6 medium strawberries, sliced

Preheat oven to 375°F.

Prepare cake mix as directed on package, adding lemon peel. Bake and cool cake as directed on package.

Combine water, sugar and cornstarch in small saucepan. Cook on medium-high heat until mixture thickens and clears. Remove from heat. Stir in lemon juice, vanilla extract and food coloring.

Alternate peach slices with strawberry slices around top of cake. Pour glaze over fruit and top of cake.   *Makes 12 to 16 servings*

Bittersweet Chocolate Truffle Squares

3/4 cup whipping (heavy) cream
1/4 cup (1/2 stick) butter, cut into chunks
3 tablespoons sugar
2 packages (6 squares each) BAKER'S® Bittersweet Baking Chocolate, broken into chunks
1/2 teaspoon vanilla
1 cup finely chopped toasted almonds

LINE 8-inch square baking pan with foil.

MICROWAVE cream, butter and sugar in large microwavable bowl on HIGH 3 minutes until mixture comes to full boil, stirring halfway through heating time. Add chocolate and vanilla; stir until chocolate is completely melted.

REFRIGERATE about 2 hours or until firm enough to handle. Sprinkle almonds in bottom of prepared pan. Spread chocolate mixture evenly over almonds. Refrigerate 2 hours or until firm. Cut into squares.
           Makes 4 dozen squares

Chocolate Cheesecake Cupcakes

CUPCAKES
2 cups (12-ounce package) NESTLÉ® TOLL HOUSE® Semi-Sweet Chocolate Morsels, *divided*
1-1/2 cups all-purpose flour
1 teaspoon baking soda
1/2 teaspoon salt
1/2 cup granulated sugar
1/3 cup vegetable oil
1 large egg
1 teaspoon vanilla extract
1 cup water

FILLING
2 packages (3 ounces *each*) cream cheese, softened
1/4 cup granulated sugar
1 large egg
1/8 teaspoon salt

FOR CUPCAKES
PREHEAT oven to 350°F. Grease or paper-line 16 muffin cups.

MICROWAVE *1/2 cup* morsels in small, microwave-safe bowl on HIGH (100% power) for 45 seconds; stir. Microwave at additional 10- to 20-second intervals, stirring until smooth; cool to room temperature.

COMBINE flour, baking soda and 1/2 teaspoon salt in small bowl. Beat 1/2 cup sugar, oil, 1 egg and vanilla in large mixer bowl until blended. Beat in melted chocolate; gradually beat in flour mixture alternately with water (batter will be thin).

FOR FILLING
BEAT cream cheese, 1/4 cup sugar, 1 egg and 1/8 teaspoon salt in small mixer bowl until creamy. Stir in *1 cup* morsels.

TO ASSEMBLE
SPOON batter into prepared muffin cups, filling 1/2 full. Spoon filling by rounded tablespoons over batter. Spoon remaining batter over filling. Bake for 20 to 25 minutes or until wooden pick inserted in center comes out clean. While still hot, sprinkle with *remaining 1/2 cup* morsels. Let stand for 5 minutes or until morsels are shiny; spread to frost. Remove to wire racks to cool completely.
           Makes 16 cupcakes

Della Robbia Cake

The publisher would like to thank the companies and organizations listed below for the use of their recipes and photographs in this publication.

A.1.® Steak Sauce

Barilla America, Inc.

Bertolli USA

Birds Eye®

Blue Diamond Growers®

Bob Evans®

Butterball® Turkey Company

California Tree Fruit Agreement

Campbell Soup Company

Cherry Marketing Institute

Colorado Potato Administrative Committee

ConAgra Grocery Products Company

Del Monte Corporation

Dole Food Company, Inc.

Duncan Hines® and Moist Deluxe® are registered trademarks of Aurora Foods Inc.

Eagle® Brand

Filippo Berio® Olive Oil

Fleischmann's® Original Spread

Fleischmann's® Yeast

The Fremont Company, Makers of Frank's & SnowFloss Kraut and Tomato Products

The Golden Grain Company®

Grandma's® is a registered trademark of Mott's, Inc.

GREY POUPON® Dijon Mustard

Hebrew National®

Heinz U.S.A.

Hershey Foods Corporation

Hillshire Farm®

Hormel Foods, LLC

The HV Company

Kraft Foods Holdings

Lawry's® Foods, Inc.

© Mars, Incorporated 2002

McCormick®

McIlhenny Company (TABASCO® brand Pepper Sauce)

Minnesota Cultivated Wild Rice Council

Mott's® is a registered trademark of Mott's, Inc.

Nabisco Biscuit and Snack Divison

National Chicken Council

National Honey Board

National Pork Board

National Turkey Federation

Nestlé USA

North Dakota Beef Commission

North Dakota Wheat Commission

Perdue Farms Incorporated

PLANTERS® Nuts

The Procter & Gamble Company

The Quaker® Oatmeal Kitchens

Reckitt Benckiser

RED STAR® Yeast, a product of Lasaffre Yeast Corporation

Riviana Foods Inc.

Sargento® Foods Inc.

The J.M. Smucker Company

StarKist® Seafood Company

The Sugar Association, Inc.

Tyson Foods, Inc.

Uncle Ben's Inc.

Unilever Bestfoods North America

USA Rice Federation

Veg•All®

Wisconsin Milk Marketing Board

General Index

Alphabetical Index

METRIC CONVERSION CHART

VOLUME MEASUREMENTS (dry)

1/8 teaspoon = 0.5 mL
1/4 teaspoon = 1 mL
1/2 teaspoon = 2 mL
3/4 teaspoon = 4 mL
1 teaspoon = 5 mL
1 tablespoon = 15 mL
2 tablespoons = 30 mL
1/4 cup = 60 mL
1/3 cup = 75 mL
1/2 cup = 125 mL
2/3 cup = 150 mL
3/4 cup = 175 mL
1 cup = 250 mL
2 cups = 1 pint = 500 mL
3 cups = 750 mL
4 cups = 1 quart = 1 L

VOLUME MEASUREMENTS (fluid)

1 fluid ounce (2 tablespoons) = 30 mL
4 fluid ounces (1/2 cup) = 125 mL
8 fluid ounces (1 cup) = 250 mL
12 fluid ounces (1 1/2 cups) = 375 mL
16 fluid ounces (2 cups) = 500 mL

WEIGHTS (mass)

1/2 ounce = 15 g
1 ounce = 30 g
3 ounces = 90 g
4 ounces = 120 g
8 ounces = 225 g
10 ounces = 285 g
12 ounces = 360 g
16 ounces = 1 pound = 450 g

DIMENSIONS

1/16 inch = 2 mm
1/8 inch = 3 mm
1/4 inch = 6 mm
1/2 inch = 1.5 cm
3/4 inch = 2 cm
1 inch = 2.5 cm

OVEN TEMPERATURES

250°F = 120°C
275°F = 140°C
300°F = 150°C
325°F = 160°C
350°F = 180°C
375°F = 190°C
400°F = 200°C
425°F = 220°C
450°F = 230°C

BAKING PAN SIZES

Utensil	Size in Inches/Quarts	Metric Volume	Size in Centimeters
Baking or Cake Pan (square or rectangular)	8×8×2	2 L	20×20×5
	9×9×2	2.5 L	23×23×5
	12×8×2	3 L	30×20×5
	13×9×2	3.5 L	33×23×5
Loaf Pan	8×4×3	1.5 L	20×10×7
	9×5×3	2 L	23×13×7
Round Layer Cake Pan	8×1½	1.2 L	20×4
	9×1½	1.5 L	23×4
Pie Plate	8×1¼	750 mL	20×3
	9×1¼	1 L	23×3
Baking Dish or Casserole	1 quart	1 L	—
	1½ quart	1.5 L	—
	2 quart	2 L	—